Postcards from the Sonora Border

POST CARDS

FROM THE SONORA BORDER

VISUALIZING PLACE THROUGH A POPULAR LENS, 1900s–1950s

DANIEL D. ARREOLA

THE UNIVERSITY OF
ARIZONA PRESS

TUCSON

The University of Arizona Press
www.uapress.arizona.edu

Printed in the United States of America

22   21   20   19   18   17   6   5   4   3   2   1

ISBN-13: 978-0-8165-3432-6 (cloth)

Cover design by Leigh McDonald
Cover photograph courtesy of the Arizona Historical Society, Tucson, Earl Fallis Photo Collection #43109.

Publication of this book is made possible in part by a subvention from the School of Geographical Sciences and Urban Planning, Arizona State University, Tempe, and by the proceeds of a permanent endowment created with the assistance of a Challenge Grant from the National Endowment for the Humanities, a federal agency.

Library of Congress Cataloging-in-Publication Data
Names: Arreola, Daniel D. (Daniel David), 1950– author.
Title: Postcards from the Sonora border : visualizing place through a popular lens, 1900s–1950s / Daniel D. Arreola.
Description: Tucson : The University of Arizona Press, 2017. | Includes bibliographical references and index.
Identifiers: LCCN 2016027349 | ISBN 9780816534326 (alk. paper)
Subjects: LCSH: Cities and towns—Mexico—Sonora (State)—History—20th century. | Urbanization—Mexico—Sonora (State)—History—20th century. | Sonora (Mexico : State)—History—20th century—Pictorial works. | Postcards—Mexico—Sonora (State)—History—20th century. | Agua Prieta (Sonora, Mexico)—History—20th century. | Naco (Mexico)—History—20th century. | Nogales (Nogales, Mexico)—History—20th century. | Sonoyta (Mexico)—History—20th century. | San Luis Río Colorado (Mexico)—History—20th century. | LCGFT: Illustrated works.
Classification: LCC HT127.7 .A775 2017 | DDC 306.70972/170904—dc23 LC record available at https://lccn .loc.gov/2016027349

♾ This paper meets the requirements of ANSI/NISO z39.48-1992 (Permanence of Paper).

"There are two ways of spreading light: to be the candle or the mirror that reflects it." This quotation, attributed to American novelist Edith Wharton (1862–1937), is a fitting expression of gratitude to one's mentors. Christopher L. Salter, Henry J. Bruman (1913–2005), and Gary S. Dunbar (1931–2015) at the University of California, Los Angeles, and Herbert M. Eder at California State University, Hayward, brightened my early path. Reflecting their light has been a joy of lifelong geographical learning. I received my first tarjeta postal from Dorothy Thatcher, a fourth-grade teacher at Will Rogers Elementary School in Santa Monica, California, who traveled to Mexico and cared enough to mail me a postcard of a beach scene in Mazatlán. She opened a door that became both a path and a passion. This book is dedicated to them and to all mentors.

Contents

Illustrations

Tables

Figures

Preface and Acknowledgments

Postcards from the Sonora Border is the second installment in a project that involves four separate books about the visual history of towns along Mexico's northern border. The inaugural publication in this ongoing research enterprise was *Postcards from the Río Bravo Border: Picturing the Place, Placing the Picture* (University of Texas Press, 2013). In that book, I studied the Mexico border towns of Matamoros, Reynosa, Nuevo Laredo, Piedras Negras, and Ciudad Acuña that face the Texas boundary along the Río Bravo/Rio Grande. The framework followed in the initial volume was thematic and used examples from the five Río Bravo border towns to illustrate landscapes within and surrounding the towns exhibited by photographic postcards from the 1900s to the 1950s. Chapters explored subjects such as gateways (bridge crossings), streets, plazas, attractions, businesses, landmarks, and everyday life to visualize how the popular photographic postcard captured peoples and places during the first half of the twentieth century.

In *Postcards from the Sonora Border*, I continue my exploration of the visual history and historical geography of the Mexican border to understand how five towns on the Sonora border facing Arizona are revealed in the photographic postcard from the 1900s to the 1950s. The framework for investigation follows a geographic template where individual chapters are presented for each of the five towns studied: Agua Prieta, Naco, Nogales, Sonoyta, and San Luis Río Colorado. Within these chapters, I develop a geographical and historical analysis of each town using text, maps, and visual imagery to narrate the particular places and events captured by the postcard photographer's lens. In this approach, emphasis is given to the towns themselves rather than to the larger geographic themes followed in *Postcards from the Río Bravo*

Border. In each instance, however, the goal is nearly the same: to understand how a popular image format shaped the way we came to see these towns as both tourist destinations and lived places. The project continues beyond these installments. In future volumes I will utilize postcards from the Chihuahua border to investigate the towns of Ciudad Juárez, Ojinaga, and Palomas and postcards from the Baja California border to examine Tijuana, Mexicali, Tecate, and Algodones.

Postcards from the Sonora Border was made possible, in part, through the generous contributions of the Comparative Border Studies program of the School of Transborder Studies at Arizona State University, which enabled field and archival study in 2012–2013, and the School of Geographical Sciences and Urban Planning at Arizona State University, which provided resources for a small publication subvention in 2016. Beyond the assistance provided by librarians and archivists at numerous institutions, the following repositories, including their staffs and resources, were especially helpful to this project: Arizona Historical Society; Douglas Historical Society; Bisbee Mining and Historical Museum; Fort Huachuca Museum; Pimería Alta Historical Society; Library and Archive, Organ Pipe Cactus National Monument; Arizona State Library and Archives; Special Collections of the University of Arizona Libraries; and the Arizona Collection of the Hayden Library, Arizona State University.

Special thanks are extended to freelance writer, researcher, and grassroots historian Cynthia Hayostek of Douglas, Arizona, who kindly shared her Douglas historic materials and who read and commented on chapter 3, "Agua Prieta"; border historian José Ramón García of Nogales, Arizona, who read and provided comments on chapter 5, "Nogales"; and two reviewers who read the entire manuscript and made valuable suggestions. Original maps were prepared from my sketches by cartographer Barbara Trapido-Lurie in the School of Geographical Sciences and Urban Planning at Arizona State University, Tempe. Scott Warren extended hospitality and shared his knowledge of resources about Papaguería during visits to Ajo, Arizona. Sue Rutman of Ajo, Arizona, generously shared her files about Ajo-Sonoyta and the histories of those communities. Thanks are extended to Kristen A. Buckles, acquiring editor; Amanda Krause, editorial, design, and production manager; and Leigh McDonald, art director and book designer, at the University of Arizona Press for their support of the project, and to C. Steven LaRue who efficiently copyedited the manuscript, improving clarity.

Preliminary findings for *Postcards from the Sonora Border* were shared in illustrated lectures and exhibitions at the School of Transborder Studies at Arizona State University in 2012; 7° Congreso Mexicano de Tarjetas Postales, Monterrey, México, in 2014; and Border-land Stories, a series of public programs in Douglas, Bisbee, Nogales, and Sells, Arizona, made possible by the School of Historical, Philosophical, and Religious Studies at Arizona State University, the National Endowment for the Humanities, and Arizona Humanities in 2015.

Writing is a private task, but authors benefit from the eyes and expertise of others who read, edit, recommend, and share. My paramount obligation is to my wife, Susan K. Arreola, PhD, who has lived with my various postcard projects for some two decades. She is both sounding board and editor, having read every word of *Postcards from the Sonora Border*. I owe her many times over for her generous commitment to reviewing my work. Across the country, friends from various quarters have shared my obsession for the postcard collecting habit, and discussions among them have sometimes lead to insights I might not have arrived at alone. I am, therefore, especially thankful to fellow Mexico postcard enthusiasts William F. Manger of Nachitoches, Louisiana, and Susan Toomey Frost of San Antonio, Texas, who have been steadfast colleagues as well as dear friends, sharing a mutual passion for postcards, *mescal y cerveza*, and our neighbor to the south.

As previously stated in *Postcards from the Río Bravo Border*, it needs repeating that postcard collecting would not be possible without the dedication and persistence of postcard dealers who work to secure material and make it available to collectors. So many have assisted my collecting over some two decades that I cannot possibly thank all of them here. I encourage readers to see the list of some of these important individuals published in the above referenced work.

Alas, two notes for readers. First, almost all of the images reproduced in *Postcards from the Sonora Border* are sourced from the Arreola Collection discussed in chapter 2. Where I know or can determine the original photographer for an image, attribution is given in the caption for each; however, many photo postcards are lacking information about the photographer, and in those instances no attribution is provided. When an image is not attributable to my collection, source information following each caption is given. Second, looking at historic postcards via the naked eye can be a challenging experience. Often, that experience is improved when a magnifying glass is at hand. As one astute reviewer of my previous postcard book advised, the very act of contemplating the details of these historic postcard images serves to transport a reader to landscapes and streetscapes of border towns past. I concur with that observation and hope your encounter with *Postcards from the Sonora Border* leads you to discover the many rich rewards of engaging the visual past.

Postcards from the Sonora Border

Introduction

The desire to see the past has been enhanced by changing technologies. In 2011, a time traveler visited Washington, DC, with a specific intent, to pose a self-photograph in the exact location where his father had posed for a snapshot more than half a century before. The photo was taken from inside the Jefferson Memorial looking out to the Washington Monument. The two photos were ultimately posted to historypin.com, a website purposed to assemble a large collection of historical photos cataloged by location and date.[1] Historypin.com encourages the public to upload images to the site, and it solicits local historical societies across the country to upload their visual archives. Historypin.com is not alone in this pursuit to join past to the present. In recent decades publishing enterprises such as Thunder Bay Press have created the Then and Now series for major cities of the world, where a photo of the past is matched to one of the same location in the present. Arcadia Publishing has become a national outlet for local authors to present photographic histories of hometowns across the country. The Ken Burns app, created by the documentary filmmaker, allows one to peruse photographs, video, and text tied to historic themes, and similar mobile devices and computer applications exist for other U.S. history sites.[2] History is not just a cataloging and interpretation of the past; it is being rediscovered and even marketed. How we possess the past and crusade for heritage is now the subject of serious intellectual discussion.[3]

The 2013 Joel and Ethan Coen film *Inside Llewyn Davis* revisited a New York that most thought was gone—Greenwich Village during the early 1960s. A *New York Times Magazine* writer asked "How do you exhume the New York of back then from under the archaeological gloss of New York, circa now?" To re-create a "visceral sense of authenticity" for 1960s New York, cinematographers were forced to use street scenes that are not part of Greenwich Village today but scattered across four boroughs of New York City. They employed long camera lens street shots to compress parts of the urban landscape that were too modern for the 1960s story. They installed signs and storefront awnings to existing buildings that shed those architectural ornaments years ago.[4] To spy an even earlier New York, the Mannahatta Project sponsored by the Wildlife Conservation Society has re-created a three-dimensional computer map of Manhattan as it appeared in 1609 when Henry Hudson first stepped on the island. The virtual exercise enables a visitor to fly above Manhattan, land wherever desired, and look around at the natural landscape that has long since been erased.[5]

Recreating a historical landscape is an everyday exercise in cinema, especially for a film charged to situate a story in a past. Yet this is a visual exercise rarely attempted by those who study the urban scene. Scholars can be adept in plumbing historical documents to reconstruct a past about a place, but few seem to have ventured into the realm of visual reconstruction.[6] After all, as is so often said by professional historians, the document is the bread and butter of their trade, and the meat of a historical revisiting rests in the textual materials of the past—records, diaries, and accounts. As a historical geographer, I concur that it would be difficult to create a viable story about a past place without the foundation of texts linked to that place's past. But does not the visual past have a role in any accurate revisiting of a place? More often than not, when visual material accompanies a historical narrative, it is supplemental, a secondary input meant to illustrate by example rather than as the source of analysis. Further, although historic imagery may be plentiful about a location, typically it is scattered in archives, and when retrieved a researcher may have one or two scenes of a place taken by separate photographers at varied times. These examples can have value as single installments, but they cannot easily re-create a place through time because the image density—the volume of images of a specific locale taken over time—is too low.[7]

Even where visual resources are robust and the technical ability to organize and present this imagery allows, it is often difficult to reconstruct scenes through time. The New York Public Library's website Old NYC: Mapping Historical Photos from the NYPL relies on a collection of some eighty thousand photographs to tell the visual history of the city.[8] It is an amazing project, but one recognizes quickly that the images that might be used to match one street corner or one block of buildings over time are hard to arrange. The difficulty is, in part, the intent of the photographer. Rarely did a photographer who captured a scene in 1910 return in 1920 or 1930 to rephotograph the same scene. Thus, an outcome of reliance on even a deep visual archive for a place can be problematic. While the repository enables many different views of a place such as New York City creating a tour de force of visual intensity, there are limitations because, in most instances, a photographer does not intentionally repeat images of the same place over generations, and there is no certainty that another photographer might return to the same site at a future date to replicate that view. This is not to say that such a massive archive of historic visual imagery cannot be used creatively to assemble a near cinematic vision of New York City through time; it certainly has that potential. However, visual archives this deep are rare for most places. How, then, can one visually study vernacular places where historic image density is limited?

There is one form of visual popular media that comes close to permitting a kind of serial imaging for a place—the lowly vintage historic postcard. Unlike historic imagery locked away in an archive, picture postcards have the unusual quality of accessibility—there were billions produced from the early 1900s through the 1950s—for places all across America and beyond. As a consequence, picture postcards, perhaps more than any other form of popular imagery, create redundancy of visual representation because commercial photographers who produced picture postcards frequently returned generation after generation to the same locations over many decades to capture views of a place, especially street scenes, landmarks, and tourist locations. Although it was never the intent of the postcard as a product, its visual redundancy has the potential to elevate image density for a location.

Postcards from the Sonora Border is primarily concerned with seeing how urban landscape (or townscape), the built environment of selected Mexican border cities, can be visualized through picture postcard imagery. The project relies chiefly on the Arreola Collection, my personal archive of more than seven thousand individual historic vintage postcards of Mexican border towns. In this exercise, the postcard as a medium of visual information is not simply illustration. Rather, the postcards—when chronologically assembled—become the narrative. The goal is to create visualizations of border town places in the past. The text is the connecting tissue that structures the narrative by elaborating the visual through supporting documentary evidence. In this way, I tell the story of border towns through selective arrangements of images that enable a distinctive viewing of these communities from the 1900s through the 1950s, the golden age of postcard photography for these places.

Postcards and Place

For several generations geographers and urban scholars have acknowledged visual inquiry that explores time and place, although not necessarily using postcard imagery to interpret places.[9] Recently, geographers especially have turned to postcard visualization to explore urban landscape.[10] Historic vintage postcards afford a kind of time travel to a multitude of places because postcards were so enormously popular in the past and so many of those places were captured by postcard photographers. In a sense, the picture postcard was the combined tweet and Instagram of an earlier era. It provided visual information on an accessible platform and was inexpensive to purchase and transmit. Through postcards, Americans came to appreciate the representation of main streets, commercial attractions, popular landmarks, institutions, and public spaces of towns and cities.[11]

Postcard collector scholars have argued this very point. In her book *As We Were: American Photographic Postcards, 1905–1930*, Rosamond Vaule demonstrates how photo postcards of the early twentieth century, especially those representing home, work, play, celebration, and transportation, depicted American town life. Vaule argues that historic postcards, particularly photographic ones, are compelling for the light they shed on mass culture and their ability to connect us with a past through the power of their imagery. "Valuable records of places, postcard views conveyed the status associated with travel and expressed pride in the local community. . . . Today, they have much to tell us, not only about how a particular place looked at a particular time but also about the period's social and cultural values."[12] Collectors Robert Bogdan and Todd Weseloh in their seminal book *Real Photo Postcard Guide: The People's Photography* chart how postcards of American towns followed a nomenclature of subjects.[13] They defined some sixteen categories for photographic postcards between 1900 and 1930 including, streets, businesses, municipal buildings, transportation, bridges, schools, churches, homes, recreational spaces, celebrations, disasters, work, and bird's-eye views. These representations of the vernacular were central to the purpose of postcard imagery to exhibit people and place. In this manner, geographer John Jakle suggests, "The postcard commodified the city as visual display" and "democratized the urban view, embracing as it did the more commonplace alongside the monumental."[14] It might be argued, then, that the picture postcard helped shape the way twentieth-century Americans viewed their domestic world before the advent of television.

The Mexican border, like American towns and cities, has been featured and chronicled through photographic postcards. The pioneering work in this area was *Border Fury: A Picture Postcard Record of Mexico's Revolution and U. S. War Preparedness, 1910–1917* by Paul Vanderwood and Frank Samponaro. Historians, not postcard collectors, Vanderwood and Samponaro imaginatively assessed how postcards came to visually represent the Mexican Revolution on America's southwestern border. The golden age of the picture postcard coincided with Mexico's Revolutionary events, so postcard photographers flocked to the border to record battles and associated activities. American soldiers stationed on the border, as well as those dispatched into Mexico in the famous punitive expedition to capture Francisco "Pancho" Villa, purchased and mailed thousands of the border postcards. Vanderwood and Samponaro speculate how postcards sent home by soldiers shaped American public opinion concerning Mexico's Revolution and Mexicans themselves.[15]

The photographic coverage of the Mexican Revolution, says historian David Dorado Romo, had all the makings of modernity in part because it attracted hordes of photographic correspondents for newspapers and magazines, itinerant portrait photographers, and postcard photographers.[16] Two photographers in particular were instrumental in producing postcards of the Mexican Revolution as well as views of towns and cities along the border: Robert Runyon and Walter Horne. Robert Runyon (1881–1968) may be the most celebrated and best-documented border postcard photographer.[17] Similar to many local photographers, Runyon operated a full-service photography studio in Brownsville, Texas, across the border from Matamoros, Tamaulipas. With the outbreak of the Mexican Revolution and battles that ensued in Matamoros, Runyon began to photograph military activities. His images sold to local and regional newspapers and ultimately became a subject for his postcard views. He produced postcards that became especially popular with the U.S. troops that were stationed in Brownsville during the Revolutionary episode, including scenes of Matamoros. Walter Horne (1883–1921), who worked out of El Paso, Texas, is another independent border postcard photographer. Horne's popular views included scenes of the Mexican Revolution in nearby Ciudad Juárez and other border towns as well as Mexican American life in El Paso. Horne's correspondence indicates that he produced some thirty thousand postcards in 1914 alone. The forty thousand troops stationed at Fort Bliss by 1916 were a primary market for Horne's Mexican Revolution postcards.[18]

Postcards are a historic visual medium well suited to an exercise that involves the reconstruction of past places, whether towns in America or on the Mexican border.

Thread

The *Postcards from the Sonora Border* project complements an earlier effort to achieve visual historical understanding for Mexican border towns along the Río Bravo/Rio Grande separating Texas from northeast Mexico.[19] In this project, however, the story shifts to the Mexican border communities along the boundary with Arizona, including Agua Prieta, Naco, Nogales, Sonoyta, and San Luis Río Colorado. Each of these towns—like all border towns—have historic themes in common as part of their twentieth-century experience, yet a town's historic past is specific to a particular location and the dynamic of peoples and events that unfolded there. For example, all Sonora border towns were affected by Prohibition, and, therefore, the history of each place includes an era of tourist flowering that emerged during the first two decades of the twentieth century. Nevertheless, the scale of cabaret entertainment stimulated by Prohibition was far deeper and more pronounced in Agua Prieta and Nogales than in Naco, Sonoyta, and San Luis Río Colorado. The reasons for this variation are diverse, but certainly access to the former locations from larger population centers in Arizona influenced the greater response to Prohibition in those towns than in the others. Similarly, both Agua Prieta and Naco experienced repeated sieges during the Mexican Revolution, and those historic events shaped town experiences in ways that were never part of Sonoyta and San Luis Río Colorado or, for that matter, Nogales, which had its own episodes of Mexican Revolutionary activity. Here again the explanation is varied. In the case of Agua Prieta and Naco, town proximity to robust mining and ranching hinterlands on each side of the boundary and the tariffs collected by railroad crossing traffic meant the customs houses in these towns were seen by contending military forces as treasure to be preserved or looted depending on the military—federal or Revolutionary—present; neither Sonoyta nor San Luis Río Colorado were viewed as strategic sites during the same period.

Postcards from the Sonora Border is organized in three parts. Part I, Places and Postcards, comprises two chapters that introduce Sonora border towns and postcards. Chapter 1 introduces the five border places and discusses their general and common historical geographies. As border towns, each was shaped by the creation of the international boundary and a distinct beginning, the influence of Prohibition and the Mexican Revolution, and post–World War II tourism. Chapter 2 explains the postcard as the critical visual medium of this project. Postcards were first popular in the United States in the early twentieth century, and the photographic postcard type is the format most used to visually capture and represent the Sonora border towns. This chapter also examines what is known about select border town postcard photographers and discusses the Arreola Collection of Sonora border town postcards and how they are used to narrate the stories of the towns.

Part II, Visualizing and Narrating Place, moves the reader to the individual stories of specific Sonora border towns. Within each chapter are sections that examine the geographic and historic setting of the border town followed by sections that assess how postcard imagery revealed the town visually over five decades. In addition, each chapter includes a vignette that exposes a special quality of the town as shown by postcard photography. Chapter 3 examines Agua Prieta; its founding and creation next door to Douglas, Arizona; its border-crossing and commercial and civic spaces; and separate vignettes on its cabaret and tourist curio store scene as well as Mexican Revolutionary battles fought there. Agua Prieta enjoyed a disproportionate popularity as a destination in what otherwise might have been thought to be an isolated corner of the border region. This was enabled in large part because Douglas was well connected by railroad and later state and U.S. highways to larger places west and east and because the Arizona border town was a copper-smelting center that generated substantial economic activity. Chapter 4 describes the tiny town of Naco across from Naco, Arizona, and downhill from Bisbee, Arizona. Founded as a railroad crossing site to serve the copper-mining hinterlands in Arizona and Sonora, Naco created, if modestly so, many of the typical Mexican border town landscape features apparent in all towns, and these, too, were subjects for the postcard photographer's lens. Naco, because of its strategic railroad position and proximity to the Mexican copper-mining town of Cananea, experienced more contestation during and even after the Mexican Revolution than perhaps any town on the entire Mexican border. Those battles and efforts to control the town by federal and Revolutionary armies are highlighted in a separate vignette.

Chapter 5 moves the story of the Sonora border towns to Nogales, the largest and without peer, the most economically important town along the Arizona-Sonora boundary. Founded as a crossing site that would eventually become a railroad and automobile gateway to the entire west coast of Mexico, Nogales served an extensive economic hinterland that stretched south to Hermosillo, the capital of Sonora state and north to Tucson, an early merchant center for mining activity in southern Arizona. This strategic location allowed the Mexican border town to develop an extraordinary merchant and cross border commerce that created multiple crossings to accommodate exchange, a condition not found in any of the other Sonoran border towns during the period of study. Further, Nogales cultivated a tourist economy unrivaled by any other Sonora border town, and that quality alone shaped Nogales in ways that were unique on the boundary. As a consequence, Nogales was a magnet for postcard photographers and easily became the most represented of all Sonora towns, not only those on the border. The high density of postcard images for Nogales allows not only an assessment of its visual townscape in many dimensions but also a gallery of themed images (for the border and fence line) beyond a vignette and the more common topical discussions.

Chapters 6 and 7 leap far west along the boundary to portray the Sonora border towns of the Gran Desierto, the desolate and isolated country of Sonoran desert that stretches from west of Nogales to the Colorado River. Sonoyta and San Luis Río Colorado are at once the oldest and the youngest of the Sonora border towns. Sonoyta, previously inhabited by native O'odham, was founded as an eighteenth-century Spanish Jesuit mission site. While the town never developed much demographically (historically, it has been the smallest of the Sonora border towns in this study), it proved a strategic oasis crossing and gateway linking travel corridors east and west, north and south. Early twentieth-century naturalists visiting the so-called Papaguería (land of the Papago, as the O'odham people were known to the Spanish and Mexican inhabitants) were some of the first non-Hispanic visitors to Sonoyta. Its American border town counterpart was Ajo, Arizona, a historic copper-mining center forty miles north of the boundary. On the Mexican side, Sonoyta was a transport hub connecting northern Sonora towns with the Colorado River settlements of San Luis Río Colorado as well as Mexicali west of the river in Baja California. In spite of its diminutive size, Sonoyta became a destination for postcard photographers once a road connected the border town to the Gulf of California fishing village of Puerto Peñasco.

Chapter 7 explores the westernmost Sonora border town of San Luis Río Colorado. Founded in the twentieth century and far from the heartland of Sonora, San Luis emerged as a major service center to the agricultural hinterlands across the border surrounding Yuma, Arizona, as well as the productive farming of the Colorado River delta in nearby Baja California. While the town developed traditional border town landscapes and activities including public spaces and residential districts, it was most often pictured in postcards by its active border crossing and surrounding commercial and tourist land uses only blocks from the gate. The vignette for San Luis Río Colorado is a visual recounting of some of the border town's most important streets and townscape features.

Part III, Sonora Border Revisited, concludes the book with chapter 8, a summary and assessment of the book's findings. The discussion underscores the five border towns, how and in what frequency they were represented by postcards over some five decades, what that panorama tells us in retrospect about this borderland, and how images from a popular lens shaped the identity of Sonora border towns.

Part I

Places and Postcards

1

Sonora Border Towns

Postcards from the Sonora Border investigates the popular visual history of five towns along the northern border of Sonora state in northwest Mexico. Sonora is the Mexican state immediately south and across the international boundary from Arizona, and it is bordered on the east and west by the Mexican states of Chihuahua and Baja California, respectively. The Sonora border towns included in this project are, from east to west, Agua Prieta, Naco, Nogales, Sonoyta, and San Luis Río Colorado (fig. 1.1). Two Sonora-Arizona border areas not examined in this project are Sásabe and Lochiel, and the explanations for these excluded areas are discussed below.

Sonora border towns are part of the larger system of north Mexican border settlements, and like all border towns they share common characteristics related to their geographic position on an international boundary.[1] On the other hand, Sonora's particular history has shaped these border towns in ways that differ from the border settlements of neighboring Chihuahua and Baja California. Further, Sonora's proximity to Arizona and the interactions of regional economies and political events further differentiate the Sonora border towns from others along the U.S.-Mexico divide. Agua Prieta, Naco, Nogales, Sonoyta, and San Luis Río Colorado share a number of historical circumstances resulting from the creation of the boundary, town founding, the Mexican Revolution and Prohibition, and post–World War II tourism.

Creating the Boundary

Before 1848 there was no boundary dividing Sonora from the United States; therefore, there were no border towns. The Mexican north including the American Southwest

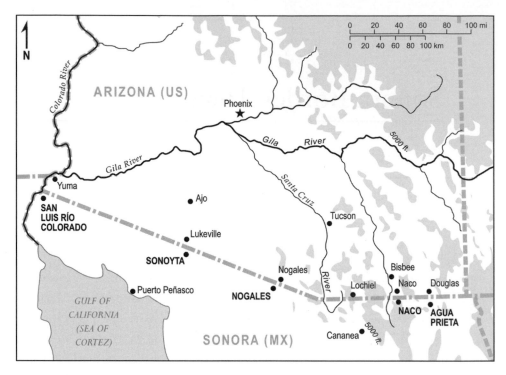

Figure 1.1. Sonora border towns and the Arizona-Sonora borderland. After Weisman and Dusard, *La frontera*, x–xi. Cartography by Barbara Trapido-Lurie.

was an inheritance from colonial New Spain, and what we today define geographically as central and southern Arizona was largely part of Sonora then.[2] Drawing the land boundary (as opposed to the river boundary along the Rio Grande/Río Bravo below El Paso/Ciudad Juárez) proved to be a protracted and contentious international issue between 1849 and 1856. The root of the controversy was the imprecise language of the 1848 Treaty of Guadalupe Hidalgo, which ended the war with Mexico. There were errors in the locations of key areas along the boundary north and west of El Paso in the document that was the geographical basis of the treaty, American James Disturnell's 1847 map.[3] The inaccuracies in Disturnell's map, discovered in the field by the first survey commissions representing Mexico and the United States, delayed acceptance of the treaty. It was not until Mexico and the United States agreed to a clarification of the Treaty of Guadalupe Hidalgo that the final land boundary was fixed. This amended treaty, approved by Mexico in 1853, was called El Tratado de la Mesilla (The Treaty of Mesilla) in Mexico because Mexico was forced to cede the Mesilla Valley in present-day New Mexico, and it was approved by the United States in 1854. It is known as the Gadsden Purchase (also Gadsden Treaty) in the United States after

James Gadsden, who was appointed minister to Mexico in order to incorporate more territory than the original Treaty of Guadalupe Hidalgo. U.S. interests were hoping to secure a lowland railroad corridor south of the Gila River, the northern border of Mexico set by the 1854 treaty (fig. 1.1). Mexico, which was ailing financially following the war with the United States, agreed to the 1854 treaty and further loss of territory for a compensatory sum of ten million dollars. The present boundary between New Mexico and Chihuahua and Arizona and Sonora is the amended border resulting from this treaty.[4] The peculiar boundary between Arizona and Sonora to the west of Nogales was a further result of this treaty. The acute angle resulted from a resolution in the final treaty that permitted Mexico to maintain land access between Sonora and Baja California. Therefore, the boundary line is a sharp turn from west of Nogales at meridian 111 degrees to a point above the mouth of the Colorado River (fig. 1.1).[5]

Almost four decades after the 1854 treaty, the United States and Mexico agreed to a resurvey of the land boundary.[6] Original demarcations were made using widely spaced stone markers, some of which had deteriorated over the years. The original survey established fifty-two monuments from the Rio Grande/Río Bravo to the Pacific Ocean, and the distances between markers varied from an eighth of a mile to ninety miles. As the areas adjoining the land border became more settled, disputes over the exact placement of the boundary line arose. Controversy was enhanced because some monuments became obscured by the growth of surrounding vegetation; others were mutilated by local residents, and some were dismantled for building material by new settlers. Further, the original monuments were not consistent in form and varied from simple rock cairns to cut stone (with and without mortar) to the occasional marble obelisk or cast-iron marker. As a consequence, an International Boundary Commission was organized between 1891 and 1896 with engineers from Mexico and the United States to resurvey the land border, relocate border monuments, and replace markers as needed. A large format atlas with maps of the terrain, settlement locations, and positions of monuments based on this resurvey was published in 1899.[7]

The resurvey of the land border increased the number of monuments from 52 to 258. The monuments were renumbered from east to west, so International Boundary Monument No. 1 begins west of the Rio Grande/Río Bravo near El Paso where Texas, Chihuahua, and New Mexico intersect, and No. 258 is south of San Diego facing Tijuana and overlooking the Pacific Ocean. The original monument No. 1 was the westernmost one at San Diego that is now No. 258. Since 1896, another eighteen monuments have been added. In order to circumvent renumbering older ones, both nations agreed to add letters to the original numbers so that several locations near town centers like Nogales-Nogales and Naco-Naco, for example, have letters A, B, C added to new monuments with the original numbers. There are now 276 monuments. Mostly, the

Figure 1.2. International monument, typical of the cast-iron forms positioned along the Sonora-Arizona boundary in the 1890s resurvey. The monument features the embossed emblem and text in Spanish on the side facing Mexico and an English-language version of the same plaque on the opposite side. Agua Prieta Curio Store, Agua Prieta, Sonora, 1900s.

monuments erected during the resurvey were six-foot-tall, cast-iron forms that tapered from a twelve-inch square base to a nine-inch pyramidal top (fig. 1.2). Some, like monument No. 1, are stone constructions, also square based with a pyramidal top but larger than the iron markers. The resurveyed monuments, whether cast iron or stone, are placed at intervals varying from one-tenth of a mile to about five miles. One hundred thirty-four monuments exist along the boundary separating Arizona from Sonora.[8]

Beginnings

Because Sonora was territory defined and settled under Spain and Mexico, the founding dates for the Sonora border towns vary significantly.[9] Tiny Sonoyta counted less than one thousand residents during most of the time period of this study (table 1.1). The settlement is, however, the only Sonora border town established during the colonial era, before the creation of the international boundary. Sonoyta was founded as a Spanish mission circa 1701, part of the system of desert communities organized by Jesuit Francisco Eusebio Kino. Its isolated location in the less populated western desert region of Sonora has limited its growth through the nineteenth and early twentieth centuries. No railroads were built to the small desert oasis, and only poor graded roads connected the town to the compass points. In the modern era, Sonoyta was chiefly a transit point between places beyond its horizon; south to the fishing village of Puerto Peñasco on the Gulf of California (called the Sea of Cortez in Mexico), north to the Arizona mining town at Ajo, east to Caborca on the Río Magdalena, and west across the treacherous Gran Desierto to San Luis Río Colorado (fig. 1.1).

Two Sonora border towns, Nogales and Agua Prieta, were founded at the close of the nineteenth century under Mexican authority. Although sparse settlement existed previously at the site, present Nogales dates, officially, to 1882, when it was organized

Table 1.1. Sonora border town populations, 1900–1960

Year/Town	Agua Prieta	Naco	Nogales	Sonoyta	San Luis Río Colorado
1900	—	519	2,738	—	—
1910	656	1,000[a]	3,177	100[b]	—
1920	3,236	1,267	13,475	483	175
1930	4,674	2,132	14,061	616	910
1940	4,106	—	13,866	—	558
1950	10,471	—	24,478	800[c]	4,079
1960[d]	15,339	2,864	37,657	1,925	28,545

[a] 1914 estimate, Ortigoza, *Ciento catorce días de sitio*, 10.

[b] 1910 estimate, Lumholtz, *New Trails in Mexico*, 176.

[c] 1950 estimate, Ives, "Sonoyta Oasis," 7.

[d] 1960 populations are for the city, not the *municipio*.

Source: Arreola and Curtis, *Mexican Border Cities*, table 2.2; Ganster and Lorey, *U.S.-Mexican Border into the Twenty-First Century*, table 6.2; Alarcón Cantú, *Estructura Urbana en Ciudades Fronterizas*, 87, 207.

as a gateway border town connecting northwest Mexico and the American Southwest by rail, the first to do so among the Sonora border towns. The founding of Nogales both extended a historic trade corridor and forged a new one. The old corridor that had linked western Sonora was a cart road from Guaymas on the Gulf of California to Tucson via an alignment following the Santa Cruz River that runs east of Nogales. When the iron rail straightened this trade route, its destination was not Tucson but Benson, Arizona, southeast of Tucson, where it merged into the main Southern Pacific trunk line connecting Los Angeles to El Paso and beyond. As a consequence, Nogales grew slowly in its first decades (table 1.1).

Agua Prieta (literally, dark water) was a small well-water stop along the border travel corridor to mid-nineteenth-century California during the gold rush era. In 1899, Agua Prieta was officially platted, and its position proximate to copper-mining settlements in Sonora and Arizona insured its gateway status, eventually leading to railroad connections among copper towns of the region. Despite the founding of Douglas, Arizona—a copper-smelting town—across the line in the early twentieth century, Agua Prieta stayed small, less than one thousand residents, during its early years (table 1.1).

The remaining two Sonora border towns, Naco and San Luis Río Colorado, emerged in the twentieth century. Naco, founded circa 1901, and similar to Agua Prieta, became a railroad gateway at the international boundary linking copper communities in Arizona and Sonora, Bisbee to the north and Cananea to the south, respectively. Like Sonoyta, early Naco was a point of transit location geographically with limited growth potential (table 1.1). San Luis Río Colorado, organized in 1917, was a military garrison site forged during the Mexican Revolution on the Colorado River frontier. Isolated west of the more settled parts of Sonora state by the Gran Desierto, San Luis Río Colorado was connected north to Yuma, Arizona, and by way of the early bridge over the Colorado River at that crossing to Mexicali, Baja California, to the west (fig. 1.1). The tiny western Sonora outpost perched on sand dunes above the nearby river would not experience substantial population growth until agricultural development of the Colorado River delta following World War II (table 1.1).

Revolution and Prohibition

A second historical situation, the Mexican Revolution (1910–20), differentially affected Sonora border towns. Sonora became a battleground circa 1913 following the assassination of Mexican president Francisco Madero and Sonora's refusal to accept his successor Victoriano Huerta.[10] Battles among federal and revolutionary armies developed in three of the five Sonora border towns, Nogales, Agua Prieta, and Naco. The erection of a border fence—the first on the boundary—between Nogales, Sonora, and Nogales, Arizona, was chiefly the result of violent outbreaks in the Mexican town. In Agua Prieta and Naco, federal forces excavated trenches and battlements surrounding the towns to withstand multiple attacks by revolutionary armies. These battles were fierce engagements involving machine guns, barbed wire, and airplane bombardments, warfare technologies equivalent to those used in Europe during World War I. Conflict was enhanced by the economic and military advantages at play in the Sonora-Arizona borderland, where access to American armaments through U.S. ports and strategies to command railroad networks and mining hinterlands raised the ante to compete for control of these border towns.[11] To the west, however, revolt and conflict were minimal, so Sonoyta and San Luis Río Colorado were largely quiet during this explosive decade in northern Mexico.

The Mexican Revolution launched a related historical process that continues to shape Sonoran border towns to the present—migration and population displacement.[12] The chaos of civil conflict in Mexico and the opportunity to seek refuge in the United States stimulated a push and pull of migrants, many of whom passed through the border towns (fig. 1.3). Between 1911 and 1920, nearly twenty-six thousand

Figure 1.3. The Mexican Revolution prompted Sonorans to immigrate to Arizona during the chaos and conflict generated by that civil war. This view shows a burro cart loaded with household goods being led across the border from Agua Prieta. The building in the background is the U.S. Customs house in Douglas, Arizona. Doubleday-Heuther, 1910s.

Mexican immigrants, some 12 percent of all legal Mexican immigrants, entered Arizona, mostly from Sonora.[13] Sonoran border towns benefited from this cross border flow in part because some migrants decided to reside in the towns. Not surprisingly, the populations of Nogales, Agua Prieta, and Naco boomed during this decade, multiplying many times over. In contrast, the western Sonora border towns, Sonoyta and San Luis Río Colorado, remained village-like during the revolution, counting fewer than five hundred residents each (table 1.1).

Perhaps no single historical period galvanized the image of the Mexican border to the American imagination as did the Prohibition era (1919–1933), and this was enhanced along the Arizona boundary because that state passed its own prohibition laws in 1915.[14] Beyond illegal domestic activities prompted by passage of the national Volstead Act, American producers and consumers of alcoholic beverages turned almost immediately to the shelter of Mexican towns where these practices remained legal. Sonora border towns, like all others along the boundary, developed adult entertainment venues including saloons, clubs, and casinos where gambling thrived. American businessmen created partnerships with Mexican investors during the 1920s so that almost every border town had its own cabaret scene. Lured by the availability of drink, Americans flocked to Sonora border towns, especially Agua Prieta, Naco, and Nogales, where entertainment activities were best developed. These border towns each witnessed population growth during the decade, in part a result of expanded economic activity and the demand for service-sector labor (table 1.1).

Both the repeal of Prohibition in the United States in 1933 and Mexico's national censure of casino gambling in 1935 slowed the flow of American visitors to Sonora border towns. Nevertheless, the door would not close completely as the years preceding and especially following World War II ushered another era of border town allure, tourism.

Postwar Tourism

The modern perception of Mexican border towns is a social construction tied to our imaginations about the nature of these places as tourist destinations.[15] The Sonora border towns, like others along the boundary, have been tourist destinations since the late nineteenth century, part of the discovery of Mexico by North American travelers. The magnetic attraction of drink, gambling, and other forms of entertainment during Prohibition certainly enhanced the border to American visitors. Following the lull of economic depression during the 1930s, tourism began to revive into the 1940s despite the years of world war. By all accounts, however, it was the explosion of the postwar era that shined the greatest light on Mexican border towns, stamping them into our experiences as places accessible and available for our enjoyment.

In late nineteenth and early twentieth-century world's fairs, Mexico shared America's fascination with the exotic, and this fed a condition of autoethnography.[16] Mexico participated officially in several early fairs in Atlanta (1895), Buffalo (1901), and St. Louis (1904), demonstrating its role as an emerging modern nation through its agricultural productivity. Beyond the economic displays at the fairs, Mexico also developed cultural exhibits such as the Mexican village theme in Atlanta, the streets of Mexico living museum in Buffalo, and the Aztecs and their artisan industries demonstration in St. Louis.[17] World fairs were increasingly seen as vehicles for advertising and mass consumption. This ideology materialized into the modern basis of tourism we know today.

During the 1920s, Mexico was discovered by a new tourist population, chiefly American artists and literati, sparking what has come to be called the Mexican Renaissance.[18] Travel to Mexico gained popularity in 1928 when the Mexican government decided to eliminate the need for a passport to visit the country; instead, visitors were required only to secure a tourist visa. In 1930, Mexico convened its first national congress of tourism and in that same year created the national commission of tourism.[19] The Mexican vogue during this period was foundational to the later development and promotion of Mexico as a tourist destination for a new consuming group, the North American middle class.

During the 1950s, tour agencies advertised travel to a romantic Mexico that included historic colonial towns such as Cuernavaca and Taxco and Pacific coast resorts such as Acapulco. For many North American tourists, however, border towns were closer. Besides, what excursionists really wanted was a chance to frolic in a Mexico of their imaginations, a place that served up a romantic streetscape, complete with artisan shops, crafts, and the illusion of being in Cuernavaca, Taxco, and Acapulco.[20]

Sonoran border towns gained popular appeal during the postwar tourism boom. Every town benefited from tourism, although Nogales gained disproportional attention because of its proximity to Arizona population centers, Tucson and Phoenix. A 1947 newspaper advertisement captures the colorful appeal of a visit to Nogales, Sonora (fig. 1.4). The town is "Just Across the Street from Nogales, Arizona"; there's "No Red Tape in Crossing the Border"; and you can "Explore Curio Shops," dine on "Fresh Sea Foods, Frog Legs, and Wild Game," dance "All Night," and take home "Alligator Purses," "Hand Made Cowboy Boots," "Silver Jewelry Made in Mexico," "French Perfumes," and the "Highest Quality Liquor." Most towns also featured seasonal bullfights in local arenas, a popular new attraction to Americans.[21]

Sonora border town populations witnessed their greatest growth in the decades of the postwar era. Nogales and Agua Prieta, the largest towns by 1960, roughly tripled

Figure 1.4. Sonora border towns such as Nogales were especially popular destinations in the post–World War II era. This 1947 advertisement captures some of the types of retail and entertainment attractions available to visitors. *Arizona Republic*, "Visit Mexico, Nogales, Sonora," February 9, 1947.

in size since 1940, Sonoyta more than doubled, and San Luis Río Colorado increased seven times its 1950 population during the decade (table 1.1). Tourism alone was not accountable for this growth because the 1950s especially witnessed extensive agricultural developments in the hinterlands of Nogales and San Luis Río Colorado, mining expansion in Sonora south of Agua Prieta and Naco, and intensified coastal fishing at Puerto Peñasco that benefited Sonoyta.[22] Nevertheless, tourism emerged as the pervasive common activity that joined all Sonora border towns by the end of the 1950s, an economic turning point that would continue to sustain these communities into the 1960s and 1970s.[23]

Excluded Border Areas

Two Sonora border locations are not considered in this project. Whereas each location has an oral history, there is a limited archival history that is accessible to the researcher. Critical to this project, there is no visual history through postcards. Sásabe is a small town west of Nogales and east of Sonoyta, across the boundary from present Sásabe, Arizona, at the southern end of the Altar Valley. Sásabe, Sonora, was founded as a small Mexican customs checkpoint several miles south of the international boundary circa 1880. It appeared on a border monuments resurvey map in 1899.[24] The site was connected by a primitive road to the Sonora town of Altar to the south. By the twentieth century, a village formed around the customs office as the crossing enabled cattle exports from Sonora to Arizona as well as contraband shipments during Prohibition.[25] Sásabe never developed a tourist economy, and thus postcard images of the place during the period of this study are nonexistent.

A second border location was the historic crossing at Lochiel, Arizona, east of the Nogales border towns and west of the Nacos. Lochiel, Arizona, like Sásabe, Sonora, was the early site of a customs house positioned to monitor transborder traffic from Sonora across the boundary through the U.S. port before the founding of Nogales (fig. 1.1). Lochiel, first known as La Noria (the well), appears on the 1899 border monuments resurvey map.[26] Sometime in the twentieth century, a Mexican customs house—previously located south of the boundary at Santa Cruz, Sonora—was positioned across the line from Lochiel, and that location was also known as La Noria. Because there was never a Mexican border town at this crossing and the outpost customs house was anything but a tourist location, postcard images are rare, if they exist at all, for the time period of this project.

2
Postcards

I n 1948 renowned photographer and collector of postcards Walker Evans penned a short essay in the popular American business magazine *Fortune*, where he was the photo editor. It was, on the one hand, a lament of sorts for the unrecognized value of a simple popular commodity—the picture postcard—and on the other hand, a tribute to the utility of historic imagery, a quality of visual documentation that Evans's own photographic work would herald years later.

> The mood is quiet, innocent, and honest beyond words. This, faithfully, is the way East Main Street looked on a midweek summer afternoon. This is how the county courthouse rose from the pavement in sharp, endearing ugliness. These, precisely, are the downtown telegraph poles fretting the sky, looped and threaded from High Street to the depot and back again, humming of deaths and transactions. . . . What has become of the frank, five-a-nickel postcards that fixed the images of all these things? . . . They are still around. Tens of thousands of them lie in the dust of attics and junk shops; here and there, files of good ones are carefully ranged in libraries, museums, and in the homes of serious private collectors.[1]

In the essay, Evans reproduced several main street view postcards from his collection, including ones showing Salt Lake City and New Haven. More so than perhaps any American artist, Walker Evans freely admits that the humble postcard and its prosaic view of the American scene inspired his photographic art. Evans's passion for postcards even led him to develop a slide show using his postcard images to entertain friends at his New York apartment during the 1950s.[2]

Postcards are the primary historic source employed in the analysis of Sonora border towns as they were represented from the 1900s to the 1950s. In this chapter, I tell, in necessarily abbreviated fashion, the story of the postcard as a visual artifact.

I explore the popularity of postcards and the influence of that popularity in shaping our view of towns and cities. I discuss the varied formats of postcard production with special emphasis on photographic postcards that are the principal postcard type used to reveal the Sonora border towns. Following this general introduction is a discussion of Sonora border town postcard photographers. Who were the authors of these many and varied images, and what photographers worked in which Sonora border towns? Selected case studies of photographers for particular towns present a local context for understanding the photographic postcard form as it emerged in and came to represent Sonora border places. I conclude the chapter with a detailed assessment of the Arreola Collection of Sonora border town postcards, the categories of imagery selected for analysis in this project, and the themes of representation that enable a historic visualization of the towns.

Postcards and Their Popularity

The origins of the postcard and its emergence as a pictorial form is a lengthy story that has been chronicled in many sources.[3] It has been proposed and is now generally accepted that the first postal cards may have been created in Austria to simplify the messages common to letter writing and to reduce the cost of mailing a letter in the second half of the nineteenth century.[4]

In the Sonora border towns project, it is the visual nature of the postcard view as a representation that is of particular value. That idea may well have started in Switzerland during the 1890s, where resorts printed views that covered the face or recto of the postcard; the verso or back of the card was reserved exclusively for the mailing address. In Germany, where advanced lithography permitted exact color separation, printers began to publish postcards with views of towns accompanied by the phrase *gruss aus*, or "greetings from."[5] In the United States, the post office permitted private postal card printing, so-called private mailing cards. Circa 1895, publishers were printing sets of postal cards with views of American cities on the recto. On May 19, 1898, Congress authorized the Private Mailing Card Act, which enabled private postal cards to be mailed at the rate of one cent; previously, government issued mailing cards cost two cents to mail.[6] By the early twentieth century, picture postcards with views of towns and cities had become a recognized and popular postal format in Europe, America, and the world.

Slight changes in the formatting of postal cards in the early twentieth century increased their popularity. Before 1907, postal card messages in the United States were restricted to the front of the card because the back was strictly assigned for the mailing address. This is why so many early cards created small margins on the recto below or alongside of the view where a short message might be penned. In 1907, the verso was modified to the so-called divided back, where half of the backside accommodated the address and half allowed space for a longer message, permitting postal cards to function as short letters according to the desires of the sender. The results created a boom in the popularity of sending and collecting postal cards. For example, Coney Island, an early recreational playground for New Yorkers, is said to have witnessed the mailing of 175,000 postal cards from its property in only four days of September 1906.[7] By 1909, close to one billion postal cards were mailed in the United States, and during the first decade of the twentieth century, one postal card company alone was producing three million cards a day.[8] A postal card craze gripped the nation.

In popular writing and reporting during this era, one author warned about "postal carditis," one of a series of collecting maladies wreaking havoc among populations across the country.

> From small beginnings the pasteboard souvenir industry has fattened upon epistolary sloth and collecting manias until there are to-day 150,000 varieties of picture postal cards. Bookstores which formerly did a thriving trade in literature are now devoted almost entirely to their sale. There were in Atlantic City last season ten establishments where nothing else was sold, and Chicago, Boston, Pittsburg and New York have emporiums where postals constitute the entire stock. . . . These wares may be seen in New York on practically every street corner and most of the drug stores, cigar stores, hotels, barber shops and department store gridirons are interested in their sale. Ten large factories are working overtime in this country to supply the demand and many smaller ones are selling their output as fast as it is produced.[9]

Another author called the picture postal card "pernicious" because it was a poor substitute for a full-fledged letter. Having received a picture postal card from a friend traveling in Europe, the author recounts his disappointment on finding the view card in his mailbox.

> With itching fingers I turned the lock; and there, displayed to my disappointed gaze, was—a picture post card! Yes, a printed picture of the Acropolis—did not I have such tame *simulacra* already by the score?—and underneath, in the narrow margin left by the egregious print, my friend's 'Greetings' and his signature . . . time was when this thing could not have been. Time was, before this futile complexity of life which we call Progress had got hold upon us, . . . Time was, when a journey was an epoch and a letter an experience. Time was, when no flying picture post cards ticked off the successive stops of a hasty "run" abroad.[10]

In localities across the nation, post offices were swamped by the volume of postal card mailings, and at one famed East Coast resort, a riot was narrowly averted when the post office ran out of one-cent stamps "to meet the demand of the victims of card-itis postale."[11]

Postcard production flourished in the United States during the first two decades of the twentieth century. Until World War I, Germany was the center of postal card manufacture for American consumption. Local photographers would snap views of towns and cities, and a local drugstore or other retail establishment often acted as the publisher, ordering cards through an American agent of a German printer. The photographs of local scenes in small towns and cities across America were sent to Germany, where illustrators using color lithography would transform the black-and-white photo image into an exquisite printed postcard that was often so detailed that it appeared to be a color photograph. Some 75 percent of American postcards produced before 1914 were made in Germany and shipped from Hamburg to Hoboken, New Jersey, on the Hamburg-Amerika Line.[12] After World War I, American companies came to dominate postcard production in the United States, and the highest quality printed cards were manufactured and vended by the Detroit Publishing Company and a handful of others. Detroit Publishing, for example, is thought to have produced greater than seventeen thousand separate postcards that were numbered in series. The company made use of the "PhotoChrom/Phostint Process" invented in Switzerland. This lithographic technique developed photographic halftone copies on stone and was capable of using nine or ten colors with each printing, thereby giving each card an accuracy of color that was unparalleled among American manufactures.[13]

View postcards, cards that show a local scene, have been at the core of postcard publishing. In the study of postcards—regardless of the scale of inquiry by country, state, or town—the local reigns supreme.[14] Main street representations of towns and cities across the United States, in particular, were an early favorite.[15] Before 1920, newspapers and magazines did not print photographs, and cameras were quite specialized—not a popular item the way we imagine them today. A picture postcard of a town or city scene was, accordingly, an extraordinary item. View postcards thereby helped shape the American urban and town imaginary, and scholars today recognize this formative influence.[16]

Photographic Postcard Format

The picture postcards used in the Sonora border town project chiefly are photographic postcards produced in Mexico and the United States between the 1900s and 1950s. Unlike printed postcards (discussed above) that are mechanically drawn on plates or screens based on a photograph, a real photo postcard is made from a negative on chemically sensitive paper and is a true photograph. The photographic postcard was especially popular in America between 1900 and 1930, and it continued to be produced into the 1950s in both the United States and Mexico.[17]

Real photo postcards were printed on postcard-size developing paper marketed by photographic companies circa 1902. Companies also made special format cameras that produced a postcard-size negative (3.25 × 5.5 inches). The earliest of these devices was the Kodak model 3A folding pocket camera, introduced in 1903, which remained popular through 1927 in a number of versions. A 1918 model 3A is described as costing approximately twenty dollars including a roll of film and a package of developing postcard paper. Armed with this simple ensemble of items, an amateur postcard photographer could then have film developed locally by a photographic company in small batches or by a larger company for greater quantities. Large companies used specialized machines that could mass-produce postcards at a rate of eighteen hundred prints per hour.[18]

The photo postcard is a particularly good format to assess the past landscape of a town or city. Unlike some printed postcards where the image is modified through the mechanical printing process, a photo postcard is an accurate rendering of a scene; the camera's eye generally captures what is seen in high fidelity. Of course, much depends on the talent of the photographer who frames, composes, and sets exposure as a camera permits. Unfortunately, attribution is problematic for many real photo postcards. In some cases this may have been the result in part because of the popularity of postcard photography in the early twentieth century and its eager acceptance by amateurs who never intended to become professional photographers and simply grasped the opportunity as a onetime business venture. This was made possible when companies such as Kodak developed technologies that were relatively easy to use. Unlike studio photographers (discussed below), who often were vested in a community through their full-service enterprise, amateurs probably dabbled in the activity for as long as it was fashionable and moved on to another business when postcard popularity declined with the Great Depression.

To understand the utility of a real photo postcard as a document and the nature of postcard photography, consider figure 2.1 below, a photo postcard of the main street, Avenida 3 (later known as Av. Pan Americana), in Agua Prieta. The view is looking northwest along the east side of the street about two blocks south of the international boundary. The image of one side of the street is focused on the façades of the Silver Dollar Bar and Café, three flat-roof adobe buildings flush to the street, the unpainted clapboard, pitched-roof Popular Café, and other buildings lining the street beyond north toward the border crossing. The painted names of the Silver Dollar buildings are visible to the naked eye, and using magnification, one can discern the names of other establishments up the street. Above street level are a series of telephone poles and the wires connecting them: even the glass resisters along the cross bars of the poles are visible. Individuals and early twentieth-century automobiles can be seen,

Figure 2.1. Avenida 3, Agua Prieta, 1920s. Real photo postcards capture a level of visual detail that is unmatched by most printed postcards. This view reveals building façades and signage, individuals, automobiles, and infrastructure along a block of the border town's main street.

Figure 2.2. Verso (back) of photo postcard shown in figure 2.1. Photo postcards can be dated by the printed clues on the back, such as the division of the card into correspondence and address and the style and type of developing paper signaled by the stamp box.

and it appears that the street is unpaved. The date for the scene is not given, but there are typically two ways to date real photo postcards. The easiest method is to interpret the scene by dating automobiles, although sometimes knowledge about building styles can prove useful, and even dress fashion can be revealing to the well-trained eye. The second way to date photo postcards is by the developing paper, including the styles of the printing on the verso and the information around the stamp box. Figure 2.2 shows a detail of the verso of figure 2.1. First, the card displays a divided back, so it is 1907 or later (see discussion above). The typeface used to spell out POST CARD and the letter font and position of the words CORRESPONDENCE ADDRESS can also be clues because styles varied and can be dated. Next, the name and symbols around the stamp box are revealing about the postcard date because AZO is the type of developing paper made by Kodak, and small squares at the corners of the stamp box signal a particular period of AZO paper production. The code described above can be identified as AZO paper, first produced between 1923 and 1926, and made through the 1930s.[19] Further, the cars shown on the recto of this photo postcard are Model T's produced in the 1920s, and the Silver Dollar Bar and Café operated in Agua Prieta during Prohibition. Given all of these clues, it is safe to conclude that the image is likely from the 1920s.

Regardless of the abundance of information discernible from this photo postcard, one still does not know the name of the photographer because there is no attribution on the recto or verso of the card. What we can infer, however, is that this image is part of a series of views taken by the photographer because #42 is visible to the left of the caption on the front of the postcard. For an advanced postcard collector, this is an important clue because one might have as part of a collection other photo postcards in this series for the town with separate numbers showing the same style of caption and type font. In the Arreola Collection, I can isolate eleven other photo postcards from my Agua Prieta file that appear to be numbered and letter captioned in this same style.[20] Because these numbered postcards are all street scenes and the stamp boxes on all cards show AZO with squares in the corners, it is likely that the same photographer made all the images during the 1920s. The next step to arrive at who that photographer might have been is to research city directories and advertising about studio photographers in Agua Prieta, Douglas, and perhaps beyond.

Typically, a printed postcard will not have the same detail as a photo postcard. Because printed postcards are halftones, the surface of the image is not continuous as in a photographic postcard; rather, it is composed of a dot matrix pattern that blurs when enlarged or magnified. While a printed postcard starts as a photograph, it is sent to a commercial printer who makes a printing plate from the photo using any number of mechanical processes. The printer then makes sheets of printed postcards that are cut, packaged, and returned to the publisher of the card. The publisher is not usually the photographer; rather, it is the individual who orders the postcards, more often than not a local retailer who operates a drugstore or other establishment where the cards might be sold. Because printers typically manufactured large quantities (five hundred to a thousand) on a single order and reordering was possible, the cost of a printed postcard was considerably less than that of a photo postcard.[21] A print postcard can have documentary utility, but its limitations of mechanical reproduction can compromise a researcher's ability to read the image for important social and cultural information.

Sonora Border Town Postcard Photographers

Two types of photographers operated between the 1900s and 1950s to produce images that would ultimately be made into real photo postcards of the Sonora border towns. Given the large number of unattributed photographic postcards in the Arreola Collection, it is safe to suggest that many postcards were likely made by amateurs rather than professional photographers. Documentation about these photographers is sketchy, and many of these individuals appear to be lost to history not only because they failed to attribute their work but also because they did not maintain records of their production. On the other hand, photographers who signed their postcards were usually established professional studio photographers in a border town whether Mexican or American. Studio photographers, whose bread and butter work was typically portraiture, took advantage of the popularity of postcards to supplement their income by snapping views of local scenes and reproducing the postcards themselves in small batches. W. Roberts, for example, who created postcards of Nogales and who operated a studio in Hermosillo, Sonora, advertised that he produced "artisticas tarjetas postales."[22] Other photographers would send negatives to larger companies that would reproduce the photos as postcards and return to the photographer who would then vend locally.

Table 2.1 illustrates the twenty-two photographers and photographic postcard companies who produced photo postcards for the Sonora border towns between the 1900s and the 1950s based on the cards in the Arreola Collection. More photographers made photo postcards for Nogales and Agua Prieta—the largest and most popular Sonora border tourist towns—but even in these towns, particular photographers appear to have worked exclusively in those places, especially Nogales; Lohn, P. M. A. (aka Francisco Saenz Aguilar), R. R. de la F., and Roberts. In Sonoyta and San Luis Río Colorado, two independent photographers—Pacheco and Haro, respectively—produced photographic postcards for the towns. Some photographers, like Osbon, worked in two towns, Agua Prieta and Naco. In one instance, a postcard photographer known for his images of another part of the Mexican border—Walter Horne (El Paso and Ciudad Juárez)—made the occasional photo postcard in a Sonora border town.[23] Other photographers, such as Cline, Cook, and Frasher, operated independent studios in Chattanooga, Tennessee; Milwaukee, Wisconsin; and Pomona, California, respectively, yet they are known to have produced postcards for many places in the western United States, including the Mexican border.[24] Finally, one enterprise, La Compañía México Fotográfico, produced photo postcards illustrating all Sonora border towns because it was a national postcard company that made and distributed postcards across Mexico.

Table 2.1. Sonora border town postcard photographers and companies, 1900s–1950s

Photographer	Agua Prieta	Naco	Nogales	Sonoyta	San Luis Río Colorado
Beffell	X				
W. M. Cline			X		
L. L. Cook		X	X		
Díaz	X				
Doubleday	X				
Frasher	X		X		
Haro Foto					X
W. H. Horne			X		
Irwin	X				
Jorschke	X				
Lohn			X		
México Fotográfico	X	X	X	X	X
Naka			X		
C. Osbon	X	X			
J. Pacheco				X	
P. M. A. (aka Saenz Aguilar)			X		
R. R. de la F. /R. R. F			X		
Roberts Foto			X		
Rochin y Méndez			X		
Stoveken	X				
Western Ways			X		
Wood			X		

Note: Includes photographers who produced photo postcards not illustrated or discussed in the text but whose photographic postcards are in the Arreola Collection.

Source: Arreola Collection.

Researching information about postcard photographers for individual towns can be a challenging project. City directories, when available for larger towns, are an important source because they list businesses and often times the proprietor of an establishment. To learn about postcard photographers who might have photographed in Agua Prieta, a survey of city directories for Douglas, Arizona, from 1904 through 1959 was conducted.[25] For the fifty-five year period, eighteen of the surveyed photographers were listed operating in Douglas, and five were resident in Agua Prieta. Table 2.1 gives the names of nine postcard photographers identified by name on postcards of Agua Prieta in the Arreola Collection. Stovekin and Jorshke appear in directories for 1912 and 1915, yet the Arreola Collection has only two postcards from these photographers. Similarly, Irwin is given in directories as the operator of a studio in Douglas from 1913 through 1942, but the Arreola Collection includes only a couple of postcards signed by Irwin. Díaz is given as a photographer in Agua Prieta in 1940, and Beffel operated a studio in Douglas from 1948 to 1950, yet the Arreola Collection has only two or three postcards from these photographers. On the other hand, Doubleday and Osbon, who each photographed extensively in Agua Prieta, never appear by name in the Douglas city directories, suggesting they did not operate studios there and most likely came to Douglas and Agua Prieta for short periods to make photo postcard images. In fact, most all of the Doubleday and Osbon photo postcards in the Arreola Collection were produced in the first two decades of the twentieth century and chiefly capture the revolutionary events of that era. The findings from this survey suggest that resident photographers were not necessarily postcard photographers and that portraiture was probably the main business of most who were listed by this profession. Further, more than a dozen postcards of Agua Prieta in the Arreola Collection are unattributed by name of photographer, so it remains even more difficult to assess who those postcard photographers may have been (e.g., fig. 2.1).

Nevertheless, some postcard photographers for the Sonora border towns are known in large part because they signed and often numbered their photo postcards. These photographers also produced many images for selected towns, and their biographies can be researched through various means.

Individual Postcard Photographers and a Photographic Postcard Company

Three individual photographers and one company are discussed to illustrate how photo postcard photographers documented views of the Sonora border towns. The individual photographers include Calvin C. Osbon, who worked in Agua Prieta and

Naco; Albert W. Lohn, who operated a studio and produced dozens of images of Nogales; and Burton Frasher, who made photo postcards of Agua Prieta and Nogales. México Fotográfico is profiled because it was the most important company to produce photographic postcards of Sonora border towns.

Calvin C. Osbon (1849–1924) was a popular postcard photographer who became known especially for his photo postcards of the Mexican Revolution in Agua Prieta and Naco. Indiana born, Osbon arrived in Tucson, Arizona, where he opened a photo studio in 1890. Between 1910 and 1914, Osbon moved about, residing for a short time in California and returning to Arizona to locate in Casa Grande. Osbon was listed as a resident of Douglas in 1923, and he died there in 1924.[26]

The Arreola Collection contains thirty-five Osbon photo postcards for Agua Prieta and two for Naco. Most of Osbon's postcards capture scenes related to the Revolutionary battles fought in Agua Prieta in the 1910s. Osbon developed a distinctive style of imagery with elaborate captions, and often the photo postcards were dated and signed Cal.Osbon, C.Osbon, and, on occasion, C.O. Photos were typically staged and sometimes included humorous captions. One of his more famous photo postcards, number 163 from February 1916, shows four local girls posed in front of a building in Agua Prieta that was hit by four separate cannon shells when Pancho Villa's army tried to secure the Sonora border town on November 2, 1915 (fig. 2.3). Each girl is seen pointing at a particular hole in the façade of the store, and in the caption there is a plea for peace now that the battle is over. Another famous Osbon photo postcard is number 662, a staged view of an American soldier standing on the U.S. side of a border monument in Douglas, Arizona, and a donkey standing on the opposite side of the monument in Agua Prieta. The caption reads, "U.S. soldier with his ass in Mexico."[27]

Some of Osbon's other Mexican Revolution photos in Agua Prieta show Mexican soldiers staged near the railroad depot, panorama views of the town taken on the eve of a battle, and a set of images depicting the town's trenches, constructed to defend against Villa's army. These latter posed photos are especially revealing as they show women washing and preparing meals for the soldiers in the trenches (see chap. 3). Beyond battle scenes, Osbon composed various street scenes and views of local landmarks. Some of my most prized Osbon photo postcards of Agua Prieta show exterior cabaret scenes during early Prohibition (see chap. 3).

Albert W. Lohn (1867–1956) was the premier studio photographer in early twentieth-century Nogales. He maintained a photo store and studio on Morley Street in Nogales, Arizona, only a block from the international border. From 1915 to 1918, Lohn advertised in the local newspaper that his shop carried a complete line of Kodak cameras and accessories and that he specialized in photographic developing.[28]

Figure 2.3. Agua Prieta after the battle of November 2, 1915. Photographer Cal Osbon frequently attached long and sometimes humorous captions to his photo postcards. Osbon, 1916.

Lohn was born in 1867 in Chicago, Illinois, the son of German immigrant parents. In 1887, Lohn moved to Los Angeles, where he formed a partnership in a photographic company with Charles C. Pierce, who became renowned for his visual documentation of Southern California.[29] In the next few years, Lohn opened his own studios, first in Los Angeles and then in Ventura, California, where he developed a successful photographic business.

In 1898, Lohn was contracted to make photographs for an article about Ensenada, Baja California, published in the popular magazine *Land of Sunshine*, edited by Charles F. Lummis. In 1901, Lohn moved to Culiacán, Sinaloa, Mexico. There he started his Mexican photography business, producing photographic and printed postcards of towns in Sinaloa, especially Culiacán. Lohn fled Mexico in 1912 following the outbreak of the Mexican Revolution, returned to the United States, and took up residence in Nogales circa 1913.[30]

In the next decade, Lohn became a recognized professional photographer in the border community, creating images of towns on both sides of the international boundary. In 1918, he purchased the Newman Photo studio at 311 Morley Avenue in Nogales, Arizona, and renamed it Albert W. Lohn Photo Supplies (fig. 2.4).[31] Lohn was hired by the Nogales Chamber of Commerce to produce photos, both studio portraits and exterior views, for a 1919 promotional pamphlet, and he was listed and pictured in the publication as A. W. Lohn, *fotógrafo oficial*.[32]

The Arreola Collection includes forty-three photo postcards of Nogales signed by or attributed to A. W. Lohn. The images range across various subjects, from street scenes and crossing gates to panorama views of the two border towns, especially the borderline. On a very few of Lohn's photo postcards, the verso of the card was ink stamped with his name and studio (fig. 2.5). More often than not, however, Lohn only

Figure 2.4. A. W. Lohn photography supply store and studio on Morley Avenue in Nogales, Arizona, was one city block from the international boundary and Nogales, Sonora. Courtesy Arizona Historical Society, Tucson #61964.

signed his name to the recto of the photo card, typically Lohn Fot. or Lohn Photo (fig. 2.6). Although Lohn used a numbering system for his photo postcards, many of his views found their way into the printed postcards of other publishers without attribution. Figure 2.7 is a printed postcard published by A. O. Boeres Company of Los Angeles and Phoenix, a 1920s printing of Lohn's "Aduana de Nogales" (customs house of Nogales, Sonora) number 21 (fig. 2.6). Whether Lohn sold the right to reproduce his image to this company is not known, but pirating of postcard images was common in the first two decades of the twentieth century. The Arreola Collection includes some two dozen printed postcards of Nogales, Sonora, that are known or likely to be originally A. W. Lohn photographic postcards.[33]

Lohn stopped producing postcards of Nogales during the Great Depression. He apparently continued to operate his studio photography and supply business in Nogales until his death in 1956.

Whereas postcard photographers Osbon and Lohn concentrated on one or two Sonora border towns, Burton Frasher (1888–1955) of Pomona, California, was a prolific postcard photographer who ranged across much of the southwestern United States and the Mexican border to capture roadside and town scenes. From the 1920s through the 1940s, Frasher capitalized on the growing popularity of the American desire to travel by automobile. He smartly realized that postcards of the American

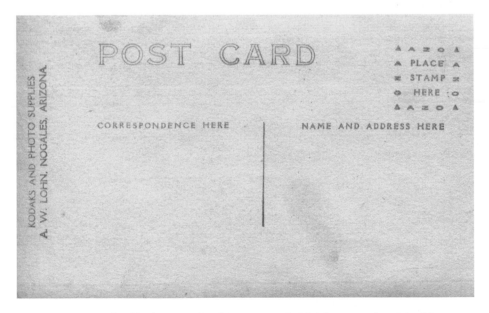

Figure 2.5. Verso (back) of A. W. Lohn photo postcard with ink stamp advertising his Kodak photo supplies store in Nogales, Arizona. Lohn would typically sign his name to the recto (front) of his photo postcards and only rarely ink stamp the back.

Figure 2.6. Lohn photo postcard number 21 of the customs house (*aduana*) along the railroad track in Nogales, Sonora. Lohn 21, 1910s.

MEXICAN CUSTOM HOUSE (ADUANA),   NOGALES, SONORA, MEXICO

Figure 2.7. Printed black-and-white postcard published by A. O. Boeres Company from a 1910s Lohn photo postcard (fig. 2.6). Many of Lohn's Nogales photo postcards were reprinted without attribution to the photographer. A. O. Boeres, 1920s.

roadside and views of towns and cities would be popular attractions to complement the explosive embrace of travel by personal car. By the 1930s, "Frashers Fotos" was one of the largest photographic postcard publishing businesses in the nation. In 1948 alone, more than 3.5 million Frashers Fotos postcards were sold in the United States.[34]

Burton Frasher (pronounced Frasier) was born in Aurora, Colorado, in 1888, the same year George Eastman coined the word *Kodak* and began to market his cameras to the world. Frasher started his commercial photography business in California in 1914 and moved to Pomona, California, in 1921, where he established his studio.[35] Photographers were beginning to use the popular Graflex single-lens reflex camera, but Frasher persisted in the use of a tripod-mounted view camera to compose most of his photo postcard views. This enabled Frasher to use low ASA-rated, slow-speed film that preserved a lengthy tonal range and very fine grain exposure in his photographs. Unlike many commercial postcard companies that produced large volumes in each printing, Frasher preferred the production of small lots to achieve clarity in the quality of his images. The result was often a superior photographic print, rich in detail, permitting an enhanced level of readable information in the postcard.[36]

The Arreola Collection includes fifteen real photo postcards of Nogales, Sonora, made by Frashers Fotos, most of the views taken in the 1930s. Burton Frasher was known to seek out the unusual view for his photo postcards, and in Nogales, he typically would venture off the beaten path to capture an unusual scene. The postcard in figure 2.8, titled "Birdseye View of Nogales, Sonora," shows a group of neighborhood boys stopped on a footpath in one of the west side *colonias*, hinged on the hillside above the commercial and residential center of the town.

La Compañía México Fotográfico was the largest photographic postcard production company in Mexico between 1925 and 1967. México Fotográfico became recognized by its distinctive "MF" logo and by its exclusive production of photographic postcards during this period. La Compañía operated as a clearinghouse for independent photographers called *agentes viajeros* (traveling agents). These freelance photographers were hired in towns and cities all across Mexico to send photographs to the company headquarters in Mexico City, where the images would be formatted to photo postcards and returned in batches to locations where the images were made to sell as postcards. This enterprise was enormously successful in part because the Mexican national government promoted the tourism industry during the period when México Fotográfico operated.[37]

More photographic postcards made by México Fotográfico are included in the Arreola Collection than any single postcard photographer or company: some 54 percent of the Nogales photo postcards in the collection are attributed to MF. While La Compañía produced photo cards for tourist areas such as the Mexican border, it also produced

Figure 2.8. Burton Frasher sometimes photographed atypical scenes not always captured by more conventional postcard photographers. This image was one of a series snapped in a hillside residential neighborhood on the west side of Nogales, Sonora. Frashers Fotos, 1937.

tens of thousands of postcards for places everywhere in Mexico. Collecting and sending MF photo postcards was not simply for American tourists; rather, the largest market for the company's postcards was Mexicans who traveled throughout their homeland.

Sonora Border Town Postcard Collection

The Arreola Collection includes postcards, photographs, and related ephemera for all the north Mexican border towns. The Sonora border town postcard collection alone includes some 1,041 individual cards, and that sum amounts to perhaps 15 percent of the total Mexican border town postcard collection. About 716—nearly 70 percent—of the Sonora border town postcards are photo postcards (table 2.2). The greater number of photo postcards over printed cards may be explained in part by the late development of postcards for places along the border compared with the abundance of printed cards—so-called Golden Age postcards from the 1900s to the 1910s—produced earlier for places in the interior of Mexico.[38] In addition, México Fotográfico (discussed above), a premier postcard producer of the twentieth century, printed and distributed exclusively photographic postcards from the 1920s through the 1950s, the era that witnessed the most significant growth among the Sonora Mexico border towns.

Table 2.2. Sonora border town postcards in the Arreola Collection

	Postcards	Photo postcards	Percent photo postcards
Agua Prieta	266	205	77
Naco	63	60	95
Nogales	638	403	63
Sonoyta	27	18	67
San Luis Río Colorado	85	30	35
Total	1,041	716	69

Among individual Sonora border towns, the larger towns were major tourist attractions, and those places appealed to more postcard photographers who produced more postcards. In the Arreola Collection, for example, there are more Nogales postcards than for any other town, and greater than half are photo postcards (table 2.2). Similarly, Agua Prieta, another popular Sonora border destination, counted many postcards, and although fewer than Nogales, an even higher percent are photographic postcards. Two of the smaller Sonora border towns, Naco and Sonoyta, count many fewer postcards, respectively, yet they also are predominantly real photo cards. San Luis Río Colorado has the lowest representation of photo postcards. Most of the San Luis Río Colorado postcards in the Arreola Collection are so-called chrome cards, color postcards with a shiny surface similar to the style popular still today, which appear to be photographs but, in fact, are printed cards made from a color photo. The prevalence of chrome postcards for this town is explained, perhaps, by the late popularity of San Luis Río Colorado as a tourist town and the coincidence of chrome postcard photography made nearly universal by the 1960s.[39]

The images reproduced for this project were selected first for the subject represented in the postcard and second for the quality of the photographic or mechanical image. While the quality of an image is important, the subject of the postcard is most critical in my study because this writing is about how the repetitive imagery of places comes to shape socially the popular view of that place. Repetition can be an important check on the accuracy of border town representation because many views over time of the same scene reinforce the authenticity of what is seen.

The Sonora border town postcard project is primarily concerned with seeing how the built landscape of the border towns is visible through postcard imagery. Scholars have privileged this form of visual inquiry for many generations, although not necessarily using postcard imagery to interpret the landscape of a town. In this project, as in my previous border postcard project, particular views were selected to illustrate how spaces in and around the border towns were represented.[40] Many postcard views are shown, but three general types dominate. Street scenes are the most common type and the richest form of postcard view for this story. Streets capture the nature and pulse of a place, and these types of views reveal a host of elements critical to my purpose, from activity levels to building types and landscape density. Street-level views were made for many parts of the border town, from the gates and crossings to the main streets of a city. Panorama postcard views are a subtype of street view from above, and this perspective was especially important for the Sonora border towns of Agua Prieta and Nogales. Landmarks, typically buildings both public and private, are a second type of postcard view. Structures in border towns and their architectural features telegraphed sophistication to visitors, creating a sense of urban modernity. Buildings could be a business such as a bar, eatery, or curio store; a residence; or a public structure such as a customs house, railroad depot, or municipal palace. A third type of view captured local residents in pose or at work. People make place, and human representation is an important compositional element for photographers. In the border towns, postcard views that highlight people enable visitors and consumers of postcard images to glimpse the natives of a city who through their presence reinforce the authenticity of place. Examples in the chapters to follow illustrate these selective view types.

A final word about dates assigned to postcards used in this project. Although collectors have established protocols for dating real photo postcards as discussed above, I have chosen to use decadal dating rather than interval or precise dating. In this system, I will typically record a date for a postcard by the decade identified according to the elements of the image on the front of the card as well as the printing codes on the back of the card. For example, if automobiles and other clues suggest a 1920s view and the back matter suggested by the developing paper assigns a date of 1926, I will still identify the postcard as 1920s. I do this even if the postcard is posted and the stamp date can be read, or the sender dates the message on the card. Following this system sacrifices some precision but it generalizes the ambiguity that can occur from differences in paper dating as well as disconnection between when a postcard image was made and when the card was mailed. The exceptions to this rule are as follows. First, some postcard photographers put actual dates for the image in the title of the postcard. This is rare but it does happen and thereby gives unequivocal precision to an assigned date for the image. A second exception is when I can point to an exact production date for a postcard image, for example as given above for figure 2.8, which has been dated by the archival records for Frashers Fotos. In most cases, this is rare, because even where studio photographers might have made records of their postcards by some numbering and dating system, the records themselves that might substantiate such a claim have not been preserved.

Part II

Visualizing and Narrating Place

3

Agua Prieta

A story reported in the *Douglas Daily Dispatch* in 1927 described Agua Prieta across the international boundary from Douglas: "Agua Prieta, the cleanest little city on the Mexican side of the border line between this country and the southern republic, is situated just at the end of G avenue and is really a continuation of Douglas, with a few vacant lots and a barbed wire fence between."[1] The notion that the Mexican town was simply an extension of the American town was not entirely accurate, yet it reveals an important theme in the long history of Sonora-Arizona border town evolution. Mexican border towns were typically settlements in symbiosis with their American counterparts—and sometimes with others not on the boundary—where codependent social and economic activities enabled the survival of each community.

In 1903, just a few years beyond the founding of Agua Prieta, the governor of Sonora announced that a substantial sum of money had been set aside for improvements to the town. New buildings, including a city hall, jail, hospital, and customs house, were contracted to a lumber company in Douglas. At the same time, hundreds of the "sons of Montezuma [*sic*]" from Agua Prieta were employed in Douglas copper smelters on the American side of the boundary.[2] The role of an early landmark in Agua Prieta, the bullring, exemplifies the American economic and social involvement in the Mexican town and the Mexican government role in sanctioning the activity. The Douglas Amusement Company, formed by three Douglas promoters in 1902, received initial permission to build an arena from the governor of Sonora and set about raising capital by selling stock certificates to investors.[3] The organizers wanted to build a prizefight arena to capitalize on the then early twentieth century popularity of that sport. In connection with the fighting stage the promoters planned for two dance halls and two large gambling rooms, a veritable Monte Carlo on the Mexican border. Caught between changing political administrations, however, the partners lost their bid for the project when a new governor would not approve the original concession. Instead the promoters won the right to build a bullring rather than a boxing arena.[4]

The Agua Prieta bullring was inaugurated on July 4, 1903. The arena, designed by American architect S. F. Forbes in a Spanish architectural style, was constructed of adobe brick and wood (fig. 3.1). It was located on the southeast side of town about six blocks from the border crossing and could be accessed by rail from Douglas via a spur line extended along Calle 6 (fig. 3.2). The arena was said to accommodate several thousand attendees and was larger than the old bullring in nearby Naco. In the years that followed, bullfights were supplemented by cockfights, prizefights, and rodeos.[5] During the opening ceremonies, one of the local dignitaries praised the Douglas Amusement Company for its enterprise and "providing a place where people of both cities could enjoy good sport."[6] The bullring was transformed by the Revolutionary activities and battles at Agua Prieta that ensued in the decade. It served as a military barracks, was heavily shelled, and was largely left to ruin.[7] In 1917, the arena was demolished and never rebuilt. Nevertheless, through this cooperative venture, Agua Prieta and Douglas forged a bond where cultural activities and economic relationships between the border communities were cemented. That melding would survive the twentieth century, demonstrating how border towns coexisted by mixing traditions and creating cultural landscapes that benefited one another.

In this chapter, I reconstruct the popular cultural landscape history of Agua Prieta by combining documentary and historic visual evidence to narrate how the town appeared from the early to the mid-twentieth century. While the story might be told for each town, my purpose is to illustrate how the Mexican border town was shaped largely by the American imagination and to some extent American capital. Visitors came to this part of the border to do business in Douglas but also to experience Agua Prieta. In the course of the early century, the Mexican Revolution, a civil war of multiple contending regional and national interests, ignited battles to control Agua Prieta and its customs house revenue that could be used to purchase arms across the boundary. Throughout the century the Mexican town enabled American visitors to partake in activities denied or unavailable in the States. Prohibitions from alcohol to gambling and the peddling of a romantic idea of Mexico via curio crafts and exotic entertainment became mainstays that insured Agua Prieta's appeal. All these events and activities were captured and promoted through postcards, a popular media of the era. Selected visual reconstruction permits a nearly unique view of Agua Prieta from the early 1900s to the 1950s.

Figure 3.1. The Agua Prieta bullring was built by Douglas investors and remained popular to residents of both border towns from 1903 to the 1910s. The arena, constructed of adobe brick and wood, suggests an adaptation of the early twentieth-century Mission architectural style inspired by California's Spanish colonial era. Doubleday, 1910s.

Figure 3.2. The Agua Prieta bullring was located along Calle 6 near Avenida 7 on the immediate southeast edge of town east of the main plaza. This view shows the Mission-style façade and the bleachers of the ring in the background to the right of center. Visitors from Douglas as well as surrounding towns of southeastern Arizona could ride the rails into Agua Prieta because a spur line off the main track ran along Calle 6 to the ring. Doubleday-Patton, 1910s.

The story begins with an overview of Agua Prieta's geographical context, including a mapping of the place to highlight themes developed. The bulk of this chapter uses postcards to view and narrate the town's landscapes frozen in time by photographers who visited the place. This visualization explores panoramic views of the town, the border crossing between Agua Prieta and Douglas, the town's main street (the most visited part of the community), selected landmark buildings, and the main plaza of the border town that attracted both local residents and visitors. Two vignettes then illustrate how Agua Prieta gained national and regional fame, one concerning a set of Revolutionary battles that catapulted the Mexican border town to early notoriety, and the other about cabaret businesses spawned by Prohibition and later replaced by tourist curio establishments that appealed to a materialized American conception of Mexico as it transitioned to a post–World War II era.

Geographic and Historic Setting

The town that would become Agua Prieta is positioned where the Valle de la Agua Prieta from the south intersects the Sulphur Spring Valley on the north side of the boundary. This lowland has an elevation of nearly four thousand feet, and historically, it was drained by the Río Agua Prieta and Whitewater Draw, respectively. The meeting of these drainages is a topographic sink where water seasonally collected on surface ponds, hence the naming of the Mexican settlement, Agua Prieta—dark water; it is, perhaps, ironic that Douglas, the American town built north of the line, also means dark water in Scottish.[8] On the eastern flanks of these valleys are mountain ranges typical of the basin and range terrain in this part of the borderlands (fig. 1.1).

When this area was mapped as part of the boundary resurvey between 1882 and 1896, there were no settlements.[9] Nevertheless, since Spanish colonial times the water that would collect seasonally at Agua Prieta permitted a *puesto de parada* (stopping place) along the route of a cordon of presidios (forts) linking Janos in Chihuahua with Fronteras in Sonora. From early in the nineteenth century, the site had been visited and described by a host of explorers and travelers. Circa 1899, a small settlement emerged on the site that would become Agua Prieta. A cluster of tents and *jacales* (brush shacks) were built around the low point where water would collect, perhaps to shelter squatters who might have serviced wagon and later freight traffic between the mines at Nacozari to the south and Bisbee to the northwest. By 1902, the settlement boasted a handful of adobe dwellings, and a year later there were perhaps fifty houses in the vicinity.[10]

The principal economic agent in the industrial development of this border region was the Phelps Dodge Corporation, which began to exert its early influence in Bisbee,

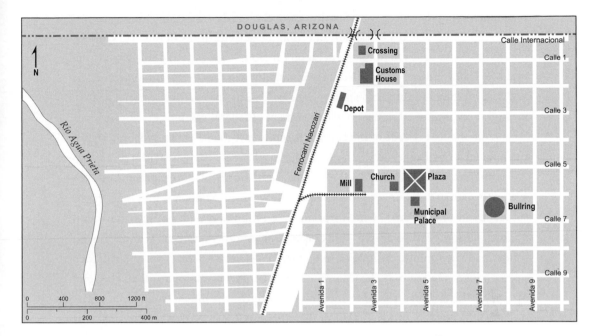

Figure 3.3. Map of Agua Prieta, 1900s–1940s, showing the approximate extent of the street grid with key locations mentioned in the text. After Gobierno del Estado de Sonora, *Agua Prieta Regiones: 1 y 2*, 1946. Locations given in Sandomingo, *Historia de Agua Prieta*. Cartography by Barbara Trapido-Lurie.

Arizona, in the 1880s. In 1897, the company purchased the Pilares copper mine in Nacozari, Sonora, with the intent of building a railroad to the border that would ultimately link to its operations in Bisbee, where it also mined copper. Sufficient ground water at the Whitewater Draw location at the end of the Sulphur Spring Valley southeast of Bisbee proved accommodating to the construction of a copper smelter to service the Bisbee mines. In 1900, James Douglas, under the employ of Phelps Dodge, founded and managed the building of both a smelter and the American border town that would bear his name.[11]

In 1903 the government of Sonora decreed the formal creation of the town of Agua Prieta. Whereas settlers had been accumulating at the site since 1899, the new town, or *fondo legal* (municipality), was laid out east of the original site and beyond the present railroad tracks in classical grid fashion with streets (*calles*) oriented west to east and avenues (*avenidas*) north to south (fig. 3.3). The plan was designed by Tomás Fregoso and surveyed by A. Mendoza.[12] In 1904, the completion of the railway Ferrocarril Nacozari linking the mines at Nacozari to Agua Prieta and the border at Douglas, the construction of two copper smelters in the American border town, and the launching of the El Paso and Southwestern Railroad connecting Douglas to Bisbee and El Paso created a crossroads of economic activity at the boundary. Workers flooded to Agua Prieta to fulfill the demand for labor.[13] An early report summarized that Mexican residents in Agua Prieta were mainly workers in the Douglas smelters and a sprinkling of officials including state and municipal police, customs guards, immigration patrolmen, and a small detachment of federal troops.[14]

During the first decade of the twentieth century, Agua Prieta and its hinterlands were characterized as a frontier transitioning to a border. There was little restriction on immigration from Mexico until 1917, and population was fluid across the boundary, with many from Sonora moving north to work in Arizona mines and on the construction of railroads.[15] One historian called the bond built between northeast Sonora and southeast Arizona a "web of economic interdependency," where Douglas residents owned mines, businesses, and stores in Sonora towns, Arizona cattlemen owned ranches in Sonora, Mexican ranchers lived part of the year in Douglas, and Mexican smelter workers lived in border barrios across the line in Douglas.[16]

Given the position of Agua Prieta at the junction of two relatively flat basins—the Valle de Agua Prieta and the Sulphur Spring Valley—one might not imagine that the border town would be visually captured from the air or from an elevated vantage point. Nevertheless, in the early part of the twentieth century, photographers made aerial and oblique views of the border town from above, and some of those images were made into photo postcards. The images provide a means to see both the aerial extent of the border town and the material landscape of structures, dwellings, and spaces that figured prominently in the twentieth-century history of the Sonora town. The images and the descriptions of the landscapes presented in those views provide an initial glimpse of the town in its first decades.

Figure 3.4 is an aerial view of a part of Agua Prieta taken in 1928 by E. D. Newcomer (1896–1973), a press photographer for the *Arizona Republican*, then Phoenix's largest daily newspaper. Newcomer is best known for his aerial imagery, and in 1928 he participated in a project to photograph scenes of Arizona from a biplane.[17] This view looks west from near the border crossing above Agua Prieta and captures a part of the border, railroad corridor, the town's main street, and proximate residential areas.

The international boundary is seen in the upper right side of the image running between a cluster of buildings and the black slag pile north of the line created as a by-product of the copper smelters in Douglas. All buildings visible in the view are in Agua Prieta. The railroad tracks run south from the boundary alignment and divide the older section of Agua Prieta settled in 1899 from the area east of the tracks that was created with the *fondo legal* in 1903. The broad street on the right of the image and perpendicular to the railroad tracks is Calle 1 (First Street); Calle Internacional (International Street)—the border street—is not visible in this view but is situated

Figure 3.4. Aerial view of a part of Agua Prieta photographed by E. D. Newcomer in 1928. Courtesy E. D. Newcomer Photograph Collection PC 196, Arizona Historical Society, Tempe.

one block north of Calle 1. South of Calle 1 are Calles 2 and 3 (fig. 3.3). All streets in Agua Prieta at this time were graded but unpaved.

The structures east of the railroad track and north of Calle 1 are the border-crossing offices of the Mexican immigration authorities. Several ground-anchored billboards are visible (with magnification) across the street from the offices. The street they face, which extends south, is Avenida 3 (3rd Avenue), the principal street of Agua Prieta that was renamed Avenida Pan Americana in 1942.[18] The prominent structure surrounded by trees and facing Avenida 3 between Calles 1 and 2 is the *aduana*, or customs house, built in 1918. Behind the customs house is a depot with a separate rail siding, and south of that building along the tracks is the formal depot for Agua Prieta. Another significant building visible between Calles 1 and 2 and facing Avenida 4 is the Club Social de Agua Prieta. Originally built in 1921, it is surrounded by a new wall enclosing the property and its remodeled tower still under construction. The *Douglas Daily Dispatch* reported on the progress toward completion of this building and its compound in the same year the aerial photograph was made. "The improvements and addition to the Club Sociale [*sic*] are being rushed to completion. This project involves the building of a high adobe wall around the club grounds. This wall is nearly complete and the arched entrances are being installed. The effect is that of exclusiveness and beauty, as the wall makes a good appearance and the arches add to the artistry of the design."[19]

On the west side of the tracks, there are several tents visible, suggesting that a circus was in town on the day Newcomer snapped his photo from above. Outside of the commercial signs visible (with magnification) on building façades along Avenida 3, most of the remainder of Agua Prieta seen in this panorama is residential, chiefly single-story adobe structures built flush to the street and open behind, creating back patios and yards and being typical of the Mexican building tradition of this era.[20] The townscape is peppered with ornamental trees, and the backyard areas of some homes show evidence of gardens and cultivation.

In 1915, Venustiano Carranza's Constitutionalist Army, fighting against Revolutionary Francisco "Pancho" Villa, occupied Agua Prieta in anticipation of Villa's plan to attack and capture the Sonora border town. Carranza's forces built several searchlight towers strategically positioned in Agua Prieta to illuminate the battlefield surrounding the town should Villa attack at night.[21] Photographer Cal Osbon positioned himself atop one of the towers to snap figure 3.5, a panoramic view looking north with Agua Prieta in the foreground and Douglas in the background. Osbon's photo postcard shows the border-crossing buildings described above (see *x*) and the boundary line separating Agua Prieta from Douglas (see *o* with dot in center). This view reveals the large swath of open area—a no-man's-land—buffering the town of Agua Prieta from the boundary and to the right of center a horse-drawn carriage and driver can be seen parading across this zone. North of the border line in the upper left and center of the image are faint views of some of the industrial facilities that supported the copper economy of Douglas and the Arizona border during this era. This district lies entirely west of the railroad alignment that crosses the border from Agua Prieta into the Arizona town.

The foreground is chiefly the first four blocks of Agua Prieta south of the crossing. The road coming south from the crossing is Avenida 3. Osbon's lens captures the makeshift early twentieth-century townscape of the emerging Sonora border town, showing a mix of traditional adobe structures as well as a sprinkling of wood buildings resulting from the work of a lumber company in Douglas that was contracted to build some early dwellings in Agua Prieta. Wood construction, however, proved problematic to the first customs house in Agua Prieta because it caught fire and was destroyed in 1903; the present *aduana*, built of brick in 1918 (not pictured here), has survived into the present.[22]

Figure 3.5. Panoramic view looking north to the international boundary and Douglas beyond from one of Calles's searchlight towers in Agua Prieta. Osbon, 1910s.

Figure 3.6. Vista looking south along Avenida 3 taken from the roof of the Agua Prieta customs house, 1920s.

Another panoramic view from the 1920s, figure 3.6 is taken from the roof parapet of the Agua Prieta customs house looking south along Avenida 3. At least two prominent cabaret establishments are visible: in the foreground the Brookhill on the corner of Calle 2 and Avenida 3, and farther down the main street on the left is a two-story, balconied, pitched-roof building, the International Club, also an early cabaret.[23] Scanning the skyline from left to right and east of Avenida 3 is the tower of the Agua

Prieta Servicios Públicos (Public Utilities) facility (dark cone shape) that provided electrical power, well water, and ice; the town's tall *molino* (mill) is visible to the west of Avenida 3 near the middle of the image.[24]

Townscape

The postcard landscape of Agua Prieta was a selectively represented set of areas, not the entire town. Photographers generally captured those elements of townscape that would be experienced by tourists and, occasionally, landmarks outside of the visitor's world, including areas frequented and important to the residents of the border town. In Agua Prieta, the commonly pictured parts of town included the crossing, selected streets and buildings, and the plaza.

Border-Crossing Views

Crossing the border is officially regulated through ports of entry on the Mexican as well as the American side of the boundary. In the early twentieth century, the crossing was a rather informal space where immigration authorities sanctioned passage, and the documentation needed to cross might depend on circumstances. Unlike travel into the interior, which required a passport and or tourist visa, passage into Agua Prieta from Douglas to seek services or entertainment was loosely enforced. Often times, Mexican immigration authorities would recognize locals and permit entrance. During Prohibition and the post–World War II tourist era, access was allowed as long as visitors remained in Agua Prieta.

Because the crossing meant leaving the United States for Mexico, even if only for a short visit, the activity was charged with anxiety and the excitement of foreign adventure. The exotic nature of this process enabled postcard photographers to create a visual fixe of the crossing space and the actors involved. Consequently, the crossing was photographically documented each decade from the 1910s through the 1950s by the souvenir postcard. This redundancy of visual representation creates a near cinematic view of how the crossing changed over time and its evolution as a symbolic landscape of Agua Prieta.

During the 1900s, crossing the international boundary at the border was a simple affair. Visitors to the Mexican town from the American town simply passed a guardhouse or office manned by a Mexican official. Figure 3.7 shows the crossing early in this decade, looking south from the American customs house to a crowd gathered around the Mexican guardhouse near the boundary. Figure 3.8 illustrates the improvements made to the Mexican crossing by the 1910s. A new wood-frame

Figure 3.7. Agua Prieta guardhouse looking south at the border crossing in the early 1900s. Attributed to Doubleday-Heuther, 1900s.

Figure 3.8. Improvements to the Agua Prieta border-crossing buildings in the 1910s.

checkpoint precedes a more substantial masonry immigration building that signals visitors to present passports. In the foreground, a U.S. Customs officer is comically posed atop a concrete pillar on the boundary, and a wire fence is visible on either side of the crossing entrance. There is no gate, suggesting that access could be achieved every hour of every day.

Figure 3.9. Agua Prieta and Douglas crossing, 1920s. Circular structures in the background are natural gas storage tanks. México Fotográfico 20, 1920s.

Figure 3.9 is a 1920s view looking back at the crossing from the Agua Prieta side of the line. The Mexican immigration office and guardhouse as well as the U.S. Customs building across the boundary are now visible in their respective visual alignments. Flagstaffs appear in front of each structure to designate symbolic authority, and in front of the Mexican immigration office is a sign signaling automobiles to stop for inspection. Although the sign reads "customs" (*aduana*), this stop was largely perfunctory because the official customs house was a much larger building that housed records and tariff revenue that might be levied on goods trafficked across the boundary, especially by rail.

By the 1950s, the Agua Prieta *garita* (gate) shows considerable enhancements to the architectural façades of the buildings at the crossing (fig. 3.10). The old guardhouse (behind) has been completely rebuilt as a frame and stucco structure; there is also an automobile portico extended from this new building. The old Mexican immigration office (front) has a new canopy extending from the original masonry structure, and this building now monitors vehicles entering and leaving Agua Prieta.

Streets and Buildings

Street scenes including building façades were the bread and butter of postcard photography. Invariably, a town's identity is captured in a view of a main street and

Figure 3.10. Agua Prieta *garita* (gate) during 1950s, showing substantial enhancements to the architectural façades of the buildings at the border crossing. México Fotográfico 55, 1950s.

prominent landmark structures. In the Arreola Collection, 37 percent of all postcards for Agua Prieta are street and building views. Chiefly, the street views are of Avenida 3—Pan Americana.

Postcard photographers typically photographed Avenida 3 from both street level and building rooftops. Figure 3.11 is a ground-level view of the main street looking north during the 1920s. The street is alive with young men and boys. South of the tower of the *aduana* or customs house on the upper left, Avenida 3 is lined with single-story buildings, bars, and an ice cream store (Neveria Central) on one side and market and general store (La Competencia and El Nuevo Mercado) on the other. Figure 3.12 is a rooftop view of the same street, also in the 1920s, focused on the west side of Avenida 3 to reveal several businesses, including a gas station on the corner of Calle 3 with a large Goodrich Tire advertisement painted onto a proximate wall. The open lot on the right side of the street exposes a building wall of adobe, a common construction material for the Sonora border town. Figure 3.13, shows the same street, now Avenida Pan Americana in the 1940s, from two blocks south of the previous 1920s views, again highlighting a corner gas station, a hearse with men standing about, and various adobe wall exposures also visible. Figure 3.14 gives a final glimpse of this stretch of Avenida Pan Americana during the 1950s, revealing changes to building façades, signage, and automobile styles over three decades when compared to previous views.

Figure 3.11. Agua Prieta street view of Avenida 3 near Calle 3, looking north toward the border, 1920s.

Figure 3.12. Agua Prieta rooftop view of Avenida 3 near Calle 3, looking north toward the border, 1920s.

Figure 3.13. Agua Prieta rooftop view of Pan Americana near Calle 5, looking north toward the border, 1940s.

Figure 3.14. Agua Prieta elevated street view of Pan Americana near Calle 4, looking north toward the border, 1950s. México Fotográfico 32, 1950s.

Figure 3.15. Mexican Independence Day (September 16) parade in Agua Prieta on Avenida 3, in front of the 1918 customs house. Attributed to Osbon, 106, 1910s.

Streets, however, were more than commercial arteries, and during special celebrations they transformed into stage sets for parades and displays. Figure 3.15 captures a large parade in front of the customs house on Avenida 3 during Mexican Independence Day (September 16) sometime in the 1920s. The Agua Prieta *aduana*, built in 1918, was the most important landmark along the main street and is featured in many postcard views. The flags of Mexico and the United States are displayed in the parade, suggesting that residents from Douglas likely participated in this event as well as those from Agua Prieta. Mutual celebratory activities were common in Agua Prieta and Douglas. A local report from the 1940s commented how both towns cooperated jointly to observe the Cinco de Mayo (5th of May) in Agua Prieta and the Fourth of July in Douglas, while the merchants of Douglas sponsored *fiestas patrias* (independence holidays) in Agua Prieta into the 1950s.[25] At other times, streets became the occasion of theatrical performances. In November 1932, a group of soldiers from the Second Company of the Sixteenth Battalion of the Mexican Army placed a concrete tablet with gilt lettering over the entrance of Alice Gatliff's Curio Café on Calle 5 and Avenida 2 to commemorate the historic role of the building during several

Figure 3.16. Mexican soldiers performing on the street in Agua Prieta to celebrate commemoration of Alice Gatliff's Curio Café, 1932.

Revolutionary battles in Agua Prieta.[26] The soldiers performed feats of gymnastic entertainment on the street to celebrate the dedication of the building (fig. 3.16).

Landmark buildings were at once functional structures and on the other hand symbolic of progress and modernism in the border town. In 1917, Agua Prieta built a two-story lodging, Hotel Moderno on Calle 4 one block east of Avenida 3. The hotel was modern for its time, sporting a Mission Revival façade and decorative Moorish window trim. It included a dining room, a cantina offering domestic and imported liquors, and an auto park next door (fig. 3.17). The Agua Prieta *molino* (mill), a three-story structure on Calle 5 west of Avenida 3, was a signature building visible in several panorama postcard images from the 1920s. The mill had a railroad spur that connected it to the Ferrocarril Nacozari (fig. 3.3) and a general merchandise store attached to the operations (fig. 3.18). In 1946, the Cine Alhambra was opened in Agua Prieta at the corner of Calle 4 and Avenida 4 (fig. 3.19). This twelve-hundred-seat theater included a ground floor dry goods store visible through large plate-glass windows and a twelve-room hotel. The landmark has an art deco façade and marquee, is built of cement block and stucco, and has "air conditioning" (evaporative cooling). The opening performance featured the English-language film, dubbed to Spanish, *Between Two Worlds*, starring John Garfield, Paul Henreid, Sidney Greenstreet, and Eleanor Parker.[27]

Figure 3.17. Hotel Moderno, a 1917 addition to Agua Prieta's retail service economy. México Fotográfico 22, 1920s.

Figure 3.18. The Agua Prieta mill circa 1910s, a prominent structure at three stories, was a landmark visible across the town.

Cine y Calle. Agua Prieta, Son. Mex.

Figure 3.19. Agua Prieta's Cine Alhambra, a twelve-hundred-seat theater that combined a general store with a small hotel in art deco splendor. México Fotográfico 12, 1940s.

Plaza

The plaza has been called the heart of every Mexican town because it is typically the social and symbolic center of a community. Agua Prieta's main plaza is called Azueta, named after a heroic captain who defended the port of Veracruz during the United States occupation of that city in the early twentieth century.[28] The space is positioned five blocks in from the border crossing between Calles 5 and 6 and Avenidas 4 and 5 (fig. 3.3). An early view of the plaza from 1913 shows the space surrounded by residences as well as small businesses (fig. 3.20). In the center of the plaza was a *kiosco* or bandstand, here decorated with bunting and portraits of Mexican patriots as part of the Cinco de Mayo celebration. There are trees and benches on the perimeter of the space, and the open areas between appear to be dirt. Not shown in this view is the church at the southwest corner of the space.

In 1929, Agua Prieta received state funds for civic improvements, and Plaza Azueta as well as the church benefited. The plaza was crosscut by concrete walkways, new trees were planted, new benches were installed, and the open spaces were seeded with grass, giving the area "an air of neatness and prosperity."[29] The church originally

Figure 3.20. Agua Prieta's main plaza during a Cinco de Mayo celebration, 1913.

Figure 3.21. Agua Prieta's Plaza Azueta, handsomely decorated with rebuilt kiosco (bandstand), concrete walkways, fenced lawn, benches, and light standards. Across the street and fronting the plaza is the church with its newly installed bell tower. México Fotográfico 6, 1950s.

built of adobe and lacking a stucco exterior was plastered inside and out. In the 1940s, Plaza Azueta witnessed further changes. The *kiosco* was rebuilt as an elevated feature with a stair to an upper platform open to the air but covered by a tile roof, and window openings for vending *abarrotes y refrescos* (snacks and soft drinks) were created at ground level. By the 1950s, the church added a large bell tower (fig. 3.21).

Vignette: Battles of Agua Prieta

Agua Prieta figured prominently in some of the earliest battles of the Mexican Revolution (1910–1920). Two memorable engagements were staged at Agua Prieta, one in 1911 and another in 1915. The Sonora border town was considered a prize in part because it was a railroad crossing between Mexico and the United States, and that position meant not only access to goods and supplies, especially armaments, but also a ready market to sell appropriated property such as livestock, which was often rustled in the region during this era. Further, Agua Prieta contained a large customs house that collected tariffs from rail traffic, and those resources could be captured by rebel groups to purchase weapons in the United States.[30]

The Mexican Revolution incited by northerner Francisco Madero in 1910 spilled into Sonora, where sympathetic Revolutionaries took up arms against federal forces loyal to Mexican dictator Porfirio Díaz.[31] One rebel group, commanded by Arturo "Red" López (fig. 3.22) and operating in northeastern Sonora, briefly captured towns with Mexican federal garrisons. On April 13, 1911, López and some 150 rebels commandeered the train that operated between Agua Prieta and the Sonora mining town of Nacozari to the south. As the train pulled into the Agua Prieta depot, rebels fired on federal troops, a full-fledged battle erupted, and within hours López's rebels captured and chased the federal soldiers from Agua Prieta's *cuartel* (garrison) across the line into Douglas, where they surrendered to U.S. Army forces camped in the American border town. López secured his control of Agua Prieta by erecting defenses on the eastern perimeter of the town. On April 15, additional federal forces arrived at Agua Prieta to recapture the town, and the battle resumed when these forces attacked López's army from the southeast.[32]

Residents in Douglas were captivated by the battle, and regardless of the danger of stray bullets crossing the boundary, they thronged to high points near the border to witness the fighting. Sightseers congregated along the boundary on the Douglas side expecting to view the battle.[33] One popular location was a two-story house at the corner of 5th Street and D Avenue only blocks from the boundary on the east side of Douglas, close to but across the line from Agua Prieta and near much of the action (fig. 3.23).

Figure 3.22. Arturo "Red" López, an early Revolutionary, lead rebels against federal forces in the 1911 Battle of Agua Prieta. Lopez's troops held the town for several days before retreating to the U.S. side of the boundary and dispersing. Doubleday-Heuther, 1910s.

Figure 3.23. Douglas residents gathered on the roof of a home located near the boundary and proximate to the fighting during the 1911 Battle of Agua Prieta. Doubleday-Heuther, 1910s; Courtesy Douglas Historical Society, CCHS Collection #53–34.

By April 17, López and his *insurrectos* (rebels) slipped out of Agua Prieta, and the first battle for control of the town ended with federal troops regaining authority. The battle, however, was significant because it gave Francisco Madero leverage in his negotiations with Mexican dictator Porfirio Díaz, who abdicated the presidency in the middle of 1911. Madero was elected president at the end of the same year.[34]

The assassination of Madero in 1913 created chaos and uncertainty in the Mexican north, including Sonora, when rival leaders refused to acknowledge Victoriano Huerta, the successor to the Mexican presidency. One of the most inflamed rivalries pitted Venustiano Carranza's Constitutionalist army, led by Sonoran Generals Álvaro Obregón and Plutarco Elías Calles, against Chihuahuan rebel leader Francisco "Pancho" Villa and his army of Villistas. During the next two years, Villa's army began losing ground to the armies of Carranza, directed by Obregón in northcentral Mexico, and Calles, representing the Sonoran governor and commanding a state militia sympathetic to Carranza, who occupied Agua Prieta when the local federal garrison forces fled the Sonoran border town. Villa was also losing the support of the United States, which had backed his efforts by providing arms early in the Revolution. Villa decided to invade Agua Prieta to secure a border port that might enable his army to be supplied via arms merchants in Arizona. Unknown to Villa, U.S. president Woodrow Wilson decided to support Carranza after numerous reports of Villistas raiding American mining and railroad interests in Chihuahua. As a result, Wilson enabled Carranza's forces stationed in Coahuila and Chihuahua to cross into the Texas border towns of Eagle Pass and El Paso to board trains that would carry the armies west to Douglas, Arizona, where they would then reenter Mexico at Agua Prieta to reinforce the Calles army stationed in the Sonora border town (fig. 3.24).[35]

Awaiting Villa, Calles's troops, including reinforcements totaling some seven thousand strong, were dug in at Agua Prieta, encircling the town with trenches and barbed wire and several strategically situated machine-gun emplacements.[36] Because he anticipated that Villa would attack at night, Calles installed searchlight towers in town to illuminate the battle lines (fig. 3.5). The trenches and encampments around and inside Agua Prieta became not only fortified sites but also domestic spaces where women prepared food for the troops and executed daily chores such as washing clothes (fig. 3.25).

Villa led his army of an estimated five thousand soldiers and camp followers overland from Chihuahua, and this group merged with existing Villistas already in Sonora, having recently taken over the towns of Naco, a border town west of Agua Prieta, and Cananea, a mining settlement south of Naco. As expected by Calles, who commanded Carranza's army in Agua Prieta, Villa attacked the town at 1:30 a.m., November 1, 1915, following an artillery barrage that did some damage to the town (fig. 2.3). The searchlights lit up the night, Calles's barbed wire stalled any Villista

Figure 3.24. Carranza's soldiers having been permitted by U.S. president Woodrow Wilson to travel by train via Texas border ports of entry disembark at Douglas, Arizona, to march across the border and reinforce Calles's troops in Agua Prieta anticipating Villa's invasion and the battle of 1915. Osbon 30, 1910s.

Figure 3.25. Women washing clothes—using water piped to the trenches—for Carranza's troops after the Agua Prieta battle in 1915. Osbon 14, 1910s.

Figure 3.26. Yaqui camp at Agua Prieta following the battle in November 1915.

penetration of Agua Prieta, and machine-gun crossfire repelled the invasion. Villa retreated, and Agua Prieta remained a defensive site throughout 1916.[37] Following the buildup to the 1915 Battle of Agua Prieta, Carranza, with the cooperation of the Sonora governor, recruited and shipped hundreds of Yaqui soldiers to Agua Prieta to fight against Villa.[38] Postcard photographers were keen to identify these specialized troops and document their presence through popular imagery (fig. 3.26).

Vignette: Cabarets and Curios

Early in its history, Agua Prieta was a destination, especially the bullring that lured Douglas residents and others to its events for the first decade after the Sonora border town was organized. While the battles of the Mexican Revolution brought international attention to the town, it was the passage of the Volstead Act and Prohibition in the United States in 1919 that launched Agua Prieta's popularity in the American imagination, although Arizona had declared prohibition to alcohol earlier, in 1915. Between 1920 and the early 1930s, Agua Prieta was host to a dozen or more drinking and gaming establishments called cabarets, many owned by non-Mexican residents of Douglas, Arizona. These businesses were easily accessible to stateside visitors, who simply crossed the line to enjoy. Although never completely erased with the repeal of Prohibition in 1933, the cabaret industry slowed in Agua Prieta through the era of the Second World War. Fortunately, a new industry, day tourism and the curio crafts trade, blossomed in the postwar period, and Agua Prieta emerged as a leading destination for Arizonans and others drawn to the romantic Mexico of their imaginations. Each of these developments, cabarets and curios, were magnetic attractants to postcard photographers, enabling an unusual visual documentation of Agua Prieta during its wide-open and tourist-popular historic phases.

Agua Prieta's cabaret and curio businesses were largely located along Avenida 3, later known as Avenida Pan Americana (fig. 3.3). This was, as discussed above, the main street of the town and connected directly to Douglas across the border. In Agua Prieta's first decades, Avenida 3 housed the major concentration of commercial activities, and this part of the town became known as *el centro* (the center), the popular designation for the commercial core of a Mexican town. By the late 1920s, domestic commerce featuring grocers and other retail services were now competing for space with cabaret businesses, shown as entertainment in figure 3.27. Whereas local commerce still dominated, some of the largest properties along Avenida 3 were clubs and bars. That Avenida 3 was the principal tourist destination during Prohibition is reinforced by figure 3.28, a map postcard illustrating the automobile roads of southern Arizona, southwest New Mexico, and west Texas leading to Douglas and the immediate street grid of Agua Prieta, with arrows highlighting the main street beyond the border crossing. The Curio Café offered "Everything to eat and drink" with Fred Girard dispensing "cheer." Another map, chiefly showing Douglas in 1928 and created by the same artist—Emory Cobb—who drafted the postcard in figure 3.28, shows a piece of Agua Prieta and the locations of several cabarets in the district nearest the crossing.[39]

In the Prohibition years 1915–1933, cabaret businesses were generally divided between small and large operations, although exceptions to this likely existed. The smaller cabarets were essentially bars or saloons. They included, for example, the Arizona Club and Saloon, Gadsden Bar, Silver Dollar Bar, Crystal Palace Bar, Curio Café, and Volstead Bar (fig. 3.29). Typically, bars were drinking establishments with some food service but without significant entertainment (fig. 3.30). The large cabarets such as the International Club, Social Club, Manhattan Club, White House Club, Aztec Club, White Horse Club, and Brookhill Café and Cabaret included upscale food service, live orchestras, and dance floors. The White Horse Cabaret, for example, issued an advertising postcard created by Emory Cobb in 1927 that asserted "Follow the White Horse over the line: The Music is 'Steppy,' Refreshments are 'Peppy,' Go to the White Horse to have a good time." In one corner of the front of the card is an inset

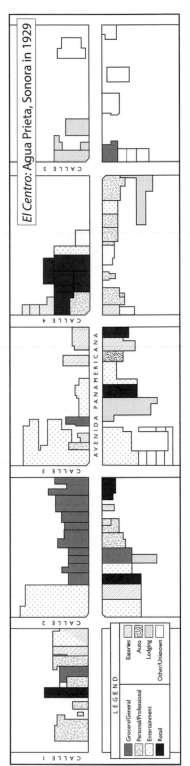

Figure 3.27. Land use in Agua Prieta's business district, 1929. Cabaret businesses, labeled entertainment, operated on some of the largest properties along Avenida 3 toward the end of Prohibition. Sanborn Map Company, *Agua Prieta, Sonora, Mexico, 1929*. Cartography by Nick Burkhart.

Figure 3.28. 1928 postcard map illustrates the location of Agua Prieta on the border between Tucson and El Paso and across the line from Douglas, Arizona. Arrows direct visitors down Avenida 3, the main street of the Sonora border town. Emory Cobb, 1928.

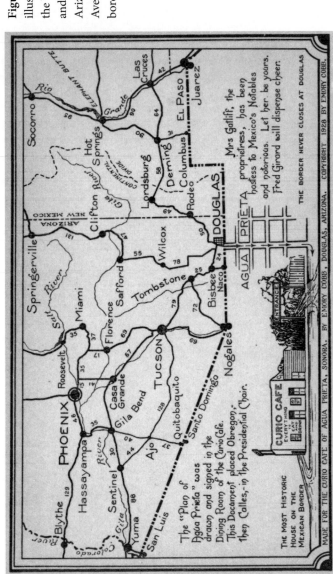

Figure 3.29. The Volstead Bar in Agua Prieta during the 1920s was an example of a small cabaret where drinking without entertainment was typical. Note the sign that announced beer served in steins and stacks of beer kegs down the street. This photographic postcard may have been given away to patrons, evident from the sign above the main entrance, "Free Postal Cards Come in."

Figure 3.30. The Silver Dollar Bar in Agua Prieta, operated by C. [Curley] E. Lester, who rented the building from Chinese businessman and property owner Jim Joe. The Silver Dollar was destroyed by fire in 1932. Attributed to Osbon, 24, 1920s.

drawing of a lady in sombrero who proclaims, "Venga a Ver Las Señoritas Bonitas" (Come to see the pretty ladies). On the back of the postcard is a menu for food served at the White Horse Grill, including venison, duck, quail, and bear; oysters, shrimp, lobster, and turtle; and Mexican fare as well as French, Italian, and American cuisines.

Whether bar or club, drink was certainly the principal attraction. A 1925 promotional brochure for Douglas, Arizona, advised that entertainment in Agua Prieta was "happily pre-Volsteadian," golf was possible year around, and its "19th hole" was Agua Prieta, Mexico, serving old-fashioned cheer.[40] Bars in the Mexican town featured domestic beer such as Pacifico, brewed in nearby Mazatlán, and High Life, a popular Sonoran cerveza. Large cabarets, often called clubs, prided themselves on full liquor service. The White House Club, operated by proprietors U. S. Williams and A. T. Sammarcelli, maintained a cellar of fine wines and spirits purchased in France, Scotland, and Germany.[41]

The Prohibition cabaret industry in Agua Prieta was decidedly owned and operated by people other than Mexicans. A review of a Douglas city directory in 1930 listed eleven of twelve Agua Prieta club proprietors as residents of the Arizona town. By contrast, a post–Prohibition 1938 directory listed six club proprietors, and five resided in Agua Prieta.[42] Ownership of a club, however, did not mean building ownership. Typically, proprietors were multiple partners who owned the business but rented a building from an Agua Prieta resident. During Prohibition most cabaret operators rented buildings owned by Chinese merchants. One of the popular cabarets in Agua Prieta was the International Club, located at the corner of Avenida 3 and Calle 5 (see two-story, balconied building in the background of fig. 3.29). This club was owned and operated by three different proprietor partners during the 1920s, yet the building was owned entirely by the Chinese Society of Agua Prieta.[43]

The Chinese presence in Agua Prieta, as in much of Mexico, was enhanced, in part, by the U.S. passage of the Chinese Exclusion Act of 1882, which restricted legal immigration of Chinese laborers. Although the exclusion in the United States was exempted for certain merchants, many Chinese entered Mexico to seek opportunity. By 1910, 52 percent of all Chinese in Mexico resided in northern states, and Sonora counted the largest population—4,486—among all states of the republic.[44] In Agua Prieta, Chinese gained a foothold as grocers, and the success of those businesses allowed them to purchase real estate, including buildings along Avenida 3 (table 3.1). Other Chinese were consistently employed in clubs as kitchen cooks and service personal. Perhaps the most celebrated Chinese in Agua Prieta during the Prohibition era was Jim Joe. He opened the Crystal Palace Bar in 1923 and remodeled the building, adding a large dance floor and renaming the cabaret the Manhattan Club in 1928. The club occupied the southeast corner block at the intersection of Avenida 3 and Calle 3

Table 3.1. Selected Agua Prieta businesses, 1930 and 1948–1949

	Grocers/ general stores	Personal/ professional services	Bars/ cabarets/ clubs	Curio stores
1930 (total = 45)	25[a]	8	10	2
1948–1949 (total = 67)	18	17	16[b]	16

[a] Twenty of the grocers and general stores given were owned and operated by Chinese merchants.
[b] Includes some restaurants that served alcohol and advertised as bars.
Sources: Douglas City Directory 1930, 139–46; Douglas City Directory 1948–49, 156–60.

Figure 3.31. The Manhattan Club in Agua Prieta, owned by Chinese merchant Jim Joe, was opened in 1928. Originally, the cabaret was called the Crystal Palace Bar. It was expanded to add a dance floor and orchestra pit and full food service as well as spirits, wine, and beer. Note how a separate "Family Entrance" (*left of main door*) enabled patrons who simply preferred food service to enter without having to pass through the bar.

(fig. 3.31). Jim Joe also owned the Agua Prieta property on Avenida 3 that housed the Silver Dollar Bar, and he was engaged in other businesses in Mexicali, a Baja California border town that was home to many Chinese.[45]

Chinese property owners and merchants like Jim Joe suffered mightily in 1931, when the state of Sonora instituted a series of expulsion laws that decimated Chinese-run businesses and Chinese labor, forcing many Chinese to relocate to other northern states and others to return to China. The anti-Chinese movement in Sonora started in 1916 with the organization and campaigning of Mexican businessmen disgruntled with the economic success of the Chinese.[46] In Agua Prieta, twenty Chinese

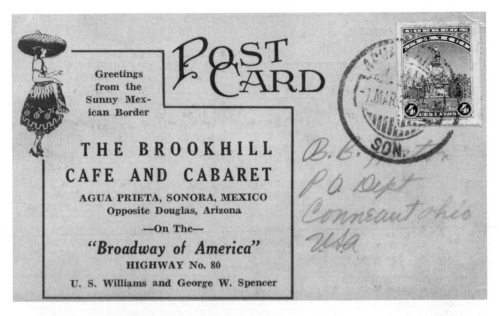

Figure 3.32. Many Agua Prieta cabarets distributed free postcards to their patrons. The Brookhill Café and Cabaret advertised its location in the "Sunny Mexican Border" and on the "Broadway of America, Highway No. 80."

merchants, mostly grocers, were listed in a 1930 city directory; by 1935, not a single Chinese name was given as a resident or merchant in that year's directory.[47]

Two of the most successful cabarets in Agua Prieta during the 1920s were the Brookhill Café and Cabaret and the White House Club. The Brookhill was strategically situated within walking distance of the border crossing, across the street from the customs house on the northeast corner of Avenida 3 and Calle 2, and included an enclosed car park behind the cabaret (fig. 3.6). The club, operated by U. S. Williams and George W. Spencer, advertised on postcards given free to patrons (fig. 3.32). The café that was part of the club specialized in wild-game dinners. When the building was remodeled, the proprietors installed a large walk-in refrigeration unit capable of storing 30–50 deer (hunted locally) so that venison steaks could be offered regularly.[48] The White House Club was opened for business in 1921 by the partnership of Ross, Wasserman, and Sammarcelli, and shortly thereafter U. S. Williams bought out Ross's and Wasserman's shares.[49] The original White House Club was, like the Brookhill, located across the street from the customs house but on the northeast corner of Avenida 3 and Calle 2 catercorner from the Café and Cabaret. The brick façade over original adobe and painted white made a gleaming statement so close to the border crossing, and its roof-mounted billboard with its faux capitol silhouette gave the structure presence in early Agua Prieta (fig. 3.33). When a fire destroyed the White House Club in

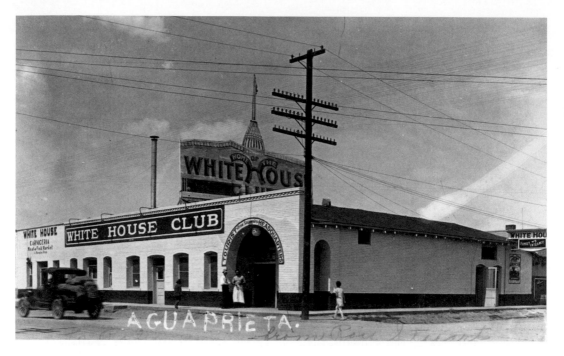

Figure 3.33. The White House Club opened in 1921 and operated as one of the most popular cabarets in Agua Prieta for nine years until it was completely destroyed by fire in 1930.

1930, liquor stored in the basement exploded, creating a disaster that lured a crowd of onlookers in Agua Prieta but also in Douglas, where residents from the Arizona town lined the border near the crossing to witness the catastrophe. In addition to the total loss of the building, fifty-nine slot machines melted because of the intensity of the conflagration, and Mexican soldiers from the local garrison stood guard to protect the curious spectators.[50] Four years later, U. S. Williams, whose interests ranged widely in the Agua Prieta cabaret industry, raised sufficient capital with investors to purchase the Social Club of Agua Prieta, a former private club that was renamed the New White House Club and open to the public. The original Social Club was one of the most distinctive structures in Agua Prieta, a blend of Mission and Romanesque styles designed by Los Angeles architect Carleton M. Winslow (fig. 3.34).[51]

The repeal of Prohibition in the United States, the enforcement of Chinese exclusion laws in Sonora, the Mexican national government removal of casino gambling privileges, and the Great Depression in the 1930s combined to spell the near total collapse of the cabaret industry on the Mexican border.[52] In Agua Prieta, tourist visitation waned until the post–World War II era explosion in border activity. When economic prosperity returned to the Sonora border, the curio trade especially led the way to revived business enterprise; city directories listed two curio stores in 1930 and

CLUB SOCIAL DE AGUA PRIETA   SOCIEDAD ANONIMA
AGUA PRIETA   SONORA   MEXICO
OPPOSITE DOUGLAS   ARIZONA

Figure 3.34. The Social Club of Agua Prieta, designed by Los Angeles architect Carleton M. Winslow in a Mission-Romanesque style, was one of the most distinctive buildings in the border town. It was sold to a cabaret owner in 1934 and became known as the New White House Club.

sixteen in 1948–1949 (table 3.1). A few revitalized establishments and new clubs such as the Royal Night Club were part of this postwar phase, but the curio store became the steadfast tourist lure attracting a new class of visitors to Agua Prieta.[53]

The earliest curio store to operate in Agua Prieta was probably that owned by Alice Gatliff (née Smith), a Mormon and the spouse of Charles W. Gatliff, who owned property and ran retail and service businesses in Nacozari and Agua Prieta. The Agua Prieta store, located on the northeast corner of Avenida 2 and Calle 5, was a saloon and hotel circa 1904. In 1907, on the passing of Charles, Alice converted part of the Agua Prieta property to the Curio Store (fig. 3.35). The store later became known as Gatliff's Curio Café, an early landmark in the town because the Plan of Agua Prieta—in which Álvaro Obregón and Plutarco Elías Calles declared their break with Venustiano Carranza near the close of the Mexican Revolution—was signed in the café on April 23, 1920 (fig. 3.28).[54]

Gatliff's Curio Café advertised itself as an eatery and a shop where visitors might purchase Mexican handicrafts (fig. 3.36). A shrewd businesswoman, Gatliff catered to American tastes in food selection—chiefly Mexican items but also American

Figure 3.35. Alice Gatliff's Curio Store, the earliest curio store in Agua Prieta circa 1911. Gatliff, at left, flew the American flag over her store during the early battles of Agua Prieta to designate her neutrality between rebels and federal forces.

dishes—and in arts and crafts by offering an array of handmade items that were symbolic of Mexican curios during the period, especially drawn work popular with female shoppers. She also reproduced postcards—chiefly print postcards made from photographs of local scenes in Agua Prieta—including ones of her own store, and made them available in the café (fig. 3.37). For some three decades, the Curio Café remained a tourist destination; it was noted in guidebooks and became a location where locals would take out-of-town guests.[55] Alice Gatliff died in 1936 when an accidental stove explosion occurred in her café. A story on the front page of the *El Paso Herald-Post* called Gatliff a "Friend of Mexican Statesmen," relating her relationships with Plutarco Elías Calles and Álvaro Obregón, both presidents of Mexico in her lifetime.[56]

Alice Gatliff was a pioneer in the evolution of the curio trade industry in Agua Prieta. Nevertheless, the slow economy of the 1930s meant few stores emerged that would specifically cater to the dwindling numbers of visitors. Advertisements in city directories give evidence of pharmacies and cigar stands where a visitor might find curios and postcards but mention only two curio stores, Gatliff's Curio Café and La Perla Book Store and Curio Shop, located on Calle 4 somewhat outside the tourist strip of Avenida 3 (fig. 3.38).[57] Another, La Azteca, opened in 1935 when Agua Prieta's main street was known as Avenida 3, then moved two doors down the street to a larger building when the main street had been renamed Pan Americana. Proprietor José

Figure 3.36. Curio Café advertisement announcing food service and Mexican handicraft products. *Douglas City Directory 1923, 4.*

Figure 3.37. Alice Gatliff, proprietor of the Curio Café, reproduced and sold postcards of local scenes in Agua Prieta, including views of her own store. Note advertising slogans on left—"Within this hive we're all alive, We sip the sweetest honey, If you are dry, Step in and try, But don't forget, The money"—and on right—"You may go east, You may go west, When you pass this place, You passed the best." Published by Curio Café, Agua Prieta, Mexico, 1920s.

Figure 3.38. La Perla Book Store and Curio Shop in Agua Prieta advertised in a local city directory in 1930 that it sold Mexican souvenirs, handsome postal cards, and Mexican "zarapes." Note the rack of postcards on the wall of the open door to the left. México Fotográfico, 1920s.

Figure 3.39. Curio stores replaced cabarets as the primary visitor attraction to Agua Prieta during the post–World War II era. Many stores, such as La Azteca Curio, Agua Prieta Curio Shop, El Sarape Curio Shop, and La Competencia Curios, located along Avenida Pan Americana proximate to the border crossing for easy access by pedestrian tourists. México Fotográfico 3, 1950s.

Figure 3.40. American tourists were the mainstay of curio businesses in Agua Prieta in the post–World War II period. Shoppers inspect wares in La Azteca Curio, owned and operated by José Castellanos. Courtesy Douglas Historical Society, CCHS Collection #62–5.

Castellanos offered standard Mexican curios such as jewelry and pottery as well as imported perfumes and Swiss watches.[58]

Soon stories began to appear in the Douglas press about the expansion of tourist services available across the line, to wit, "Agua Prieta, the friendly, romantic city across the border, invites residents of Douglas to shop or seek amusement and entertainment. There are articles of merchandise to be found in Agua Prieta which cannot be found on this side of the border, especially native products and curios which are unique and peculiar only to Mexico."[59] In the early 1940s there were only three curio stores in Agua Prieta, but by the close of the decade there were 16 (table 3.1).[60] Through the 1950s, the border town was known for its curio shopping, with many stores crowded along the first few blocks of Pan Americana near the border crossing to insure easy access to visitors who only had to walk into the Sonora border town from neighboring Douglas (fig. 3.39).[61] Curio store merchants catered exclusively to American shopping tastes, presenting their shops and merchandise as an exotic experience (fig. 3.40). Curio shopping had replaced cabaret hopping in the new postwar visitor economy as the landscape of Agua Prieta once again shaped itself to satisfy American desires.

4

Naco

Naco, Sonora, identified as a "notorious border village astride the line" in a 1920 popular account, is sometimes confused with the Arizona community of the same name immediately north of the border and facing the Mexican town. Even the origin of the town name is unclear, with one account suggesting it derives from the last two letters of Arizona (Na) and the last two letters of Mexico (co) and another noting that Naco means "bear hills" in the language of the Ópata, a native group of Sonora.[1] The two towns are equally small even today. Partly, this can be explained by geography: the Nacos are situated in the shadow of larger Sonora towns—Agua Prieta to the east and Nogales to the west—and the more historically famous mining towns of Cananea, Sonora, to the south and Bisbee, Arizona, to the north. A local testament to the obscurity of the border towns comes from one resident who claimed that "Our peak was 1950," because the primary tourists who once visited the Nacos—U.S. military personal stationed at nearby Ft. Huachuca, Arizona—no longer visit the border and instead get what they need next door in Sierra Vista, Arizona.[2]

Notwithstanding its diminutive condition, Naco, Sonora, "wasn't always that sleepy little border town."[3] Few would associate the place with aviation history as the site of the world's first aerial dogfight or the first place a bomb was dropped from the sky onto American soil. Like its neighbor Agua Prieta, Mexican Naco was besieged during the Mexican Revolution, and it continued to stage military engagements into the late 1920s as regional skirmishes raged in Sonora. Beyond its so-called bizarre excitements,[4] Naco displayed many of the same qualities of place found in other Mexican border towns. It was a formal port of entry between Mexico and the United States, and it maintained a railroad crossing for much of its history. It created a small plaza as the social center of the community, and it roared with the best of the border towns during Prohibition. Although Naco continued to attract visitor attention during part of the post–World War II era, it slowed considerably by mid-twentieth century. Nevertheless, these events and circumstances made the town appealing to postcard photographers, who documented a visual record of Naco from the early 1900s through the 1950s.

In this chapter, I resurrect Naco, Sonora's, past landscapes as a visual narrative to appreciate how the border town looked in its first half century. The town is mapped, districts are revealed, and landmark places are revisited. Postcard views capture the borderline and crossing and the immediate community and touristic spaces that were the principal subjects of visual representation during the first half of the twentieth century. The chapter concludes with a vignette of the battles at Naco that were reported by visiting journalists and pictured by postcard photographers.

Geographic and Historic Setting

Naco, Sonora, is situated west of Agua Prieta along the international boundary and south of Bisbee, Arizona (fig. 1.1). Unlike Agua Prieta, however, the site is not perched at the junction of two large valleys; rather, the border town is hinged at circa forty-six hundred feet on the lower slopes of the San José Mountains, which reach to greater than seven thousand feet elevation. To the northwest across the border are the Mule Mountains, which climb above five thousand feet, nestling Bisbee, Arizona, and to the west are the Huachuca Mountains, which rise above eight thousand feet, the highest elevation in the local area. The San Pedro River is the largest drainage in the vicinity, flowing north from Mexico across the boundary between the San José and Huachuca Mountains (fig. 4.1).

The site where Naco, Sonora, would rise straddled two mining districts, the Bisbee works in Arizona and the Cananea operations in Sonora. By the 1890s, freighting was a major enterprise where railroads had yet to penetrate. Figure 4.1 illustrates many of the trails that stitched the area together in 1896. Mexican freighters hauled food and mining supplies between the districts on each side of the international boundary. The crossing where Naco would emerge is high desert grassland, and teamsters staged at the site where natural feed and water from the San Pedro River were available for their animals.[5]

As the Phelps Dodge Company began to cement its control of copper mining and smelting in southeast Arizona and northeast Sonora, there were speculations about extending a railroad from Bisbee to Nacozari (south and east of Cananea). In 1898, a line was built to the border at Naco, Arizona, and once a concession was secured from

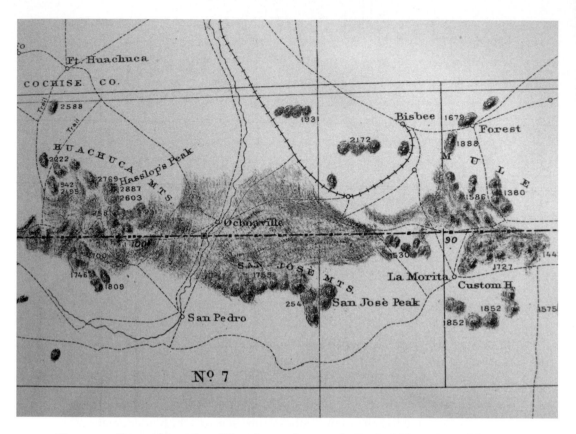

Figure 4.1. Geographic setting of Naco, Sonora, between the San José Mountains and the Huachuca Mountains (*elevations on this map are in meters*). When this map was made, the town had not yet been created. The future site would be on the international boundary northwest of La Morita and north of San José Peak. The San Pedro River is shown on the map but not labeled, flowing north between the San José and Huachuca mountains. International Boundary Commission, *Boundary Between the United States and Mexico*, detail from map Index Sheet A.

the Mexican government, plans were drafted to extend the rails south to Nacozari. Plans were aborted once Phelps Dodge realized the challenges of construction across the rugged Sonora topography to their mines at Nacozari from the border at Naco. Near the turn of the century, the El Paso and Southwestern Railroad connected El Paso to Douglas, and the line continued west to the border crossing at Naco.[6] This spurred the Cananea Consolidated Copper Company, owned by Tombstone rancher William Cornell Greene, to initiate construction of a railroad connecting Naco to Cananea. Greene obtained a concession from the Mexican government in 1900 to build a railroad between Naco and his copper-mining operations at Cananea, some forty miles beyond the border crossing. In 1903, the Southern Pacific Railroad obtained the railroad built by Greene.[7] By 1904 the Nacos were linked by steel rails

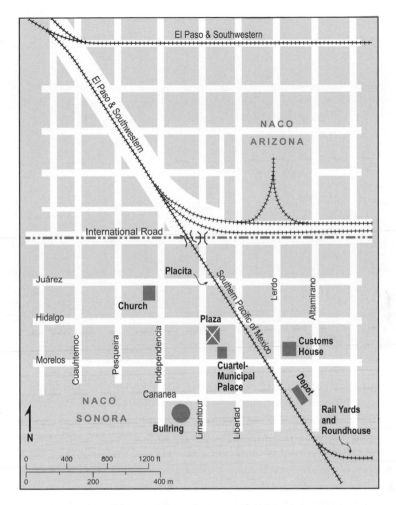

Figure 4.2. Map of the two Nacos, Sonora and Arizona, circa 1910s.
Sanborn Map Company, *Naco, Cochise County, Ariz., 1909*; International
Boundary Commission, *Proceedings Relating to the Placing of Additional
Monuments.* Cartography by Barbara Trapido-Lurie.

on each side of the border to mining and processing hinterlands beyond. The border
towns arose side by side, complementary settlements situated at a critical junction in
the emerging industrial landscape of the Sonora-Arizona borderland.[8]

The urban plan that was crafted for Naco, Sonora, in 1899 initially coincided with
the plan for Naco, Arizona (fig. 4.2). Blocks were mapped in symmetry, and streets,
although with different names, were aligned on each side of the border. The earliest buildings at Naco, Sonora, were both wood-frame and traditional adobe construction. Fearing that a haphazard plan might emerge, American property holders
who controlled land in Naco, Sonora, convinced the state of Sonora to reorganize

Figure 4.3. Aerial photograph of Naco, Arizona, and Naco, Sonora, 1924. The El Paso and Southwestern railroads intersect on the northwest side of Naco, Arizona, at the lower right of the image. The rails cross the international boundary at a diagonal to become the Southern Pacific Railroad of Mexico that extends into the background en route to the Mexican mining town of Cananea. A spur extends east of this line on the southeastern outskirts of Naco, Sonora, where a rail yard and locomotive roundhouse are visible at the middle left of the image. The cluster of quadrangles and associated buildings in Naco, Arizona, north of the railroad intersection, is Camp Naco. U.S. Army Air Service, "Aerial Photograph, Naco, Arizona, and Naco, Sonora, 1924." Courtesy Fort Huachuca Museum.

the initial plan. Sonora dispatched engineer Ignacio Bonillas to modify the plan to incorporate space for public buildings and a central plaza in the Mexican tradition and to reduce lot size to accommodate an expanding population. By 1907, infrastructure improvements heralded the growth of the Mexican town with the expansion of railroad yards to include machine shops and a water system extended from Naco, Arizona, to Naco, Sonora.[9]

Because the Nacos were developed as a railroad junction, the tracks cut diagonally across the grid of streets (fig. 4.3). At Naco, Arizona, the Arizona and South Eastern (after 1901, this rail segment became part of the El Paso and Southwestern) entered on the northwest side of town, where it intersected the El Paso and Southwestern, which

Figure 4.4. Railroad workshops and roundhouse at Naco, Sonora. The railroad and its facilities were constructed by Mexican operations of the Southern Pacific Railroad, which obtained the railroad from the Cananea, Yaqui River and Pacific Railroad in 1903. México Fotográfico 13, 1920s.

entered from the east. When the rails crossed the international border, the line initially belonged to the Cananea, Yaqui River and Pacific Railroad, the renamed Naco-Cananea line built by Greene in 1900, and eventually incorporated into the Southern Pacific Railroad of Mexico.[10] On the Arizona side of the border, spurs extended along the boundary, and on the Sonora side the rails peeled off to a roundhouse for locomotive service and railroad yards on the southeast edge of town (fig. 4.4).

The initial census taken for Naco, Sonora, recorded fifty-nine residents, chiefly Mexican men who worked for the railroad and the *aduana*, or customs office. Small numbers of French nationals and Americans were also counted in the first census. Naco, Sonora, attracted merchants, including several who operated stores in Nogales, Sonora, and who hoped for commercial success at the border crossing.[11] A 1904 map shows one property as a Chinese restaurant.[12] Because merchants depended on American shoppers, the signs in stores, cantinas, and hotels were typically in English, and American dollars were the preferred currency of exchange (fig. 4.5).[13] Although the Mexican border town grew rapidly from the beginning, its population hovered between five hundred and one thousand in its first decade (table 1.1).

Figure 4.5. 1900s view looking west along the boundary between the Nacos. Early buildings in Naco, Sonora, were wood frame, and merchants typically advertised in English to attract Americans. This view shows three kiosks where Mexican inspectors regulated official transit across the border, which was without a fence. The railroad cars on the right are positioned on the siding parallel to the boundary in Naco, Arizona. The railroad crossing to the Mexican side of the line is behind the horse-drawn cart that straddles the boundary in the middle of the image. In the far background is the shadowy outline of the Huachuca Mountains.

Crossing

Before the platting of the Nacos, two separate customs houses controlled official traffic across the boundary in the area. The American office was located in Bisbee, Arizona, whereas the Mexican customs was at La Morita, southeast of the future crossing (fig. 4.1). The La Morita customs was a regular stop for the stage service between Nacozari and the border. In 1900, both Mexico and the United States agreed to relocate customs facilities to the border at the respective Nacos.[14] The Mexican customs house in Naco was located near the railroad depot several blocks in from the boundary (fig. 4.2). Unlike more substantial structures at Agua Prieta and Nogales, the Naco customs house was a simple wooden structure (fig. 4.6). Nevertheless, the significance of the customs house as a repository of revenue from rail crossing traffic made the facility a key pawn in the many Revolutionary engagements where one army tried to protect it while the other army was trying to possess it.

Examination Station
of the Mexican Custom House
Naco, Sonora.

Figure 4.6. The first customs house in Naco, Sonora, is shown here in detail from a multi-view postcard of the early 1900s. The customs house was located proximate to the railroad line and near the depot several blocks in from the international boundary.

The Naco crossing was an open border without a fence until the late 1910s. The reminiscences of one former resident recalled that "the casual observer might not have noticed where Naco, Arizona, ended and Naco, Sonora began. . . . The Line is simply a monument here and there along the miles."[15] Figure 4.7 reveals the open border crossing during the 1900s and the Mexican *municipio* (municipal palace) and *cuartel*, or garrison building, several blocks in from the line along the main street, with a clock tower and flagstaff visible. This building at Naco, constructed sometime in the 1900s, was a grand architectural icon in the early border town, testimony to the need to quarter soldiers in the town to protect its economic position gained from rail traffic revenue (fig. 4.8). Border crossings were controlled at the ports of entry once a fence was constructed. Figure 4.9 shows the section of wire fence looking east from the railroad crossing with the main gate crossing just beyond. The adobe walled building with a pyramidal roof and animals and men in front is the Mexican crossing inspection station (often confused with the *aduana* or customs house).

Some three decades later the Naco crossing station became the immigration office, where Mexican officials were responsible for inspecting vehicles that enter Mexico through the port of entry and issuing visas for transit beyond the free border zone (fig. 4.10). In the 1950s, a new combined Office of Migration and Customs House,

Figure 4.7. View looking south into Naco, Sonora, from the U.S. side of the border before the boundary fence circa late 1900s. On the far left is a boundary marker, and behind and to the right is the crossing inspection, a simple wood-frame structure. On the right is the railroad alignment, a diagonal line crossing into Mexico. In the far background, with a flag flying above its cupola, is the Mexican *municipio* (municipal palace) and *cuartel*, or garrison.

Figure 4.8. *The municipio-cuartel* at Naco, Sonora, was indicative of the town's symbolic importance as a revenue station for railroad traffic crossing the international boundary and the need to defend the site. A grand architectural statement, the building was more elaborate than any single structure in the small border town. This view dates from the first decade of the twentieth century. In succeeding years during Revolutionary conflicts, the building would serve as a hospital. It also served as a school and, ultimately, returned to its role as the municipal palace, although greatly modified from its original grandeur.

Figure 4.9. View along the border fence between the Nacos circa 1910s. The building on the Mexican side with animals and men in front is the crossing inspection station. Osbon, 1910s.

Figure 4.10. Oficina de Migración (Immigration Office) is the primary inspection station for autos entering Naco during the 1940s. Immigration officers issue tourist visas to travelers driving into the interior of Mexico beyond the border zone. México Fotográfico 24, 1940s.

Figure 4.11. A new immigration and customs station was built at the Naco crossing during the 1950s. The two-story structure of concrete and glass in the boxy International style suggests the broader embrace of a modern architectural aesthetic in Mexico. México Fotográfico 14, 1950s.

a two-story structure of concrete and glass in boxy International style with covered bays for entrance and exit, appeared at the crossing (fig. 4.11). During this period, the Mexican national government passed a law that required visitors to Mexico who were not residents of an American border town to pay a fee to enter Mexico. This legal requirement caused some confusion at the crossing, and Mexican immigration officials in Naco refused to enforce the ordinance, believing the fee would compromise local tourism.[16]

Tourist Places

Prohibition initiated the construction of cabarets in Naco, Sonora, although this industry was small compared to the entertainment activity at nearby Agua Prieta. The drinking, dancing, and gambling businesses that opened in Naco were chiefly operated by American entrepreneurs from Bisbee, Arizona, whose saloons in Brewery

Naco - Border town near Bisbee

Figure 4.12. During the Prohibition era, drinking establishments that included Chinese-run restaurants were chiefly crowded near the border crossing. In this 1920s view, two American-operated businesses—Del Monte Café Bar and Arizona Club Café and Dining—are visible to the left and right respectively. San José peak looms in the background, and the spur line of the railroad in Naco, Arizona, is seen in the foreground. Courtesy Arizona Historical Society, Tucson #508.

Gulch closed in 1915 with passage of Arizona Prohibition that preceded the Volstead Act.[17] The Mexican border town was, in the vernacular of the era, "wide open," where American enterprises paid Mexican officials, and Mexican workers enabled full operation of the cabarets that were visited often by Bisbee residents.[18] There were perhaps five or six saloons, and all included a Chinese-operated restaurant serving steaks and wild-game dinners (fig. 4.12).[19] One of the more popular cabarets was the Foreign Club, which occupied a long set of buildings fronting the Mexican border town and squarely facing the international boundary (fig. 4.13). Inside, the Foreign Club had a large dance floor with live orchestra stage and decorative lanterns and wall hangings inspired by the Chinese who ran the café (fig 4.14).

Beyond cabaret, Naco operated a bullring that predated the one opened in Agua Prieta in 1903 and introduced American visitors to the traditional Mexican blood sport, which enabled gambling. Like the *plaza de toros* in Agua Prieta, the American-owned

Figure 4.13. The Foreign Club Café and Foreign Club Casino were popular venues for Americans visiting Naco, Sonora, during the town's "wide open" era.

Figure 4.14. The large ballroom with Chinese-inspired lamps and wall hangings inside the Foreign Club Café at Naco, Sonora, where Prohibition-era visitors could while away the night with drink, dance, and live music.

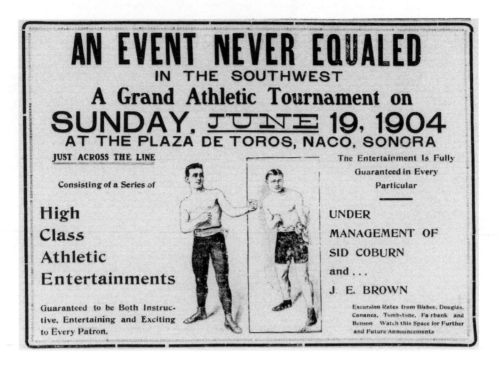

Figure 4.15. The bullring at Naco was a stage for prizefights as well as bullfights during the first decades of the twentieth century. Visitors from the American side of the line could ride by train to the ring in Mexico. *Bisbee Daily Review*, "An Event Never Equaled in the Southwest," advertisement, June 11, 1904.

and operated bullring—it was called the Plaza de Toros, Mazzantini, after its operator in 1901—was also a stage for prizefights and other activities (fig. 4.15).[20] The ring was five blocks from the crossing at the southern edge of town, accessible by rail from the American side of the border (fig. 4.2). The bullring persisted beyond Prohibition and into the post–World War II period as a tourist attraction.

With the repeal of Prohibition in 1933, American cabaret owners in Naco, Sonora, closed their enterprises and returned to saloon businesses in the United States while Mexicans assumed the cabaret operations, which slowed considerably with the Great Depression. Naco, Sonora, revived somewhat in the post–World War II era when cabarets reopened to attract principally U.S. military personnel on leave from nearby Ft. Huachuca.[21] Perhaps the most popular attraction during this period was the Monterrey Bar, which opened near the crossing where the previous Arizona Club Café and Dining had operated during the 1920s (fig. 4.16). While the Monterrey Bar offered drinking, dancing, and live entertainment on its outdoor patio (fig. 4.17), Naco also catered somewhat to the emerging curio crafts trade that expanded with border

Figure 4.16. The Monterrey Bar in Naco, Sonora, was perhaps the most popular post–World War II cabaret establishment drawing American tourists to the small Mexican border town. The bar was within walking distance of the border crossing, and it offered drink, dinner, dancing, and curios. México Fotográfico 16, 1950s.

Figure 4.17. A principal attraction of the Monterrey Bar in Naco, Sonora, was the outdoor patio, where locals as well as tourist visitors could gather. The patio included sheltered seating, a tile dance floor, and a small covered bandstand. In this image there appears to be a soldier seated at one of the tables; Naco's proximity to Ft. Huachuca made it a favorite entertainment venue for military personnel.

tourism after the Second World War. However, this was not an entirely new activity. Naco, Sonora, did have curio shops before as evident by advertisements in Bisbee newspapers. The Three Republics store, for example, promoted itself in 1907 as being, "Just Across the Line," selling Mexican serapes, silk shawls, carved leather, baskets, pottery, and Veracruz cigars.[22] Ironically, however, Naco likely generated greater revenue from the cattle-crossing trade than curio and cabaret businesses during this era, but the ranching business seemed less alluring to postcard photographers than tourist activity, and consequently no popular images of the cattle operations were created.[23]

Civic Landmarks

Although a small border community compared with neighboring Agua Prieta, Naco typifies Mexican towns across the republic with its plazas, church, and municipal palace, or city hall. Postcard photographers were especially engaged by the plazas and surrounding land uses that were close to the crossing and accessible to visitors. While Naco maintains a Catholic church, the structure is modest compared with most towns, and significantly, it is not situated near other public spaces; rather, it is located on a residential side street (fig. 4.2).

The principal plaza of Naco is called Plaza Pública; it bears no honorary name and thereby contains no statuary celebrating any Mexican historical figures.[24] This may be the result of the late modification of the town layout as described above, and it suggests the heritage of American property ownership in the border town. The plaza was located only two blocks from the border crossing at the intersection of Limantour and Hidalgo (fig. 4.2). By the 1940s, the small plaza sported dirt walk paths leading to a central elevated wooden covered *kiosco* (bandstand) surrounded by benches and sparse ornamental vegetation including cottonwood trees (fig. 4.18). Next to the plaza on the same block was the municipal palace (fig. 4.19). The palace, or city hall, is the same building that once served as the *cuartel*, or garrison (fig. 4.8), although greatly modified following the battles at Naco during the 1920s. Naco, like many border towns, regularly celebrated Mexican holidays called *fiestas patrias* in Mexico, and often these festivities were celebrated on the plaza and surrounding streets.[25] During the 1950s, Naco's plaza and municipal palace were remodeled. The plaza walkways became concrete, and the *kiosco* was elevated and rebuilt with stone and concrete. The entrance to the palace facing the plaza and street was modified, and older columns were removed (fig. 4.20). Also in the 1950s, a second, smaller plaza was constructed in Naco on the triangular block across the street and facing the border crossing (fig. 4.2). This *placita* (small plaza) was designed in art deco style popular during the era (fig. 4.21).

Figure 4.18. Plaza Pública in Naco, Sonora, with its dirt walk paths leading to a central small wooden *kiosco* surrounded by benches and spare ornamental vegetation. México Fotográfico 22, 1940s.

Figure 4.19. The municipal palace or city hall in Naco, Sonora, flanked by the main plaza of the town. México Fotográfico 23, 1940s.

Figure 4.20. The Plaza Pública in Naco, Sonora, was remodeled in the 1950s, adding concrete walkways and elevating and rebuilding the *kiosco*. Next door, the municipal palace entrance was also remodeled; cf. fig. 4.19. Plazas were sometimes the settings for fiestas and circus rides (note Ferris wheel in background) that would occasionally visit border towns. México Fotográfico 9, 1950s.

Figure 4.21. Placita (little plaza) constructed in Naco, Sonora, on a small triangular parcel between the border crossing (*background*) and the main plaza (*out of picture*). México Fotográfico 23, 1950s.

Vignette: Battles at Naco

Beyond its significance as an international railroad crossing and the implications of that position to the regional economies of northeastern Sonora and southeastern Arizona, Naco, Sonora, was the stage of numerous military engagements in the first three decades of the twentieth century. While these encounters strictly involved Mexican forces in combat with one another on the south side of the border, American military on the north side of the boundary at Naco, Arizona, were typically put on high alert. In the case of one protracted engagement where Mexican Naco was under siege for months, American diplomatic involvement was necessary to quell the violence. The battles at Naco, however, were not simply civil wars; they also became theater for American observers north of the line who flocked to the boundary to witness the fighting. These engagements drew news reporters, even a movie production crew, and, not surprisingly, postcard photographers. Images were the illustrated media of the day, and similar to border conflicts on other fronts of the Mexican American boundary, postcards were a popular means of representing the events and visual consequences of battle.[26]

Between 1910 and 1929, Naco was occupied and or attacked on four separate occasions. In 1911, rebel leader Arturo "Red" López, sympathetic to Francisco Madero's Revolutionary cause, led his small army into Naco, Sonora—then held by federal forces—to sack the *aduana* of its monetary resources collected through tariffs at the international railroad crossing. Rebel attempts to sack the customs house in Naco were common. In one instance in 1910, the Mexican customs officials relocated important documents and funds to Naco, Arizona, for temporary safe keeping, and in another instance, the customs house revenue was shipped to Mexico City to keep it out of rebel hands.[27]

In 1913, following the assassination of President Francisco Madero, Naco was again held by Mexican federal troops under General Pedro Ojeda, who was ordered to defend the railroad border town by newly ascended president Victoriano Huerta. In opposition to Huerta's rule, Constitutionalist rebel armies directed by Plutarco Elías Calles and Prefecto Bracamonte invaded Naco. Ojeda ordered defensive trenches dug on the outskirts of Naco, and a siege lasted for more than a month before Ojeda surrendered his troops. During one of the final engagements, however, Constitutionalist forces launched bombs at the federal barracks (the *cuartel*), customs house, and other buildings, and the result was a fire that ravaged much of the town. It was the 1913 battle that was filmed by an American cinematographer, and the documentary was released and shown in the same year.[28]

Perhaps the most revolutionary event of the battles at Naco was the appearance of biplanes used by both armies in 1913. While airplanes in battle chiefly to drop explosives appeared during the Mexican Revolution starting in 1911, Naco's confrontation may be the first instance of an aerial dogfight. The federal forces had been harassing Constitutionalist armies trying to invade Naco, Sonora, by commanding a Christofferson biplane to fly over the rebel troops every few days to drop small bombs. American soldier of fortune Dean Ivan Lamb, a veteran of several Latin American revolutions, convinced Constitutionalist General Benjamín Hill that he could assist the rebel cause if he could somehow secure an airplane. Hill wired contacts in the United States to confirm Lamb's claims and then ordered a Curtiss Model D biplane to be railway express shipped to Douglas, Arizona. Flying out of Naco, Arizona, on aerial reconnaissance, Lamb encountered the Mexican federal biplane and immediately recognized the pilot as Phil Rader, a reporter for the *San Francisco Examiner*. The pilots drew their pistols and exchanged gunfire, but there were no recorded hits. Out of ammunition, the pilots separated and returned to their respective landing strips. In a later memoir, Lamb testified that Rader's first shot was not actually aimed at him and that after mutual agreement the two pilots continued to fire at anything on the ground that seemed fair game, providing the onlookers below a ringside seat to what the press later called the "world's first aerial duel."[29]

The most celebrated battle at Naco occurred in 1914 and 1915, when Constitutionalist forces under Venustiano Carranza refused to abide Madero's successor, Victoriano Huerta, who had become implicated in the former president's assassination. In Sonora, Governor José María Maytorena, resenting Carranza's attempts to depose him by supporting rival generals Elías Calles and Benjamín Hill, invaded Naco, then controlled by Hill-Calles forces in 1914.[30]

In October 1914, as Maytorena prepared to invade, Hill and Calles amassed some two thousand troops at Naco. The Constitutionalist generals excavated lines of formidable trenches and defensive battlements surrounding the town on the east, south, and west, planted land mines outside the lines of trenches, erected barbed wire on the perimeter, and installed a light on top of the town's bullring to illuminate any nighttime attack, thereby transforming the small Mexican border town into a virtual fortress (fig. 4.22). Anticipating the battle, the U.S. government in Washington ordered Colonel John F. Gilfoyle, commander of a cavalry unit in Douglas, Arizona, to proceed to Naco, Arizona, to defend against any encroachment on American soil. Gilfoyle erected American flags along the north side of the international border and advised General Hill in Naco, Sonora, and Maytorena, who was camped outside of town with four thousand troops, including many Yaqui soldiers, that "no firing into American Naco would be tolerated."[31] For several days, light skirmishing between the armies ensued, but no major attack on Naco transpired. Little time passed before American spectators—thrill seekers wanting to witness the battle—began to arrive in automobiles from Bisbee.

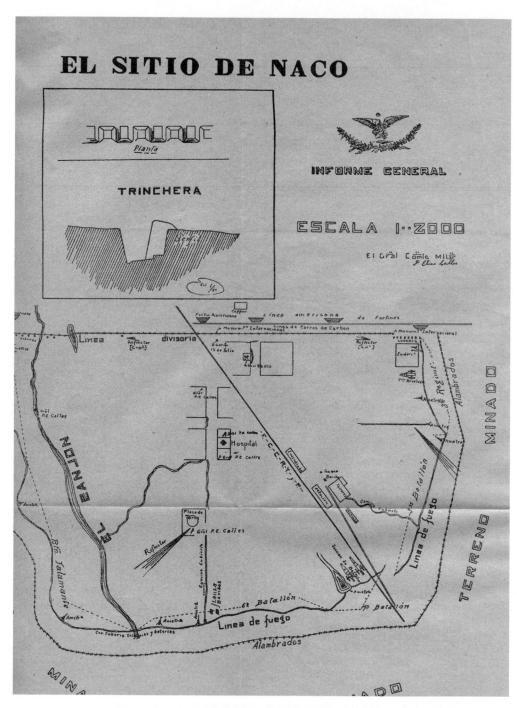

Figure 4.22. Calles map showing the Hill-Calles defenses surrounding Naco, Sonora, during the protracted siege from 1914 to 1915. Trenches, battlements, land mines, barbed wire, and an electric light atop the bullring to defend against night attack transformed the small border town to a virtual fortress. Elías Calles, *Informe relativo al sitio de Naco*, 1914–1915.

Maytorena finally let loose a full attack on Naco, Sonora, at midnight, October 11, rushing Yaqui soldiers toward the defensive trenches. The night battle resulted in some Maytorena forces crossing into Naco, Arizona, to attack Hill's army from the undefended international border in defiance of American neutrality. Some of Maytorena's canon fire also crossed the boundary, striking but doing little damage to American Naco. The next day, Maytorena withdrew to attack Agua Prieta, also held by Constitutionalist forces, allowing Hill's army a reprieve that likely cost Maytorena victory. Although Maytorena attacked Naco, Sonora, again on October 15, Hill's forces repelled the attempt, and soon the battle slowed to an impasse despite repeated attempts by Maytorena's army to penetrate Naco's defenses.[32] Over the course of the stalemate, which ensued for more than one hundred days, photographers emerged to capture images of Hill's defenses, and some of these appeared as photo postcards.[33]

In December 1914, American diplomatic efforts convinced both forces that retreat from Naco was in the best interest of all. Calles and Hill were advised to relocate east to Agua Prieta and Maytorena west to Nogales. The Constitutionalist armies agreed, but Maytorena remained intransigent. Finally, Francisco "Pancho" Villa, who by this time had broken with the Carranza Constitutionalists, advised Maytorena to retreat, and in January 1915 his army evacuated. Almost immediately, order was restored to Naco, and a plan to rebuild destroyed buildings was put in place.[34]

The final episode of twentieth-century battles at Naco was a post–Mexican Revolution event known as the Escobar Rebellion. The revolt, led by General José Gonzalo Escobar under the banner of the Plan of Hermosillo, called for the overthrow of Mexican president Portes Gil in 1929. Gil's administration was announced to be the instrument of former Mexican president Plutarco Elías Calles, accused of exercising corruption to impose his will on the nation. The Escobar Rebellion has been judged, thereby, as an anti-Calles movement.[35] The revolt was especially centered in north Mexican states, including Sonora, where Governor Fausto Topete supported the Plan of Hermosillo. Topete ordered his armies to invade Naco, which was then held by federal troops that supported president Gil. As in all previous battles at Naco, the Sonora border town was prized because it was an international port of entry and a railroad junction linked to a resource-rich economic hinterland of mining.

Naco was still surrounded by trenches from the 1914–1915 siege, and the federal troops holding the town made ready these defenses in anticipation of the rebel attack in April 1929 (fig. 4.23). Many residents flocked to the international line to seek refuge in American Naco. One American customs inspector recalled the haste created by the thought of another battle. "The threat of an immediate rebel attack alarmed the civilian population of Naco, Mexico. . . . They stormed this office seeking refuge in this country. They resembled refugees from some storm or flood stricken area, with their blankets,

Figure 4.23. Federal trenches surrounding Naco, Sonora anticipating a rebel attack during the Escobar Rebellion in 1929.

Figure 4.24. Naco, Sonora, residents created fortifications to protect their homes from anticipated shelling during the Escobar Rebellion battle of 1929. Courtesy Bisbee Mining and Historical Museum, Valenzuela Collection, #A-241–37.

household goods, cooking utensils and in most cases, parrots, chickens and the ever present dog."[36] In town, those residents who decided to remain erected fortifications around homes, recalling the destruction delivered from previous battles (fig. 4.24).

The 1929 battle was especially noteworthy because aerial bombardment by airplanes rained down on both Mexican and American Naco.[37] Pilots manning the World War I vintage biplanes were Americans contracted to each army. The federals maintained an airfield south of Naco, Sonora, and the rebels used the airfield in Naco, Arizona. Rebel aircraft chiefly bombed the outskirts of Naco where federal troops were concentrated, but bombs also fell on the Southern Pacific Railroad yards, again inflicting significant damage to the facilities that had previously been destroyed (fig. 4.25).[38] At times, rebel pilots were confounded by the accuracy of their targets and on several occasions actually dropped bombs on American Naco. "All during the battle rebel airplanes bombed the town of Naco, Mexico, and one bomb fell on the U. S. side of the line, a full block north of the Customs House. Bullets were continually flying on this side of the line and this office [U.S. Customs] was hit many times, although the officers remained on duty during the entire day."[39]

One of the most celebrated accidents was a car destroyed by aerial bombs; it was quickly photographed and made into a postcard that has been widely reproduced in

Figure 4.25. Railroad yards and roundhouse on the south edge of Naco, Sonora, were regularly subject to destruction during the border town's repeated Revolutionary struggles. This photographic postcard shows burned railroad cars and warehouses at the Southern Pacific Railroad yards on the southeast outskirts of the town circa 1910s.

Figure 4.26. American tourists gather at Naco, Arizona, on the international boundary (note the boundary monument and wire fence) to view the trenches where Mexican federal troops defended Naco, Sonora, from rebel invasion during the battle in 1929. Courtesy Bisbee Mining and Historical Museum, Lockridge, Myrtle Collection, #211–14.

historical accounts.[40] Another postcard that gained popularity was an image of one of the federal pilots, American R. L. Andrews, standing between two pieces of aerial ordinance, a twenty-five-pound bomb and a one-hundred-pound bomb.[41]

The 1929 battle, like previous engagements, attracted an audience of American curiosity seekers, again chiefly from Bisbee, Arizona. News reporters and tourist observers gathered especially at the Naco Hotel on the Arizona side of the border where second-story rooms with windows facing Naco, Sonora, enabled daily viewing of the battle.[42] When the engagement was declared a draw and a truce signed about one month after it started, tourists made their way to the border and even into Naco, Sonora, to inspect the trenches (fig. 4.26). Following the 1929 battle, the trenches on the outskirts of Naco were filled in and never used again for a defensive campaign.[43]

5

Nogales

T he site that would emerge as Ambos Nogales—Nogales, Sonora, and Nogales, Arizona—was known as Rancho Los Nogales, a large tract of land that straddled both sides of the international boundary when the line was surveyed in 1853. In the local Spanish vernacular, *nogales* are walnut trees that grew along the arroyo where the towns would be built. The surrounding lands had been owned by several *hacendados* (large property holders) with family names such as Elías and Camou, surnames that would later be attached to prominent streets in the Sonora town. As settlement developed, different names became associated with the respective towns. The Sonora side settled on Nogales, although it was early called Villa Riva, and in at least one instance there was a failed attempt to rename the community Ciudad Dublán after a Mexican finance minister. The American settlement was first called Issactown, bestowed by an early resident, but popular consensus preferred the name Line City because the town hugged the international boundary.[1] In 1883, the American town name was changed to Nogales, a symbolic gesture that "underscored the growing interrelationship between the towns."[2] Ambos Nogales, the two Nogales, thereby share both a physical proximity and social identity along the Sonora-Arizona border.

In this chapter, I chart the visual landscape of Nogales, Sonora, as presented chiefly through postcard imagery. Because the Sonora town grew as a railroad crossing and the most significant economic node along the Arizona boundary, Nogales was frequently captured through the lenses of local as well as itinerant photographers, more so than any other Sonora border town (table 2.2). The high density of photographic postcard imagery enables attention to a host of subjects. Like other border towns, Nogales can be assessed through views of its crossing, its plaza, and its streets, activity spaces that drew postcard photographers. Beyond those nearly universal border allures, there were spaces unique to Nogales that allowed photographers to create different views that might not be found in other Sonora border towns. Nogales, for example, is the only Sonora border community with a high-rise building, the multistoried Fray Marcos de Niza Hotel completed in 1950. Also, because Nogales has been the most populated Sonora border town since the late nineteenth century, it supported multiple crossings, another unique quality. Further, while other Sonora border places have or had customs houses, none could rival the Neoclassical façade and grandiose nature of the Nogales *aduana*, a landmark structure that symbolized the town for generations of Nogalense (residents of Nogales). Finally, Nogales's location in a narrow ravine surrounded by hills creates a setting unusual among Mexican border towns. This position meant postcard photographers could compose images looking down on the town from surrounding vantage points to create panoramic vistas. That imagery enabled postcard views of Nogales's hillside residential development as well as unique perspectives on the boundary, and later fence line, dividing the Mexican from the American town.

This chapter, similar to chapters 3 ("Agua Prieta") and 4 ("Naco"), includes a separate vignette that documents one of the most celebrated landmarks of the Sonora border, the Cavern Café, which graced Nogales and attracted patrons from around the world. Unique to this chapter is a separate gallery to illustrate the changing nature of the boundary and fence separating Nogales, Sonora, from Nogales, Arizona.

These viewpoints, however, require a spatial context. Before exploring streets, landmarks, and tourist places, I situate Nogales on the Sonora-Arizona border. Maps informed by discussion based on documents provide a first glimpse of the geographical setting of Nogales, Sonora. I then use visual perspectives from panoramas and border crossings to anchor a geographic understanding of the largest Sonora border town.

Geographic and Historic Setting

Nogales, Sonora, sits at an elevation of almost four thousand feet between the Patagonia Mountains to the east and the Pajarito Mountains to the west (fig. 5.1). The natural path that cuts between these ranges is the Santa Cruz River, which flows south from the Patagonia Mountains, across the international boundary, and then turns north to flow across the border again immediately east of Nogales. Before the creation of the international border, passes between the Patagonia and Pajarito Mountains such as the Santa Cruz River were access points linking the principal settlements of Sonora to the south with the border region and beyond. This corridor was part of a nineteenth-century wagon route linking Sonora and its historic port of Guaymas

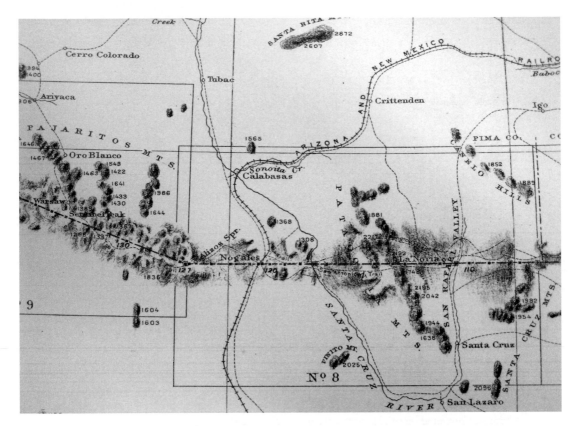

Figure 5.1. Nogales is situated at circa four thousand feet elevation between the Pajarito and Patagonia Mountains (*elevations on this map are in meters*). The Santa Cruz River crosses the international boundary two times before flowing north east of Nogales. This map also shows the path of the railroad north and south of Nogales. International Boundary Commission, *Boundary Between the United States and Mexico*, detail from map Index Sheet A.

on the Gulf of California to the northernmost outpost of Mexican settlement in the region at Tucson on the banks of the Santa Cruz River in present Arizona.[3]

When the decision to route a railroad across the international boundary was made in the late 1870s, Mexican engineers for the Sonora Railroad (part of the Atchison, Topeka and Santa Fe—ATSF—system) selected a path through a narrow arroyo west of the Santa Cruz River. North of the boundary American engineers extended the Arizona and New Mexico Railroad (also part of the ATSF system) from Benson, Arizona, south to intersect the Mexican line at Nogales (fig. 5.1). The two lines joined in 1882, creating a rail link that would later be incorporated into the Southern Pacific Railroad system.[4]

Engineers Ignacio Bonillas and Charles E. Herbert were commissioned by the governor of Sonora to plat the municipality of Nogales after contractual agreements with

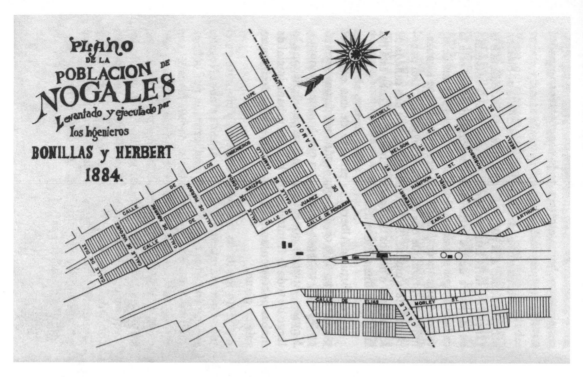

Figure 5.2. Bonillas and Herbert 1884 plat map showing Nogales, Sonora, and Nogales, Arizona. This was the first official map of the surveyed towns. Unattributed, see Piñera Ramirez, *Caminando entre el pasado y el presente de Nogales.*

private property owners were arranged to create the *fondo legal*.[5] The 1884 Bonillas and Herbert map shows the distinctive grid of city blocks west of the railroad tracks that contrast with the truncated irregular blocks east of the tracks (fig. 5.2). The street east of the tracks on the Mexican side is Calle Elías, which is especially constricted by a steep hill, hence the tight arrangement of smaller blocks along that alignment. Also visible on the plat is a property setback from the boundary line along Calle de Camou on the Mexican side, whereas town blocks on the American side are flush to the borderline. The map also shows the early railroad depot as a single structure straddling the international boundary. A decade later, in 1894, Mexican historian F. T. Dávila commented that Mexican Nogales and American Nogales were face-to-face separated by a single street: "La villa Mexicana de Nogales, está colocada frente á frente de la ciudad Americana de Nogales. Están divididas por el espacio de una calle."[6]

The populations at Nogales, which before the railroad consisted of a few scattered residents on each side of the boundary, exploded with the meeting of the rails. In 1884, the population in Nogales, Sonora, reached one thousand, and in 1900, nearly three thousand. It would persist throughout the twentieth century as the most populated

Mexican town on the boundary with Arizona (table 1.1). Nogales, Arizona, by comparison, counted less than two thousand residents in 1900, and through succeeding decades would never surpass the Sonora town in population.[7]

Figure 5.3 is the Gustavo Cox map of 1888, which captures the material landscape of Nogales, Sonora, on the eve of the twentieth century. Whereas the Bonillas and Herbert plat of 1884 showed the skeleton of the town's ground plan, the Cox map highlights with dark shading how blocks were built up and, thus, where residents lived and used spaces. Most of the Mexican town population hugged the border with the greatest density of settlement inside three blocks of the boundary. Beyond Calle Pierson, only scattered blocks along Calle Arizpe appear built on, and most of the town, while platted, was not yet occupied. Calle Elías is densely built up, as are the blocks adjacent to Calles Pesqueira, Campillo, and Juárez. The large rectangular structure on the southeast corner of Calle Campillo and Avenida Juárez and jutting out toward the railroad alignment is the customs house. The map also reveals in light shading three separate channels of the town's arroyo that converge along Calle Camou immediately west of the railroad depot that straddles the boundary. These drainages created a deep trench along the borderline—Nogales Wash—that would not be filled until the early twentieth century.

From 1910 through the post–World War II era, Nogales grew to become the most populated town on the Sonora border (table 1.1). The border town emerged as a transaction center for surrounding ranching and mining interests, and merchants became wealthy importing and distributing goods to local and regional consumers. In a 1919 publication by the Camaras de Comercio (Chambers of Commerce), Nogales was called La Ciudad Llave (Key City), boasting of its strategic location, rail connections, and aggressive entrepreneurial spirit.[8] In the following year the *Nogales Daily Herald* published its Sixth Anniversary and Industrial Edition, "Replete with Information Relative to Progress, Industry and Opportunity Offered by the Key City to the West Coast of Mexico."[9] Entire sections of the fifty-four-page special edition boasted about the cities of Nogales, Sonora, and Nogales, Arizona, as well as west coast Sonora towns such as the port of Guaymas and the capital of Hermosillo.

While economic prosperity brought geographic expansion to Nogales, the town enlarged only slightly from 1888 to 1924.[10] Because the principal built up area of Nogales was restricted by its confinement to a narrow corridor, physical growth was chiefly limited to flat land. From the 1930s to the 1950s, and especially after the Second World War, however, the population almost doubled in size from nearly fourteen thousand to greater than twenty-four thousand residents (table 1.1). Some of the growth in Nogales during this two-decade era resulted in greater residential encroachment into surrounding hillsides, a process captured by historic postcard photography.

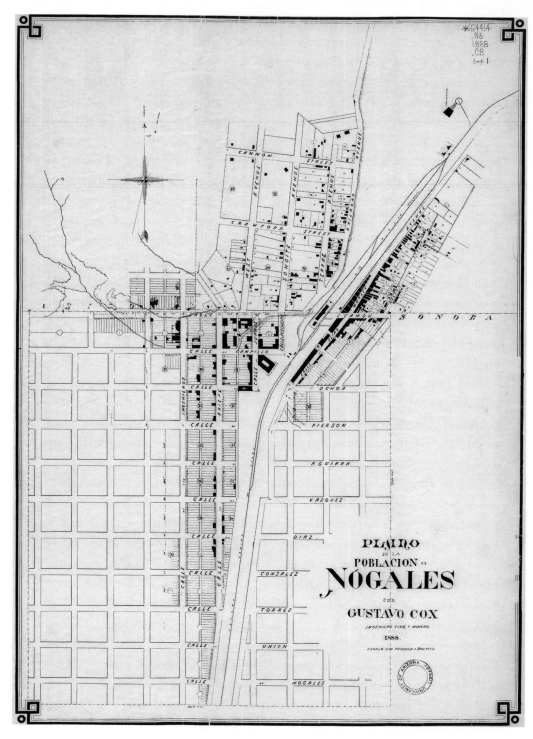

Figure 5.3. *Plano de la Población de Nogales*, Gustavo Cox, 1888. Courtesy Special Collections, University of Arizona Libraries.

Panoramic Views

Nogales is unusually positioned in a narrow pass surrounded by hills, and that condition alone enabled postcard photographers to capture views not possible in any of the other Sonora border towns. Figure 5.4, a detail from an 1889 boundary resurvey map, suggests how the original plat of the town was nestled in a narrow bottomland encircled by steep hillsides (tight contour lines). The illustration captures Nogales, Sonora, situated inside a twelve-hundred-meter contour line east and west of the plat and railroad corridor. Beyond the boundaries of the plat are two separate clusters of dwellings that indicate residential building, even then, progressing up slope. One group of structures is shown east of the railroad track about three blocks south of the international boundary. These dwellings were likely the initial buildings that would eventually form a separate *colonia* (suburb) called Buenos Aires (Good Airs), named for the hill zone immediately east of the town center. A second cluster of dwellings is evident on the map at the southwest edge of the town positioned chiefly above the twelve-hundred-meter contour line, suggesting another early suburban concentration. These early hillside residential zones are visible in photographic postcards and other images made between the 1890s and 1950s.

The Arreola Collection includes fifty-seven postcards that are panoramic views of Nogales, Sonora (not including the panoramic fence line views discussed in the gallery below). Six of these views from the twentieth century are used to illustrate some of the panoramic viewpoints and hillside housing surrounding Nogales over six decades.

A series of postcard views looking south from Nogales, Arizona, into Nogales, Sonora, for the 1910s, 1930s, and 1950s reveals the sequential development of dwellings on the hillsides immediately east of the Mexican downtown area. Figure 5.5, a 1910s view, shows little to no building on the hill zones east of the town center and beyond. Two decades later, in the 1930s, dwellings are seen scattered along these same hillsides, and two decades hence, in the 1950s, these same areas suggest slightly greater housing density (figs. 5.6, 5.7). One of these hillside districts (Colonia Buenos Aires) was captured in close-up, and thereby illustrates how dense some of these suburban communities had become (fig. 5.8).

Houses built in the hill zones around Nogales vary in quality and style depending on time of construction and the general wealth of the residents. While it is sometimes assumed that only the poorest residents choose to live in hillside areas, from the early twentieth century, some Nogalense have built homes on the surrounding slopes of town (fig. 5.9). Largely inaccessible by automobile, these neighborhoods were linked by steep footpaths and later by primitive staircases. Nevertheless, hillside *colonias* and

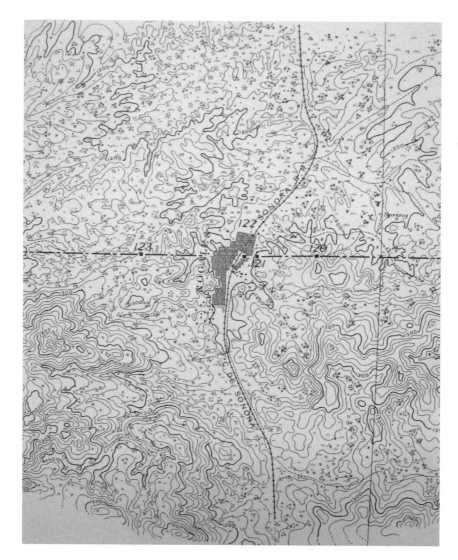

Figure 5.4. Nogales was joined by railroads from the north and south in 1882. The flat land along the narrow pass enabled initial construction of towns divided by the international boundary. Boundary markers 120, 121, and 122 are positioned east of the railroad alignment (*elevations on this map are in meters*). International Boundary Commission, *Boundary Between the United States and Mexico*, detail from map no. 12.

the dwellings that make up these neighborhoods have always reflected the well-being of residents, including those in lower-income households (fig. 5.10). From its earliest beginnings, Nogales, Sonora, was really two towns: a conventional concentration of homes and businesses on flat land—Nogales *abajo* (lower)—surrounded by a perched town of homes and small businesses strung like pearl necklaces across nearby hills— Nogales *arriba* (above).

Figure 5.5. Panoramic view looking south from Nogales, Arizona, to Nogales, Sonora, circa 1910s, with border visible near the center, where a crossing-guard kiosk is positioned at the north edge of Calle Arizpe. Hillsides to the east of the town center are chiefly without buildings. Lohn Fot., 1910s.

Figure 5.6. Panoramic view looking south from Nogales, Arizona, to Nogales, Sonora, showing early hillside residential development east of the Mexican town center in the 1930s.

Figure 5.7. Panoramic view looking south from Nogales, Arizona, to Nogales, Sonora, circa 1950s, showing intensified housing development on hillsides east of the Mexican town center. W. M. Cline, 1950s.

Figure 5.8. Bird's-eye view of Colonia Buenos Aires east of the town center of Nogales, Sonora, 1950s. Note density of housing development here compared to views of previous decades (fig. 5.5, 5.6). México Fotográfico 15, 1950s.

Figure 5.9. Many hillside residents in *colonias* surrounding Nogales walked to their homes on narrow paths. While electricity might have been available, water was likely hauled uphill before municipal systems extended into these zones. This view also shows that outdoor privies were common before sewerage systems were constructed. Frashers Fotos, 1937.

Figure 5.10. Primitive dwellings of Nogales hillside residents. Lohn Fot., 30, 1910s.

Crossings

Compared to other Sonora border towns, Nogales is unique as well in the number of official crossing sites connecting the Mexican to the American town. Four separate crossings have linked Nogales, Sonora, to Nogales, Arizona, since the late nineteenth century. Two of these crossings were neighborhood points of access on the west side of Ambos Nogales that were closed by the late 1920s. The two surviving commercial crossings have been the Elías-Morley gate and the main gate that also includes the railroad crossing. Like border crossings in other towns along the Mexico–United States boundary, gates are active social and economic sites where pedestrian and automotive transit are suspended by immigration authorities. As a consequence, crossings have historically attracted postcard photographers who document the to and fro of human mobility at these nodes of border transaction. The Arreola Collection includes almost one hundred individual Nogales gate-crossing postcards.

Figure 5.11 is a 1920s view looking west along the borderline that reveals the four crossings. Starting at the bottom of the image and moving toward the top of the photo postcard, one can discern the Elías-Morley gate with two guardhouses flanking the opening through the simple wire fence, a small guardhouse at the main gate and railroad crossing, and a guardhouse beyond at the intersection of Calle Camou (parallel to the boundary on the Mexican side) and Calle Arizpe. Not visible in the shadow of the image is a fourth guardhouse on the south end of the Bonillas Bridge that spans the arroyo—Nogales Wash—between the railroad crossing and the Arizpe crossing.

The Calle Elías and Morley Avenue gate was the most prominent crossing of the early decades in part because it linked the two oldest commercial streets of Ambos Nogales (fig. 5.3). Figure 5.12 captures a street-level view of this gate looking north into Nogales, Arizona, along Morley before the construction of the border fence. The man in the chair is sitting next to a Mexican guardhouse, while the man on horseback is across the line in the United States; the telephone poles are the approximate location of the international boundary. Figure 5.13 is a 1920s view looking into Nogales, Sonora, along Calle Elías snapped from the American side of the line. In this image, the metal poles (near the Lohn signature) of a short wire fence are visible to the right of the Mexican guardhouse near boundary monument 122 (the white obelisk), and the American guardhouse is positioned like a chess piece in the middle of International Street to monitor movement across the line.

West of the Elías-Morley gate is the railroad crossing. Since 1884, one railroad depot spanned the international boundary (fig. 5.2), but in 1904, fire destroyed the landmark that once physically joined Ambos Nogales. By 1906, separate depots set back from the international boundary were constructed in Sonora and in Arizona. A

Figure 5.11. Prohibition-era vista along the Nogales boundary. Border-crossing locations inserted here—Calle Elías-Morley Avenue, Main Gate and Railroad, Bonillas Bridge, and Calle Arizpe—are not evident on the original postcard. Lohn, 1920s.

Figure 5.12. 1910s street-level view looking north on Morley Avenue from Calle Elías at the Nogales border. Boundary is shown before the border fence with guardhouse on right in Sonora and buildings positioned north of the line in Arizona. Attributed to Rochin y Méndez, La Industria Mexicana, 1910s.

Figure 5.13. 1920s street-level view looking south from the Nogales, Arizona, border across the boundary down Calle Elías. Boundary is shown after the border fence that runs near the Mexican guardhouse on the right. The American guardhouse is positioned in the middle of International Street so traffic can enter Mexico on the right and exit on the left. Lohn, 48, 1920s.

small guardhouse was built parallel to the track to monitor railroad crossings moving north into Nogales, Arizona, and south into Nogales, Sonora (fig. 5.11).

West of this guardhouse and the railroad track is the arroyo of the Nogales Wash that runs parallel to the boundary on the Sonora side (fig. 5.11). The arroyo is spanned by a stonemasonry bridge, which connects to Calle Pesqueira and Mexican Nogales. Figure 5.14 is an early view of this crossing and the Mexican guardhouse positioned at the end of the Bonillas Bridge. The Neoclassical façade of the Mexican customs house can be glimpsed in the background, and the large two-story structure to the right of the bridge is the American consulate in Nogales, Sonora. The arroyo was filled in 1918, and drainage along this part of the boundary was diverted into an underground culvert that crossed into Nogales, Arizona. As a result, the Bonillas Bridge was removed and with it the guardhouse crossing at Calle Pesqueira.

Three blocks west of the former Bonillas Bridge site was another neighborhood access point at the intersection of Calle Camou and Calle Arizpe (fig. 5.11). The guardhouse here survived the drainage improvements made to the arroyo along the boundary (fig. 5.15), but, like the Bonillas Bridge, the crossing was permanently closed once the channel became concrete lined in the late 1920s.[11]

Nogales, Sonora.

Figure 5.14. 1910s view looking south into Nogales, Sonora, across the Bonillas Bridge. A Mexican guardhouse is positioned at the end of the bridge to monitor access along Calle Pesqueira. The Neoclassical façade of the Mexican *aduana* is partly visible in the background, and the large two-story structure to the right of the bridge is the U.S. Consulate in Nogales, Sonora. Attributed to Rochin y Méndez, La Industria Mexicana, 1910s.

Taken half way donw west hill so as to show more in detail the improvements made in 1927 in Mexico. The International Line is closer to the arroyo wall and not where fence is located.

Figure 5.15. 1928 view of the Mexican guardhouse at the intersection of Calle Arizpe and Calle Camou. The crossing was permanently closed once drainage improvements were made to the arroyo that parallels the international boundary. Courtesy Arizona State University Libraries, Arizona Collection CTH-649.

Figure 5.16. The Elías-Morley gate was transformed with the addition of decorative stone pillars topped with electric lights in the late 1920s. This view looks south into Calle Elías. In the foreground is a Mexican woman who appears to be showing her border-crossing card to U.S. Customs officers as she walks into Arizona. Frashers Fotos, 1937.

Improvements made to the surviving border crossings in the late 1920s resulted in the erection of stone pillars topped with light standards at the Elías-Morley and main gate crossings. Starting in the 1920s, crossing the boundary became a more formal process than in previous decades. Figure 5.16 captures a Mexican woman draped in shawl displaying a border-crossing card to U.S. Customs officers as she passes the American sentry house at the Morley gate. The new stone pillars flank the crossing, which combined pedestrian and automotive access. By the 1950s, the Elías-Morley gate would include a sliding fence so that the crossing might be closed in the evenings (fig. 5.17). The Mexican guardhouse has been modified to a boxy, modern aesthetic in keeping with the era, but the 1929 stone pillars persist at this gate. South of the line along Morley are signs of American commercial prosperity associated with the post–World War II decade. Ville de Paris (with the Eifel Tower sign) and Bracker's (several properties beyond) were two of the most popular upscale department stores that lured wealthy Mexican shoppers to the street that became known all across Sonora as "La Morley." To the west of Elías-Morley, a separate crossing is created that becomes the new main gate, also with stone pillars flanking the portage (fig. 5.18). A second railroad gate crossing is on the east side of this new guardhouse (cf. fig. 5.11).

Figure 5.17. The Elías-Morley gate circa 1950s allowed regular access to the fashionable shopping street on the Arizona side of the boundary. Generations of shoppers from all across Sonora knew the district simply as "La Morley." México Fotográfico 123, 1950s.

Figure 5.18. Cars in line to cross into Mexico at the new main gate. Like the Elías-Morley gate, this crossing was decorated in the late 1920s with lighted stone pillars. This perspective makes visible the sliding metal gate immediately east (*right*) of the Mexican guardhouse that would be opened when trains crossed the border. Beyond where the older main gate Mexican sentry house stands is the original railroad crossing. Across the line and situated between the two railroad tracks is the Arizona depot. México Fotográfico 40, 1920s.

Figure 5.19. Panoramic view of the main gate crossing and the train station plaza circa 1940s. A new sentry house has replaced the previous Mexican guardhouse (fig. 5.18), and the activity level in spaces around the crossing is heightened compared with that of past decades. Across the line on the Arizona side west of the main gate is the U.S. Customs house, newly opened in 1934, in sparkling Spanish Revival style with tiled roof and arched breezeway. R. R. F. Foto 16, 1940s.

In the decades during and following World War II, the main gate was transformed yet again with the construction of new guardhouses to accommodate the increased crossing traffic. Figure 5.19 is a 1940s panoramic vista of the main gate that shows a modern and enlarged Mexican guardhouse (cf. fig. 5.18) and a long fence-enclosed park called Plaza del Estación because it served the nearby train depot. The activity level around the main gate captures street vendors, auto traffic, and pedestrians. The fence-enclosed building left of center with an elevated signed entrance on the corner is the Cavern's Beer Garden that faces the town plaza just out of view on the far left. One decade later, the main gate would witness further changes. Figure 5.20 reveals the expanded Mexican guardhouse and the replacement of the beer garden with the two-story Tropical Garden Exposition featuring Mexican Curios Arts and Crafts, signaling the explosion of tourist activities that energized Nogales, Sonora, during the 1950s. Finally, figure 5.21 looks east across the main gate from the Arizona side during the same decade. Billboards on buildings across the railroad tracks and on the hillside behind draw roadside attention to lure visitors to shopping and entertainment possibilities in Nogales, Sonora.

Figure 5.20. Main gate west of the railroad tracks during the 1950s reflects the expanding tourist activity that gained Nogales, Sonora, its enviable popularity as the principal auto and rail U.S. portal to western Mexico during the era. The Safeway supermarket visible across the line in Arizona earned a reputation for high-volume sales in the region because of the large number of Sonorans who would regularly shop across the border. México Fotográfico 48, 1950s.

Figure 5.21. View looking east across the main gate reveals a plethora of billboard advertising intended to lure visitors to entertainment and shopping possibilities in Nogales, Sonora. The 1950s may well have been the golden era of visitor crossings into and through the Mexican border town. Auto traffic nearly doubled from thirty-eight thousand in 1954 to seventy-four thousand in 1959. L. L. Cook, 1950s.

Gallery: The Line and the Fence

"The international boundary line is a wire fence in the middle of the street and with a smile and a friendly wave of the hand, officials representing both countries bid you welcome to the pleasures that await!"[12] An appropriate gesture that trumpets the openness between Nogales, Arizona, and Nogales, Sonora, during the 1920s, when the Mexican town depended on the visiting American tourist who sought liquid refreshment in disregard of the Volstead Act. But the story of the boundary is deeper than a single cross-section in time. To understand the changes experienced at this meeting place of two nations and two peoples requires comparative visualization through time. The Arreola Collection contains seventy-two separate postcard images of the border and fence dividing Nogales, Arizona, from Nogales, Sonora. In this gallery, I use eleven views, chiefly postcards, to create a window on the transformed border at Ambos Nogales over more than six decades. Postcards enable this kind of reconstruction because postcard photographers often repeated the same views in succeeding decades, unwittingly capturing in almost cinematic fashion the changes in landscape along this historic alignment.[13] The gallery is arranged in chronological sequence with an extended caption for each image so that the view is the narrative and the text explains the view.[14]

INTERNATIONAL STREET, NOGALES.   CALLE INTERNACIONAL, NOGALES.

Figure 5.22. From the first platting of the towns in 1884, Mexico had maintained a fifty-foot setback from the original 1854 boundary survey (fig. 5.2). This 1890s view looks west from a nearby hill to show the setback. The two-story building with arched windows on the Mexican side (*south*) near the upper center of the image is positioned at the north end of Calle Elías, and across the open space fifty feet beyond is Morley Avenue in Nogales, Arizona. On the American side (*north*), all buildings are built up to the boundary. The tower of the Mexican customs house built circa 1887 is faintly visible at left background. International Boundary Commission, *Report of the Boundary Commission.*

Figure 5.23. In 1898, to discourage rampant smuggling that had persisted because the buildings in Nogales, Arizona, were tight to the boundary line, U.S. President William McKinley ordered the clearing of all structures located within sixty feet of the border, thereby creating a 110-foot open zone between Mexican and U.S. buildings proximate to the boundary because Mexico had previously declared a fifty-foot setback. A comparison of this view with figure 5.22 above illustrates the zone of the U.S. setback. All structures south of the long white building with distinctive high shuttered windows in figure 5.22 have been removed in this view, thereby creating the sixty-foot American setback. Because the original railroad depot is not visible in this image, having burned in a fire, and the new depot on the Nogales, Arizona, side was completed in 1905, this perspective is likely the early 1900s but before 1918 and the construction of the fence.

Figure 5.24. This view is a rare image of the parade and celebration on February 15, 1898, honoring Arizona governor M. H. McCord and Sonora governor Ramón Corral that took place on the fifty-foot Mexican setback then called Calle Internacional, or International Street. The two-story building at left is the Hotel Cazabón, positioned at the north end of Calle Elías, and it is the same structure identified in figure 5.22. In the middle background is the railroad depot that was built as one structure across the international boundary. The spirit of the procession symbolizes how Ambos Nogales was, indeed, one place separated by a single street. Enrique P. Célis. Courtesy Arizona Historical Society, Tucson #29035.

Figure 5.25. A ground-level view shows two men standing either side of boundary marker 122 near the intersection of Calle Elías and Morley Avenue circa 1900s. Horse-drawn carts rather than automobiles help to date the view; however, the type of paper used to print the image—CYKO 5, first issued in August 1907—suggests pre-1910.

Figure 5.26. This ground-level view was made by El Paso photographer Walter Horne looking west from the middle of the border zone, again datable not only by the absence of a landscape feature—the original cross border railroad depot—but also by the photographic paper used—AZO 4 triangles turned up in the stamp box, first issued September 1907—suggesting pre-1910.

Figure 5.27. A third ground-level view shows the boundary west of the railroad alignment focused on the Bonillas Bridge across the Nogales Wash. This bridge was removed in 1918, so this view is before then. Given the postcard paper, stamp box design, and divided back labeling—AZO 5 triangles turned up in the stamp box, and CORRESPONDENCE HERE on verso—this image is March 1910 or later.

Figure 5.28. This view looks west from a low position on the hill east of town to show the 1918 fence that was constructed by the United States following separate instances of conflict between U.S. army and U.S. Customs officers and Mexican military and customs officials in Ambos Nogales. Fearing further hostilities, Brigadier General DeRosey C. Cabell, dispatched to Nogales from his command at Fort Huachuca, Arizona, and Plutarco Elías Calles, governor of Sonora, conferred and recommended construction of the fence as the best solution to potential cross border violations that might inflame greater conflict. The fence was a simple wire affair strung to pickets along a two-mile stretch and built entirely on the U.S. side of the boundary. By this gesture, a permanent physical divide was now in place separating Ambos Nogales. Attributed to A. W. Lohn, 1910s.

Figure 5.29. Another view west from a similar vantage point to figure 5.28, but later, because the Nogales Wash has been filled, and the Bonillas Bridge is no more, so post-1918. Light standards and some curbing have been installed on the Nogales, Arizona, side of the line fence, and a new sentry box is now visible on the U.S. side where Morley Avenue meets International Street. On the Mexican side the building at Calle Elías and Calle Internacional is now identified as the Cosmopolitan Club, a Prohibition-era cabaret. The paper stock for this image is AZO 8, first issued in June 1926, so this view is very likely mid-1920s. Lohn Photo, 1920s.

Figure 5.30. The verso of this photo postcard identifies the scene as the celebration of Mexican Independence Day, September 16, 1929. A large crowd of American and Mexican men, mostly, appears to mix with soldiers representing each country. A platform, decorated with bunting and flags—American and Mexican—straddles the border and suggests dignitaries giving speeches. The view is taken from Nogales, Sonora, looking north to the railroad depot in Nogales, Arizona. The border wire fence is difficult to see, but there appears to be a space dividing the north and south sides of the boundary. Lohn, 1929.

Figure 5.31. Boundary line vista from the Mexican side of the hill east of town looking west. The late 1920s improvements to the fence—masonry pillars at the Elías-Morley and main gate crossings—are distinctive as are the remodeled sentry guardhouses at the respective ports of entry. On the Mexican side beyond the main gate is the subterranean drainage improvement made to the Nogales, Sonora, boundary alignment (fig. 5.15). On the American side west of the railroad depot is the newly constructed, in 1934, U.S. Customs house—two-story, Spanish Revival style building with arches, tile roof, and cars parked in front. L. L. Cook, 1939.

MEXICO   U.S.A.

International Street - Nogales, Arizona and Nogales, Mexico   6-Y-139

Figure 5.32. This view, which by now had become the standard postcard fix of Ambos Nogales, showing the line and fence, looks west to reveal subtle changes from previous views. The old simple strand wire fence has become a chain-link mesh fence ordered built by the International Boundary Commission in 1950 and constructed by San Xavier Rock and Sand Company of Tucson, Arizona. The chain-link fence was some two-and-one-half miles long: one mile east of monument 122 (located at the Elías-Morley crossing), and one and one-half miles west of the same monument. The fence was eleven feet high inside the Nogales, Arizona, city limits and nine feet outside of town. Light standards and the masonry posts from the previous era are still in place, but ornamental vegetation—shrubs and trees—now appear at several locations along the fence median. The guardhouses at the main gate have been rebuilt; a second story is added to the Mexican one, and the American one is completely rebuilt to be a much larger facility (cf. fig. 5.31). The eleven-story high-rise Fray Marcos de Niza Hotel is visible in Nogales, Sonora, and residential development can be seen in the hills behind. In 1950, Nogales, Sonora, counted almost twenty-five thousand residents; by 1960, the population of the Mexican border town was nearly thirty-eight thousand (table 1.1). W. M. Cline 6-Y-139, 1950s.

Townscape

Like other Sonora border towns, only parts of Nogales were captured in postcard photography. In this section, we revisit a residential neighborhood in the town center, the town plaza, and selected landmarks distinctive to the largest and most popular Sonora border town.

Arizpe-Obregón Neighborhood

Before Prohibition and the post–World War II tourist boom, Nogales, Sonora, was largely a community of quiet residential streets and neighborhoods. While Calle Elías on the east side emerged as the Mexican border town's first tourist street, neighborhoods west of the railroad tracks were principally residential and commercial, serving local populations. The heart of this district was Calle Arizpe (renamed Calle Obregón in 1934), a roughly three-block strip surrounded by several additional blocks and close to the international boundary. This neighborhood was mapped in 1917 to reveal a densely settled district of chiefly adobe dwellings with some structures built of stone and wood (fig. 5.33). In addition, there were mixed retail businesses located on Arizpe and surrounding blocks, including restaurants, drugstores, barbers, lodgings, bakeries, pool halls, jewelry stores, a tailor, coffee roaster, a theater, and a municipal market. Institutional structures included a church, city hall, and a masonic lodge. Perhaps the most recognized businesses in the area were Chinese-operated establishments—twelve grocery stores and three laundries.

Three postcard views capture Calle Arizpe in the first decades of the twentieth century. Figure 5.34 is a 1910s image that shows the concentration of chiefly residential dwellings along the street looking north toward the border. There are children playing in the unpaved street, raised sidewalks, ornamental trees, telephone poles and wires strung above, and homes built tight to the street. Figure 5.35 is a view from the 1930s also looking north to reveal period automobiles, a drugstore, and street-side gasoline pump. In this view, land use along Arizpe, now Obregón, is both residential and commercial. Figure 5.36 captures Obregón looking south from the corner of Calle Campillo at the north end of the district. The building on the right corner of this image identified as "Salon" is a saloon. It is the same building shown at the southwest corner of Arizpe and Campillo in figure 5.33 and labeled a pool hall. Figure 5.36 suggests how the main street of Nogales became increasingly commercial close to the border, where former residential buildings were converted to businesses.

Further evidence of this transformation is revealed by 1920s views of street vendors who crowded Arizpe to sell chiefly food products when the district was still

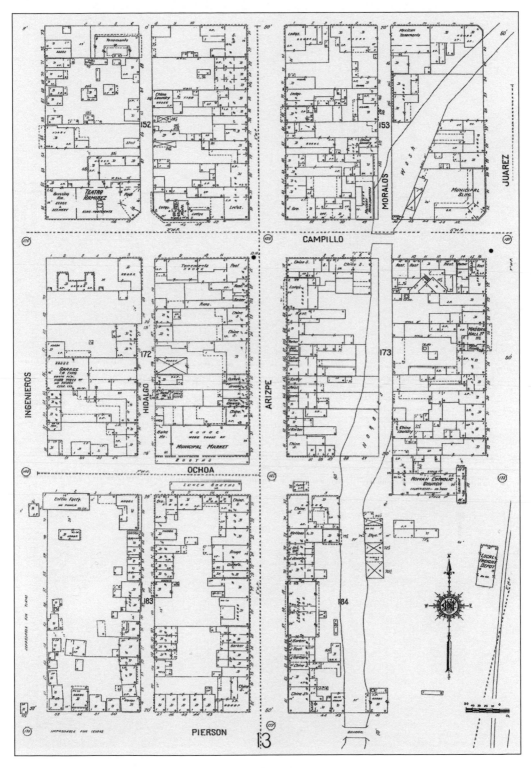

Figure 5.33. The Arizpe district. In the first decades of the twentieth century, Calle Arizpe (later Calle Obregón) was the residential and commercial spine of Nogales, Sonora. Chinese stores individually labeled "Chine S" on the map were the most common businesses in the neighborhood. Sanborn Map Company, *Nogales, Santa Cruz County, Ariz., Including Nogales, Mexico, 1917*, detail from map 12.

Figure 5.34. Chiefly a residential street, Arizpe is captured in a view looking north toward the border in the 1910s. Lohn Photo, 1910s.

Figure 5.35. In 1934, Calle Arizpe's name was changed to Obregón to celebrate the native of Navajoa, Sonora, Álvaro Obregón, who was president of Mexico from 1920 to 1924. México Fotográfico 33, 1930s.

Figure 5.36. Obregón (formerly Arizpe), looking south from the intersection with Calle Campillo, illustrates how the principal street of Nogales, Sonora, had transitioned from an early residential district (fig. 5.34) to an increasingly commercial strip. Frashers Fotos, 1937.

largely residential (fig. 5.37). Residents collected in front of dwellings to sell food products that could be consumed immediately at street-side tables or to purchase produce for home consumption. The municipal market at the northwest corner of Calle Arizpe and Calle Ochoa provided a variety of products from produce to fresh meat delivered daily from surrounding farms and ranches (fig. 5.38). The market and most grocery business in the town was controlled by Chinese vendors.[15]

The presence of Chinese merchants in Nogales during the first decades of the twentieth century parallels the story of their role in the economy of Agua Prieta (see chap. 3). Sonora became a major destination for Chinese seeking opportunity in Mexico after the United States passage of the Chinese Exclusion Act in 1882. By the early twentieth century, a state registry indicated that Chinese operated 52 of 968 businesses in 21 of 87 towns in Sonora.[16] The Arizpe neighborhood in Nogales counted fifteen Chinese-operated businesses in 1917, suggesting their dominance of grocery and laundry enterprises. The Juan Lung Tain and Company store in Nogales was part of a string of businesses owned by the Chinese merchant who resided in nearby Magdalena, Sonora (fig. 5.39). Lung Tain advertised in the *Nogales Daily Herald* that his business was both wholesale and retail and specialized in "Abarrotes Extranjeros"

St. in old Spanish quarter. Nogales, Mexico

Figure 5.37. Women vendors and street-side eateries along Arizpe reinforce the largely residential character of the street during the 1920s.

Loby.
Market. Nogales Sonora México.

Figure 5.38. Like many buildings along Arizpe, the municipal market constructed in 1909 was made of adobe brick fronted with cut stone. The market, chiefly operated and controlled by Chinese vendors, was a principal meeting area for local residents. Lohn 56, 1920s.

Figure 5.39. Shuttered Juan Lung Tain and Company store at the southeast corner of Calle Arizpe and Calle Campillo in Nogales, Sonora (fig. 5.33). Chinese merchants dominated border town grocery and dry goods trade in the first three decades of the twentieth century but were driven out of Sonora in the 1930s. Acme Photo, 1931.

(foreign groceries), "Calzado Americano" (American shoes), and "Gran Fabrica de Ropa" (clothing cloth).[17]

Nogales, Sonora continued to be a central place in the story of the Chinese on the border. The town boasted a Chinese Society Hall at the southwest corner of Campillo and Ingenieros, testifying to the influence of the group on local business. Following the restrictions on Chinese immigration into the United States, several rings of smugglers operated out of Nogales, Sonora, often with the illegal assistance of U.S. Customs officials in Nogales, Arizona. Thousands of Chinese were smuggled through the border at Nogales then directed to Chinatowns in Phoenix, Los Angeles, and San Francisco.[18]

In the blocks surrounding the Arizpe district, varied institutional structures were built to accommodate resident services into the early decades of the twentieth century. On streets east of Arizpe were the 1897 Municipal Palace (fig. 5.40) and the town's principal church, first built in 1891 (fig. 5.33). On Arizpe one block south of Calle Pierson was the Escuela Enrique Pestalozzi, designed by an American architect and built in 1912 (fig. 5.41).[19] As residential development spilled south along Arizpe,

Figure 5.40. Neoclassical façade of the Nogales, Sonora, post office. This building was originally constructed in 1887 as the Municipal Palace at the southeast corner of Calle Campillo and Calle Juárez. The building is shown at this location on the Sanborn-Perris Map Company map of Nogales, Arizona, 1898. In the 1920s, the Municipal Palace was moved to a building on Calle Arizpe that had previously served as the town jail. Lohn Foto 1, 1920s.

Figure 5.41. Escuela Enrique Pestalozzi, built in 1912 by an American architect, showcases the redbrick and white stone multitonal look common to Richardsonian Romanesque style fashionable in the first decades of the twentieth century. This building suggests the progressive spirit of early Nogales, Sonora. A comparable public school of this grandeur would not be built in Nogales, Arizona, until 1915. Attributed to Lohn, 1920s.

Figure 5.42. A showcase of elite homes in Colonia Moderna, where American architectural styles—Southwest Territorial and Neoclassical—appear as a residential district developed south along Calle Arizpe. Lohn Photo, 1920s.

wealthy Nogales merchants built custom homes in American architectural styles along a stretch that became known as Colonia Moderna (fig. 5.42).[20]

Plaza

Nogales, Sonora, was unusual in another way that is quite contrary to the tradition of town founding in Mexico. While the town was organized in 1880 and platted in 1884, it did not have a formal plaza until 1889 when then-mayor Manuel Mascareñas is said to have created the space.[21] The Gustavo Cox map of 1888 (fig. 5.3) does not show a space for the plaza; neither does the map from 1893 by the Sanborn-Perris Map Company. It first appears on the map published by the Sanborn-Perris Map Company in 1898 and is labeled a park. The 1901 Sanborn map shows the park as a rectangular space bordered on the east by the Sonora Railroad track, Calle Campillo to the south, Calle Pesqueira on the west, and two dwellings that abut Calle Camou near the international boundary on the north.[22] Albert Lohn's 1920s panoramic photo postcard captures a view of the plaza looking northwest from the hill behind Calle Elías (fig. 5.43). This vista shows the classic rectangle with diagonal crosswalks that converge on a sheltered *kiosco*, round beds for flowers flanking the *kiosco*, benches surrounding a perimeter walk path, and planted trees without leaves suggesting perhaps

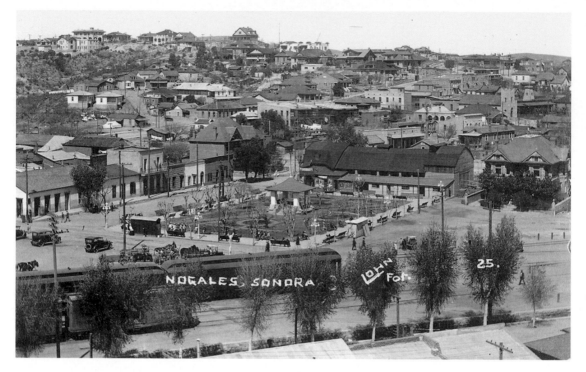

Figure 5.43. Panoramic view of Nogales plaza circa 1920s. This view looks northwest from a hill on the east side of town. Homes on hills in the background and behind the buildings on the north side of the plaza are across the boundary in Nogales, Arizona. Lohn Fot. 25, 1920s.

a winter scene. Vendor stalls (sometimes called *pequeño comercio* [small commerce]) are positioned on two sides, and a long roof-covered set of linked stalls borders the north perimeter. The railroad track with cars is seen at the bottom of the image.

Figure 5.44 is a street-level view of the west side of the plaza from the 1900s. The view is looking north on Calle Pesqueira from the intersection with Calle Campillo, and the Bonillas Bridge guardhouse on the international boundary is seen at the end of the street. The plaza is enclosed by a picket fence, and the trees, perhaps mulberry, are in leafy bloom. A 1920s view taken from close to the same vantage point but focused chiefly on the plaza shows how the 1900s fence has been removed, benches added, and globe-shaped electric lights installed on cast-iron standards that punctuated the perimeter concrete sidewalk (fig. 5.45). The trees have been pruned, and advertising bills (legible with magnification) in English promote silent films: *The Eleventh Commandment*, a 1924 full-length feature, and *Fatty's Indiscretion*, a 1914 comedy short. Both films are being shown "Hoy" (today) in a local theater. In figure 5.46, the northeast corner of the plaza is viewed two decades later in the 1940s, showing the new art deco–Spanish

Figure 5.44. 1900s photo postcard view of Calle Pesqueira looking north to the Bonillas Bridge crossing. The treed area behind the picket fence at right is the Nogales, Sonora, town plaza.

PLAZA de Nogales Sonora.

LOHN 5 PHOTO

Figure 5.45. A *kiosco* (bandstand), lighting, and walk paths highlight improvements to Nogales, Sonora, plaza made since 1900s. Lohn Photo 5, 1920s.

Figure 5.46. Northeast corner of Nogales plaza, by now called Plaza Trece de Julio. The main gate crossing is visible at right, and in the center background between the Teatro Obregón and the Cavern's Beer Gardens is the tiled roofline of the U.S. Customs house completed in 1934 across the boundary in Nogales, Arizona. México Fotográfico, 1940s.

Revival architectural façade of the Teatro Obregón, featuring Spanish-language films and next door the Cavern's Beer Gardens. The plaza grounds appear to be concrete surfaced, and benches accommodate gathering locals. The traditional outdoor social space was by then called Plaza Trece de Julio (13th of July) to commemorate the date in 1889 that the legislature of Sonora elevated Nogales to the status of *villa*.[23]

Plaza Trece de Julio, also locally called plaza *principal* (main plaza), is seen in figure 5.47 during the early 1950s looking southwest across the tree-covered space from an elevated perch. The original *kiosco* and light standards survive, but the wooden benches of an earlier era have been replaced with commemorative concrete ones on platforms. At left, a group of men gather at a corner shoeshine stand; at right is a small *refresco* (soft drink) and *abarrotes* (snacks) stand. The roofline behind the tree canopy caps many of the same adobe structures that appeared in an earlier view (fig. 5.43), especially the distinctive two-story building now identified as Jalisco Restaurant. On the left a block away at the corner of Calle Campillo and Calle Obregón is the new high-rise Fray Marcos de Niza Hotel completed in 1950. In a final farewell, figure 5.48 captures the Plaza Trece de Julio on the eve of its destruction. Trees and *kiosco* are

Figure 5.47. The plaza *principal* (main plaza), looking southwest across the tree canopy of the public space to the high-rise Fray Marcos de Niza Hotel completed in 1950. México Fotográfico 104, 1950s.

Figure 5.48. Plaza Trece de Julio on the eve of its destruction. In 1963, the plaza and the 1887 Mexican customs house (long column-supported building at left background) were razed to inaugurate the new Programa Nacional Fronterizo remake of the border town's gateway. México Fotográfico, Mexfotocolor 315, 1960s.

gone, replaced by a flagpole, and the historic globe light standards are replaced by modern outdoor illumination. Visible still are the Jalisco Restaurant building, the Marcos de Niza Hotel, and part of the classic 1887 *aduana* across the street from the plaza on Calle Campillo. By 1963, the entire plaza as well the Mexican customs house would be razed to make way for the modernist Programa Nacional Fronterizo transformation of Nogales, Sonora's, gateway.[24] A new town plaza, christened Plaza Niños Héroes, would be remade as a small local bus stop depot next to the town church several blocks in from the remodeled entrance.[25]

Landmarks

Nogales's place identity is tied to several structures that have shaped the popular view of the border town in the past. Chief among these have been the customs house and the Marcos de Niza Hotel. Each prevailed as a landmark dominating the skyline of the town in different eras. Presently, only the hotel survives. It has persisted as perhaps the most famous landmark for the city since opening at the midpoint of the twentieth century.

Customs houses in the borderland were typically located close to the boundary to regulate commerce and protect against contraband smuggling. As discussed previously in the chapters on Agua Prieta and Naco, customs houses were premier institutional landmarks for eastern Sonora border towns that were served by railroads. The lucrative copper-mining hinterlands south and north of these nodes empowered Mexican border towns to capitalize on cross border commerce, both transit into Mexico and traffic out to the United States. Tariffs on imported and exported goods were typically levied at the border, and the monetary accumulation of such transactions was considerable. Nogales, even more so than Agua Prieta and Naco, was the most trafficked border crossing along the Sonora-Arizona boundary. Its economic hinterland extended south to the Mexican state of Sinaloa and its port at Mazatlán—the so-called Wonderful West Coast of Mexico—and north to central Arizona, southern California, and western Texas in the United States (fig. 5.49).

Nogales established a customs house before the town was formally organized when the Mexican government relocated the customs station at Magdalena, Sonora, to the border. The first customs house in Nogales was a simple structure located near Calle Arizpe and the boundary.[26] As border commerce accelerated with the construction of the railroad in 1882 and later, Nogales became the site of one of the most architecturally elaborate customs houses erected along the entire Mexican boundary. The customs house was completed circa 1887 by the construction firm of L. W. Mix at a cost of nearly $84,000.[27] A Neoclassical wonder, the *aduana* faced the railroad track and was highlighted by two multicolumned front-gabled roofs with decorative

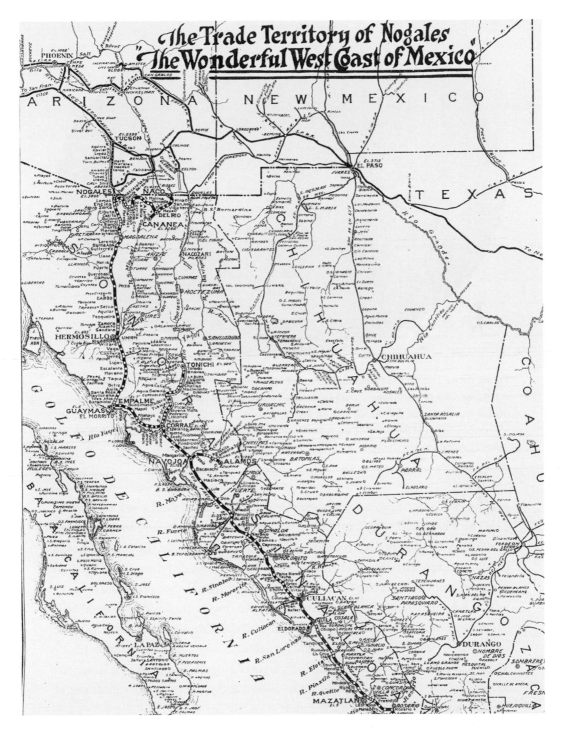

Figure 5.49. "The Wonderful West Coast of Mexico." During the 1920s, Nogales promoted itself as a key point of commerce and trade linking northwestern Mexico and the American Southwest. *The Trade Territory of Nogales, "The Wonderful West Coast of Mexico,"* (map) 1920.

Figure 5.50. The Mexican customs house (*aduana*) completed in 1887 was a landmark that symbolized the importance of trade and commerce at the border. This 1900s photographic postcard captures the full façade view of this Neoclassical, architectural wonder. The building was razed in 1963 as part of the Programa Nacional Fronterizo modernization of the Nogales gateway. Attributed to Rochin y Méndez, La Industria Mexicana, 1900s.

pediments that wrapped around each side and flanked a central clock tower bordered by a balustrade (fig. 5.50). The effect was like two Greek temples bookended to a French Second Empire tower.[28] Behind the grandiose façade, the customs house building occupied nearly an entire town block with a long side facing Calle Campillo and a shorter back aligned to Calle Juárez.[29] On the building's south wall, two long rail sidings extended to intersect the multiple railroad tracks. These sidings would later be covered and enclosed, creating a single railroad shed (fig. 5.51). The customs house was razed in 1963 as discussed above, but for half a century the building was symbolic of the economic might and landscape character of Nogales. Its tower was so adored by locals as a landmark that it was later re-created and placed as a monument east of the railroad alignment, where it still stands.

By the middle 1950s, Nogales, Sonora, was competing with Nuevo Laredo, Tamaulipas, on the Texas border, long regarded the most popular port of entry for American motorists bound for the interior of Mexico. In January and February 1955, the prime winter travel months, some 6,195 vehicles passed through Nogales en route to the

Figure 5.51. Panoramic vista of downtown Nogales with the Mexican customs house located left of center. This view shows railroad cars along tracks in front of the building and the covered and enclosed siding on the left. A small part of Plaza Trece de Julio is visible across the street (Calle Campillo) on the right, and the Fray Marcos de Niza Hotel—the new landmark in the border town—overshadows the customs house in the near background. México Fotográfico 102, 1950s.

Mexican interior; Nuevo Laredo counted 6,943 cars in the same direction in those months that year.[30] Part of the explanation of this benchmark in Nogales tourist history was the completion in 1950 of a paved highway between the border town and the port of Guaymas in Sonora and four years later the extension of that highway linking Nogales to Mexico City.[31] Auto traffic to Mexico was exploding in the post–World War II era, and border towns with good highway connections to the interior were reaping the profit of an expanding tourist industry.

Lodging at the border became a possibility, and because Nogales, Arizona, was underdeveloped to service this segment of the bourgeoning travel economy, a group of investors from Nogales, Sonora, decided to take advantage. The upshot was the construction of the Fray Marcos de Niza Hotel (named to celebrate an early Franciscan traveler-explorer of the northwest Spanish borderlands) that would cater to the growing clientele of Americans touring Mexico by automobile.

The venture, however, would span three years from gestation to the start of construction and six years of delays in the building process. In January 1941, Nogales announced plans to build an $80,000 hotel near the international boundary.[32] The

Figure 5.52. The Fray Marcos de Niza Hotel was initially conceived in 1941 to accommodate the growing tourist business of Nogales, but wartime supply shortages delayed construction for six years. This view (*detail*) looks east along Calle Campillo to the incomplete eleven-story building at the corner of Calle Obregón only blocks from the main gate border crossing. R. R. de la F., 1940s.

hotel was designed by the Mexican architectural firm of Garita y Jesus Aguirre, and the construction contractor Jesus Irastorza encountered delays over the next six years because of shortages in materials caused by World War II.[33] As a result, the shell of an eleven-story structure at the corner of Calle Campillo and Calle Obregón silhouetted the Nogales skyline during the second half of the 1940s (fig. 5.52). Completed at last in June 1950, the hotel became an immediate success with visitors as well as locals. The modern structure mirrored the boxy concrete and glass of the emerging International architecture style popular in Mexico and the United States (fig. 5.53). It included one hundred rooms, fifteen suites (all with bath and phone), two restaurants, two cantinas, and the popular Sky Room and Terrace atop the hotel, where floorshows and entertainment were staged. The hotel was air-cooled, and single rooms rented for $2 to $6 per night.[34] The Marcos de Niza was a mainstay of Nogales during the heyday

Figure 5.53. Completed in 1950, the Fray Marcos de Niza Hotel included one hundred air-cooled rooms, two restaurants, two bars, and the popular Sky Room and Terrace at the top of the building. The architecture followed the boxy concrete and glass International style then emerging to commercial success in the United States and Mexico. México Fotográfico 88, 1950s.

of tourist popularity, especially for those who continued by auto or by train into the interior. Along with other tourist venues such as the Cavern Café in Nogales, Sonora, and the Rio Grande Resort outside of Nogales, Arizona, the Marcos de Niza promoted a special Thanksgiving dinner that attracted locals and a Wednesday night Mexican dinner special for visitors and locals. All special events were offered in the popular Sky Room.[35]

Tourist Places

A 1920s promotional pamphlet titled *You'll Like Nogales, on the Border* boasted that Nogales, Mexico, offered "Cabarets! Entertainment!! 'n Everything!!! A good place to visit."[36] The Prohibition era was a time when American visitors flocked to the Sonora border. In Arizona, restrictions transpired even earlier than the national Volstead Act (1919) because the state prohibited alcohol production and consumption starting in 1915. Following the national repeal of Prohibition in 1933, businesses in the Sonora border towns turned to the curio craft trade as a substitute lure. Both cabaret and curios have survived in one form or another to the present as part of the social and economic attraction of the Mexican border town to American visitors.

In Nogales, tourist businesses were especially concentrated on two principal streets, Calle Elías and Avenida Obregón, and two additional streets, Calle Colon and Calle Campillo, that spanned the few blocks separating the primary streets (fig. 5.54). Each street emerged during specific periods of tourist attraction, Elías developing in the first part of the twentieth century and Obregón gaining popularity largely in the second half of the twentieth century. One enterprise on Calle Elías, La Caverna, or the Cavern Café, became an institution and, therefore, deserves special attention (it is discussed and illustrated in a separate vignette at the end of this chapter). Further, bullfights must be added to any treatment of the entertainment scene of a Mexican border town, and the Plaza de Toros in Nogales was, perhaps, the best-known and patronized ring along the entire Sonoran border.

Calle Elías

Calle Elías was from its beginning the principal commercial street of Nogales, Sonora, situated directly across the international boundary from Morley Avenue in Nogales, Arizona.[37] The first commercial houses, such as La Moda General Store, La Francesa Dry Goods Store, and the Hotel Pedro Cazabón, as well as other retail and wholesale businesses, were concentrated along this street tucked below a steep hill east of the railroad tracks. Many of the merchants represented the earliest families to settle Nogales, Sonora, and others were European immigrants who became powerful entrepreneurs in the growth of Nogales as a trading center. La Moda, which specialized in clothing and accessories for women, for example, imported goods from Europe and the United States, and its owners could transact business in Spanish, English, German, and French.[38]

Calle Elías during the late nineteenth and early twentieth centuries was both a commercial and residential street. An 1898 map shows that most properties in the

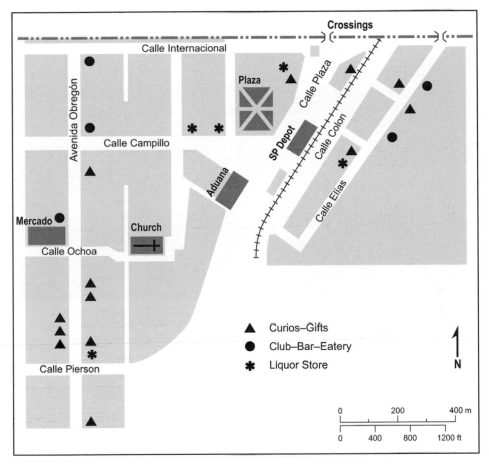

Figure 5.54. Selected tourist locations in Nogales, Sonora, 1950s. Adapted from *City of Nogales Old Mexico Tourist Guide*. Cartography by Barbara Trapido-Lurie.

first few blocks were businesses, but as one progressed south along Elías, the neighborhood became progressively residential.[39] A 1920s photographic postcard looking north to the boundary illustrates an adobe property transformed to a saloon at the south end of Calle Elías; the doorway and window openings as well as the chimneys suggest this property was originally a residence (fig. 5.55).

"When Arizonans say to other residents or winter visitors, 'Let's go to Nogales' they have one thing in mind—food and legalized refreshments across the line."[40] This 1929 testimonial might have been true even before American Prohibition, because the 1898 map discussed above shows that some ten businesses in the first few blocks below the boundary along Calle Elías were saloons at least two decades before the passage of the Volstead Act. Nevertheless, when Nogales transitioned into the

Figure 5.55. Calle Elías looking north toward the international boundary. This view illustrates the south end of the street, which was more residential, as evidenced by the adobe dwelling with chimneys at left compared to the north end of the street, which was chiefly commercial. P. M. A., 1920s.

roaring twenties, Calle Elías became the nerve center of the town's cabaret industry, prompting one postcard photographer to title an image of the street "No Prohibition Here" (fig. 5.56).

Following the repeal of national Prohibition, Nogales transitioned to a decade of tourist promotion to sustain a stream of visitors to its shops and businesses. The Nogales, Arizona, Chamber of Commerce distributed brochures at the San Francisco and New York World's Fairs boasting about the opportunities of visiting the border towns as part of any excursion along Mexico's west coast.[41] Locally, the Nogales Chamber of Commerce advertised in Tucson newspapers how picturesque Nogales—half in Arizona and half in romantic Old Mexico—was a place to visit for entertainment, excitement, and a foreign atmosphere. The ad explained that there was "No Red Tape in Crossing the Border into Mexico" and how each tourist visitor was allowed to return to the United States with up to $100 in duty-free goods.[42] Not to be outdone, the Phoenix newspapers included advertisements pitching Nogales, Sonora, as romantic and exciting, where visitors could "Get the Thrill of Setting Foot on Foreign Soil," and where they could enjoy bright cafés, delicious wild-game dinners, dancing, and entertainment.[43]

Figure 5.56. Calle Elías became a street of drinking establishments during the Prohibition era, which started in Arizona in 1915 and was followed by the national enforcement of the Volstead Act from 1919 to 1933.

During the 1930s and 1940s, Calle Elías was the hub of tourist visitor services, including clubs with live entertainment, dining, and the emerging curio crafts trade.[44] In a single advertisement in Arizona's largest circulation newspaper, the *Arizona Republic*, in 1936, seven separate businesses on Elías beckoned visitors: one restaurant (Cavern Café), two dance clubs (Concordia and Ordian), and four curio crafts stores (Casa Reyes, S. S. Aguilar, Carrasco Brothers, and La Industria Mexicana).[45] Carrasco's, which opened in 1933 at 26 Calle Elías across the street from the Cavern Café, was one of the more elaborate curio stores, selling textiles, pottery, decorative glass, wood furniture, and life-size woven straw figurines, both animal and human (fig. 5.57). Another block down the street at 33 Calle Elías was La Industria Mexicana, owned and operated by Delfina Rochin de Vergobbi, a Sonora-born businesswoman who is credited with opening the first Mexican arts and crafts store in Nogales (fig. 5.58). Educated in Sonora, Arizona, and California, and married to an Italian immigrant who came to the Mexican border via Argentina in 1898, Mrs. Rochin de Vergobbi would frequently travel to the interior of Mexico to secure art goods of the finest quality. Her curio store is listed in a 1912 city directory as the successor to Rochin and Méndez, an early producer of postcards in Nogales, Sonora.[46] Into the early

Figure 5.57. Carrasco Brothers curio store on Calle Elías, 1940s. R. de la F., 1940s.

Figure 5.58. La Industria Mexicana, Mexican Arts and Crafts, located on Calle Elías. Delfina Rochin de Verboggi, standing right, was the owner of what is claimed to have been the first curio store in Nogales. To the left of the figures (visible with magnification) on a street-facing wall is painted "Genuine Mexican Curios and French Perfumes." México Fotográfico 62, 1940s.

Figure 5.59. Curio stores, clubs, and restaurants began to crowd out residential properties along Calle Elías during the 1940s. This view looking south on the street shows two curio shops, La Cucaracha and Arte Mexicano, and several doors farther down the street, the Cavern Café. México Fotográfico 60, 1940s.

post–World War II period, Calle Elías persisted as the center of curio store enterprise in Nogales as more and more shops opened along the length of the street (fig. 5.59).

The commercial success of curio stores on Calle Elías created competition on nearby streets as some merchants expanded by opening additional stores and others opened new establishments. Along Calle Colon west of Calle Elías, Carrasco Brothers opened a second store, and other businesses began to set up on the street, such as Las Cazuelas only a block south of the second Carrasco store (fig. 5.60). Curio stores like Carioca's spilled west onto Calle Campillo (fig. 5.61), permitting advertisements from the era to boast "Curio Shops Galore . . . More Than a Score to Visit," and the favorable exchange rate of 4.80 pesos to one dollar gave the visitor "mucho dinero when you cross over."[47]

Avenida Obregón

During the 1940s, Calle Obregón (previously Arizpe) became Avenida Obregón, suggesting its elevated status as a major thoroughfare of Nogales, Sonora. The avenue was still chiefly commercial and serving residents of the community. As the century transitioned to its fifth decade, Obregón emerged as the principal tourist area of Nogales, accommodating restaurants, bars, and curio stores aplenty (fig. 5.62). Pedestrian

Figure 5.60. Nogales curio stores spilled west of Calle Elías with the expansion of a tourist economy during the 1940s. Las Cazuelas is located on the street identified as Calle Colon on the map in figure 5.54, a street sometimes called Calle Ferrocarril (Railroad Street) because it faced the tracks out of the picture on the left. México Fotográfico 38, 1940s.

Figure 5.61. Carioca's Mexican Curios located on Calle Campillo west of the railroad corridor illustrates the transition of tourist businesses away from Calle Elías toward Avenida Obregón during the 1940s.

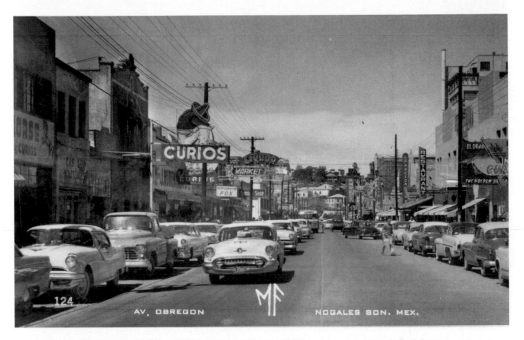

Figure 5.62. Avenida Obregón's transition to full-blown tourist street was complete in the 1950s. Restaurants, bars, and some twenty curio stores crowded four blocks of Obregón, making it the most developed tourist street among all Sonora border towns. México Fotográfico 124, 1950s.

visitors typically strolled along the three-to-four-block stretch between the international border and Calle Pierson, where most shops and tourist services were located (fig. 5.54). Shopping for silver, perfume, and assorted curios became a regular activity, with storeowners hiring sidewalk barkers to lure visitors to shops and vendor stalls (fig. 5.63). Some places became favored haunts, such as Antonio Giron's B-29 Bar with its distinctive neon airplane sign and block-glass cocktail lounge entry (fig. 5.64).

A close inspection of more than sixty chiefly photographic postcards in the Arreola Collection revealed greater than twenty separate curio stores along Obregón between Calle Campillo and Calle Pierson. A few stores, such as Maya de México and El Regalo, may have also sold curios but distinguished themselves by not using the word *curio* in their street signage. Some shops, such as Choza's, specialized in higher-quality goods and advertised several locations in Nogales beyond Obregón (figs. 5.65, 5.66). The variety of goods that might be vended in the curio stores was staggering. As a result, guide books and newspaper stories that covered the Nogales shopping scene would frequently describe in detail the types of goods, many having been imported from production centers in the interior of Mexico and sometimes

SILVER ALLEY

NOGALES. MEXICO

Figure 5.63. Silver Alley was an early tourist stop on Avenida Obregón. Located on Calle Ochoa, a side street behind the town cathedral, it started as separate stalls but was converted later to an enclosed shopping arcade called the Silver Market. Western Ways, 1940s.

Figure 5.64. Located next door to Montaños Curios was the B-29 Bar and liquor store, a popular refreshment stop on the Avenida Obregón tourist path. The B-29 was considered kitschy because of its distinctive neon sign featuring the outline of the famous World War II bomber. México Fotográfico 44, 1950s.

Figure 5.65. With three locations in Nogales, including Avenida Obregón, Choza's Gift Shop was an upscale tourist store specializing in Spratling silver from Taxco and French perfumes. *City of Nogales Old Mexico Tourist Guide.*

produced locally.[48] Tourist curio crafts might include hand-blown glassware, leather goods, silver jewelry, tin decorative goods, paper flowers, piñatas, *cascarones* (confetti-filled eggshells), pottery, decorative objects, toys, straw crafts, wood and onyx carvings, and woven textiles.

Another mainstay of the tourist street was the donkey cart mobile stage, where visitors could pose for a souvenir snapshot. In 1950s Nogales, this service was a near

Figure 5.66. Choza's perfume bar at its Obregón store featured wall and display case painting by Mexican artist Salvador Corona.

permanent fixture on Calle Ochoa across from the Silver Market (fig. 5.67). In time, other carts would appear on other side streets as the demand for this iconic memento attracted growing popularity. Not captured by postcard photographers, however, was the famous red light district of Nogales, Canal Street. Situated south of the Avenida Obregón shopping area, Canal Street was a single block zone surrounded by a low-income residential neighborhood. Five clubs identified in a Spanish-language publication from the 1950s included the Conga Nite Club, the Lobby Club, the Mambo Club, the Stork Club, and the Singapore Club.[49] Typical of so-called zonas— short for *zonas de tolerancia* (zones of tolerance)—these adult entertainment districts in Mexican cities were legally sanctioned by local ordinance, yet their unsavory character meant they never shared the limelight with other tourist activities. Foreign visitors who might venture to Canal Street were likely chaperoned to the location by taxi drivers who knew the destination well.[50]

Plaza de Toros

From the 1910s to the 1930s, bullfights in Nogales were staged in makeshift wooden ovals typically located on the southern outskirts of town (fig. 5.68). In 1939, a wooden ring with perimeter rock wall enclosures was constructed. This ring was said to have

Figure 5.67. By the 1950s, donkey carts began to appear on several side streets off Obregón. For many tourists, a snapshot posed in the cart was a standard souvenir of a visit to Nogales.

a large capacity, offered shade (*sombra*) as well as sun (*sol*) seating, entertained some of Mexico's finest matadors, and, on at least one occasion, featured Juanita Cruz, Spain's famous woman bullfighter.[51] In 1952, bullfight promoter Pedro Gonzales Duarte raised money to build the first concrete arena on the same site as the 1939 wooden plaza, and this arena became the most celebrated plaza de toros in Nogales[52] (fig. 5.69). Next door to the arena was the Foreign Club bar that could accommodate crowds on Sunday *corridas* (literally, bullbaitings) that were typically scheduled for

BULL FIGHT,   NOGALES, SONORA, MEXICO

Figure 5.68. Early bullrings in Nogales, located on the outskirts of town, were typically wooden enclosures with simple bleachers to accommodate attendees. Saenz Aguilar, 1920s.

El Forin Club y Plaza de Toros
Nogales, Son. Mex.   126

Figure 5.69. Plaza de Toros in Nogales, with the adjoining Foreign Club bar. This arena, constructed of concrete with decorative paintings of bullfighters on exterior panels, became the most celebrated bullring in Nogales during the golden age of border bullfighting, 1950s–1960s. México Fotográfico 126, 1950s.

Figure 5.70. The Plaza de Toros in Nogales could accommodate five thousand attendees at Sunday *corridas* in the spring, fall, and winter seasons. Local businesses such as Mickey Mouse and Arte Mexicano curio stores as well as the B-29 Bar advertised on the back wall of the arena. México Fotográfico 130, 1950s.

spring, fall, and winter seasons. Tucson newspapers especially helped promote bull-fighting in Nogales with stories appearing regularly during the 1950s.[53] With a seating capacity of five thousand, the Plaza de Toros became a popular venue for visitors, celebrities, and politicos until it closed in 1963, only to be sold and reopened one year later, and then permanently shut in 1972 (fig. 5.70).[54]

Vignette: Cavern Café

A restaurant-bar might well be discussed as part of a border town's cabaret person-ality, especially during the era of Prohibition, or as a tourist attraction in the post–World War II era. Rarely, does an eating and drinking establishment create a legacy. La Caverna or the Cavern Café, however, was an extraordinary establishment, one that over many decades helped shape the identity of Nogales for visitors and locals alike, earning it landmark status in the history of the Sonora border town.

The story of the Cavern Café starts with another café-bar called the Cave. In 1892, two French-born brothers, Agustín and Enrique Donnadieu, arrived in Nogales via Mexico City and opened a general merchandise store called La Ciudad de México. The brothers, who came to be known as Los Hermanos Donnadieu, developed a successful enterprise vending a variety of imported products, chief among these being wine and spirits.[55] The Donnadieus purchased property on the east side of Calle Elías and sometime in the 1900s carved at least two caves out of the steep hillside behind their storefront building, each being some twenty-five feet wide and one hundred feet deep horizontally into the rock. The reason the caves were excavated is not certain; some sources suggest that they were mine shafts, although that may be dubious given the angles of excavation. Nevertheless, the caves were used by the Donnadieus to store liquor, because inside the rock shelters the average temperature was somewhere near 72 degrees Fahrenheit.[56] In the early 1920s, one of the caves was leased or sold to businessman John Hughes, who opened the Cave, advertised as "Sonora's Most Unique Restaurant—Dining Rooms Hewn Out of Solid Rock."[57] The Cave gained popularity during the Prohibition era and advertised dancing to a five piece "jazz orchestra" on Sundays.[58] The building that fronted the Cave was a single-story, fired-brick façade on the east side of Calle Elías with a separate "Ladies Entrance" where unchaperoned females could enter without any associated stigma (fig. 5.71).

Figure 5.71. During the Prohibition era, the Cave Restaurant and Bar maintained a separate Ladies Entrance where women sans chaperon might enter the establishment without any stigma or association that could be ascribed to a single female out on the town. Lohn Fot. 37, 1920s.

In 1927, the Donnadieus leased or sold one of the caves to Chris Kerson, a Greek immigrant who created a nightclub called the Cavern, next door to the Cave (fig. 5.72). Some years later, the Cave was said to have been purchased by Kerson from proprietor John Hughes, and that space was absorbed into the Cavern so that the establishment now had two caves that were subdivided into separate rooms for dining and dancing (fig. 5.73). Chris Kerson sold the Cavern to his nephews Jim and Nick, also Greek born, who operated the nightclub-café for several decades. Nick became a U.S. citizen, whereas Jim became a Mexican citizen, changing his name to Demetrio P. Kyriakas (1907–1990). During its heyday, the Cavern was patronized by many national and internationally renowned personalities, including, for example, General John "Black Jack" Pershing, Leo Carrillo, Clark Gable, W. C. Fields, Mario Moreno (aka Cantinflas), Maria Felix, Agustín Lara, and several Mexican presidents and governors of Sonora and Arizona. In the opinion of many border residents, La Caverna (as native Nogalense called it) was the town's main tourist attraction.[59]

For the next two decades, the Cavern Café hosted locals and visitors alike with regular advertisement in local newspapers and certainly by word of mouth.[60] The building exterior continued to show separate entrances for the Cave and the Cavern (fig. 5.74). In the main room the floor was hardwood, there was an elevated stage, and

Figure 5.72. The Cave, opened in the early 1910s, and the Cavern, next door, opened in 1927. The two would later be combined into a single establishment, the Cavern Café, a landmark that survived for nearly five decades as reputedly the most popular tourist attraction in Nogales. México Fotográfico 19, 1920s.

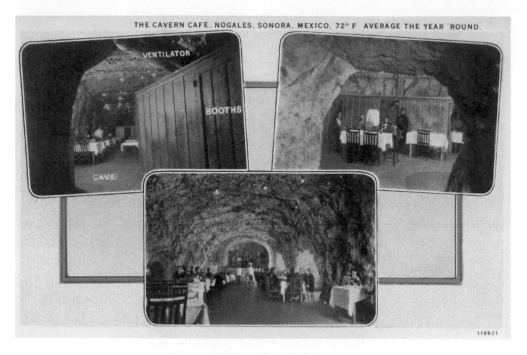

Figure 5.73. The Cavern Café comprised one large room circa 25 feet wide by 100 feet long and several smaller side rooms. The caves had been hewn out of solid rock, as one advertisement noted, and thereby maintained an average year around temperature of circa 72 degrees Fahrenheit. Dining and orchestra entertainment were considered first class, and on the verso of this print postcard it states that the Cavern Café is "Dedicated to those who Seek the Best." Curt Teich & Company 119821, 1928.

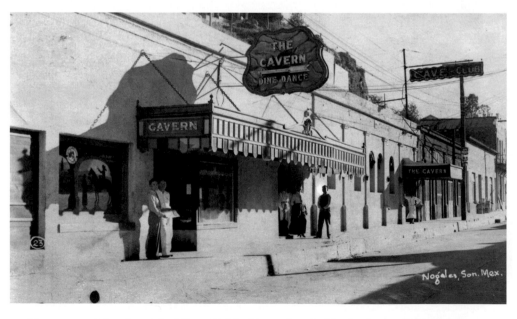

Figure 5.74. After the original Cave Club had been absorbed by the Cavern Café, the old sign from the 1920s that hung high above street level in front of the original redbrick building was replaced with a neon sign that read Cave-Club. The Cavern signs in the foreground as well as on the porticos also appear to be neon. R. R. de la F. 23, 1930s.

CAVERN CAFE, AN OLD MEXICAN PRISON
©L.L.Cook Co. 1939
MILWAUKEE, WIS.   NOGALES, OLD MEXICO   C 310

Figure 5.75. The main room at the Cavern Café included an elevated bandstand, hardwood dance floor, and linen covered tables with electric lights lined against the cave walls. One story, often repeated even to the present, is that the cave was formerly a jail that once housed Chiricahua Apache leader Geronimo. L. L. Cook, 1939.

tables for dinner lined either side of the cavern walls. Entertainment included floor-shows typically accompanied by live orchestra (fig. 5.75).

The variety of food offerings was staggering by almost any standard and would likely have been characterized as "continental" during this period. Here is the "Special Dinner" menu served daily from noon to midnight during the 1940s and 1950s.[61]

Relishes—Sweet Pickles, Mixed Olives

Appetizers—Fresh Guaymas Oysters or Shrimp Cocktail, Fresh Fruits Brandy Sauce

Soup—Fresh Guaymas Green Turtle

Choice of Entrée—Fresh Lobster ala Newbourgh, Venison Steak Wine Sauce, Fresh Frog Legs Fried or Saute, Fresh Frog Legs ala Poulette, Hommer Squabs Broiled or Fried, Broiled Lobster Drawn Butter, Fresh Shad Roe Fried or Broiled with Bacon, Fresh Shad Roe Saute Sherry Wine Sauce, Cabrilla Broiled, Fried, or ala Veracruzana, Fresh Guaymas Oysters Au Gratin, Fresh Guaymas Oysters Fried in Butter, Chicken, Shrimp, or Pork Chop Suey, Fresh Shrimps ala New Orleans or ala Creole, Fresh Shrimps ala Newbourgh or ala Bombay, Tenderloin of Trout with Tartar Sauce,

Figure 5.76. Between the street and the portal that lead to the cave rooms at the Cavern Café was the bar room, where cocktails were made on demand for patrons and where casual dining in booths was possible. R. R. de la F. 22, 1930s.

Figure 5.77. The Cavern continued as a popular tourist attraction into the 1950s. This view suggests how changes were made to the building façade and how the original neon sign was converted to what appears to be a backlighted sign that reads The Cavern Cafe Danzant. México Fotográfico 120, 1950s.

T. Bone Streak Grilled Mex. Meat, Spring Chicken Broiled or Fried, Fresh Wild Boar
Steak Hunter Style, Roast Chicken with Sage Dressing, Club Steak Mexican Meat
Manhattan Sauce, Fresh Turtle Steak Maitre D'Hotel, Breaded Pork Chops Tomato
Sauce, Roast Leg of Lamb with Quince Jam, Lamb Steak Manhattan Sauce, Lamb
Chops Grilled on Toast, Chicken Mole Poblano ala King or Spanish Style, Chicken
Livers Fried Saute or ala Brochette

Dessert—Plumb Pudding with Brandy Sauce, Green Apple Pie, Fruit Jello, Daily Cream
Pie, Casaba Melon

Coffee, Tea, Milk

Price—$2 US or $10 Pesos

The Cavern Bar outside of the Cave dining room prepared drinks on demand. It was also an area with booths for patrons who wanted a less formal dining and drinking atmosphere (fig. 5.76). Sometime in the 1950s, the hanging sign that graced La Caverna since it was founded was painted over to read The Cavern Cafe Danzant. The restaurant's exterior was changed as well with the addition of a wrought iron and tile awning with decorative hanging lamps over the bar entrance and a large evaporative cooling unit stacked on the old portico and duct that extended into a nearby window (fig. 5.77). Over the next several decades, the Cavern continued to draw tourists even as the new visitor path shifted to Avenida Obregón and away from Calle Elías.

The Cavern Café had become famous for its fine foods, orchestral entertainment, and moderate prices, and it was a longstanding member of the Duncan Hines Club, a stamp of approval for international travelers. Tragically, however, disaster struck on February 18, 1984, when fire closed the landmark. For several years thereafter plans were floated to rebuild and reopen the historic restaurant and bar, but squabbles among cave owners and operators stifled resolution.[62] To this day, it has not been rebuilt. The Cavern "was not so much a business as it was part of border heritage," said Charles Fowler, past executive director of the Nogales–Santa Cruz County Chamber of Commerce; "when La Caverna burned down, we lost a part of the heart and soul of Nogales."[63] Without the Cavern, other tourist businesses on Calle Elías, especially curio stores that had weathered the relocation of tourism to Avenida Obregón decades earlier, began to close. Luis Gerrardo Piña, who operated Patricia's Curios, was only able to open the store part-time and reported that in one three-day period after the Cavern closed, his only sale was a single postcard of La Caverna.[64] Faded glory, it seems, survives only in memories and postcards.

6

Sonoyta

William T. Hornaday, an early twentieth-century naturalist, explorer, and visitor to the Sonora Desert, captured the remote nature of the tiny border village of Sonoyta in his popular account *Camp-Fires on Desert and Lava* in 1909. "A hundred times over, as I have looked on the maps at the queer Papago-Indian name 'Sonoyta'—the *only* name printed on the long, bare stretch of 234 miles between Nogales and the Colorado River—I have wondered about that lonesome little spot. So far as I have read, no one ever has taken the trouble to write more than ten lines regarding the ensemble of the place and its people, and everything was left to the imagination."[1] While Sonoyta was certainly small and isolated when visited by Hornaday, his account included a full chapter about the village. On the footsteps of Hornaday was the Norwegian ethnographer Carl Lumholtz, whose popular account *New Trails in Mexico* published in 1912 also included a complete chapter about Sonoyta.[2] These accounts would be followed by several other writings in the first decades of the twentieth century to lend further exposure to the remote Sonora border settlement.[3]

Notwithstanding these explorations, Sonoyta has remained a small Mexican border town. To the present, Sonoyta sits largely alone on this stretch of border, and no equivalent American border town has ever developed. Through most of the twentieth century, Sonoyta was linked economically and socially to the Arizona desert mining town of Ajo some forty miles distant from the international boundary. Sonoyta's emergence as a gateway is tied to the Sonora, Mexico, town of Puerto Peñasco on the Gulf of California. That connection especially opened the remote village to increased visitors and, eventually, postcard photographers who captured its visual landmarks for tourist travelers.

In this chapter, I bring Sonoyta's geographic past to light through varied sources—narrative and visual—and particularly through the postcard images created late in its long history, freezing its landscape personality in the heyday of its renown. Like other border towns, understanding Sonoyta follows a geographical setting on the international line, an evolution of its townscape, and a visual chronicle of selected touristic landmarks. Unlike other Sonora border towns, Sonoyta's history can be traced to the Spanish colonial period and before, when it emerged as a small aboriginal settlement. Mostly, however, Sonoyta is portrayed as a place between, a stopping point and oasis for those crossing an unforgiving desert, a campsite and supply station for explorations of the Sonoran Desert, and a point of transit linking Arizona with a recreational fishing and tourist seaside settlement on the Gulf of California. The chapter closes with a vignette that explores Sonoyta's crossroads and gateway identity.

Geographic and Historic Setting

Situated west of Ambos Nogales, east of San Luis Río Colorado, south of Ajo, Arizona, and north of Puerto Peñasco on the Gulf of California, Sonoyta is the oldest of the Sonora border towns and one of the earliest Mexican settlements on the international boundary (fig. 6.1). Founded as a Jesuit mission circa 1700, the oasis site was already occupied by so-called Sand Papago (Hia-Ced O'odham) when the Spanish arrived. The name Sonoyta (also Sonoíta) is said to derive from the O'odham words *Kávortkson*, where *Kávortk* equals "rounded hill" and *son*, translated as "at the foot of," combined with *óitac*, meaning "field in a place where there is water."[4]

True to its word origin, Sonoyta is situated at the base of a small hill cradled between the volcanic Sierra de Sonoita to the north and the granitic Sierra de Cubabi on the south. The Sonoyta River that creates the oasis has its headwaters to the east of the site in ranges found in Sonora and Arizona. For much of the year—except during summer thunderstorms when surface flow can be substantial—this drainage flows underground. It surfaces at the oasis location as the result of local geologic conditions.[5] Beyond Sonoyta the stream disappears into the desert sands surrounding the nearby Pinacate Lava fields (fig. 6.1).

The seasonal presence of water in this part of the Sonoran Desert probably explains the long tenure of human occupation at the site of Sonoyta, perhaps two thousand years according to archeological excavation.[6] Nevertheless, the aboriginal population here may have never exceeded two hundred residents. When visited by Lumholtz in 1909/1910, there were some 100 Mexican residents in Sonoyta and another 100 Papagos (Hia-Ced O'odham) living one mile downstream in a separate locale.[7]

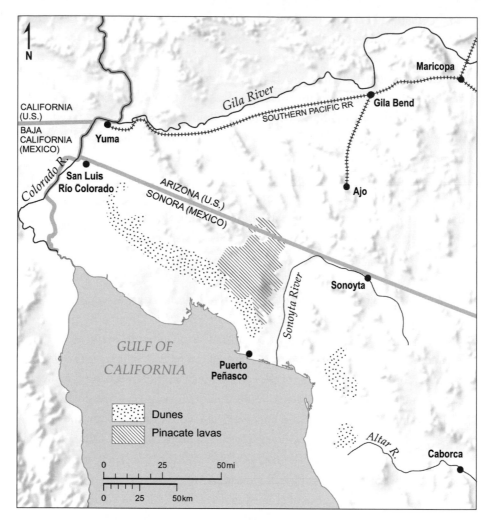

Figure 6.1. Sonoyta–San Luis Río Colorado borderlands. Adapted from Ives, "Sonoyta Oasis," fig. 1. Cartography by Barbara Trapido-Lurie.

During the Spanish colonial era, this ancient aboriginal site along the 225-mile stretch called the Camino del Diablo was the only dependable water source between the Jesuit mission settlement at Caborca and the Colorado River. Circa 1700, Eusebio Francisco Kino, a Jesuit priest who explored much of northwestern Sonora, recognized the strategic importance of the oasis and called for the founding of a mission here, where cattle could graze and irrigation farming was possible. For almost five decades, San Marcelo de Sonoydag, later Sonoíta, proved a stopping point between Jesuit missions in Sonora and the early mission settlements on the Colorado River. A revolt of Pima Indians in 1751 resulted in the destruction of the mission at Sonoíta;

however, the site continued to function as a water stop for Spanish explorations into California during the 1770s. Following independence from Spain (1821) and circa 1850, a few families from nearby Altar, Sonora, and the mining village of Zoñi, Sonora, founded the Mexican community of Sonoyta, as it came to be known.[8]

The place continued to be referenced, sometimes disparagingly, as a primitive refuge for travelers across the desert and, in the mid-1800s, especially by California gold seekers. In 1854, Andrew Gray, part of a railroad survey team in southern Arizona, visited Sonoyta and gave this account. "Sonoita . . . , a short distance below the limits of our territory, is an Indian town where the Gobernador of the Papagos resides. There are also a few Mexican families. The valley is broad, with springs, and a small stream (the Sonoita) which flows a few miles in the dry months, when it sinks, like the river of San Diego in California. During the rainy season it extends for a long distance toward the Gulf."[9]

Sonoyta was visited next by the U.S. and Mexico boundary resurvey team in the late nineteenth century. A map from that period shows the situation of Sonoyta and the locations of other rancho settlements downstream from the historic site, including El Pueblo, Rancho Romo, Ranchería del Papagos, Rancho de Buenos Aires, Rancho de Rosa de Castilla, and Santo Domingo. Some of these settlements, like El Pueblo and Ranchería del Papagos, were native sites, the former known as Akimuri (The River) by the locals. The river ranchos including Sonoyta survived by irrigating small fields to grow corn, wheat, and selected vegetables and to pasture cattle. Nearby mining camps were sometimes consumers of village surplus, but mostly what was produced appears to have been utilized locally. Downstream from Sonoyta, and chiefly under the authority of the Cipriano Ortega family, Santo Domingo was a central location in the area because it contained a *molino* (mill), a soap factory, a blacksmith shop, an *arrastra* for crushing ore from nearby mines, livestock corrals, several stores, and a church; for a time, it was also the official port of entry, with a customs office that monitored travel into the area despite its distance by road from the international boundary.[10]

Old and New Sonoyta

Two Sonoyta's existed in the immediate area of present Sonoyta.[11] Old Sonoyta was situated about a mile east of the present town on the south bank of the Sonoyta River and proximate to the original site of the mission San Marcelo de Sonoydag. Although Papagos occupied this site after the destruction of the mission in 1751, Mexican families who began to locate here gradually displaced the Papago who moved downstream to rancho sites such as El Pueblo and Ranchería del Papagos. Old Sonoyta was a small collection of adobe houses and corrals with few stores and a small school; there was no church. Agricultural life in Old Sonoyta depended on the water system of the river shared among all settlements. Water pooled in lagoons was diverted via *acequias* (irrigation ditches) to irrigate crops.

A summer storm in 1891 brought a torrent of water down the Sonoyta River. The floodwaters scoured the tranquil lagoons and deepened the river channel such that three years later, the river facing Old Sonoyta transformed to a mesquite bosk (riverine forest) that prohibited successful irrigation. Slowly, Mexican residents began to relocate about a mile downstream, founding New Sonoyta, with some residents moving seven miles down the Rio Sonoyta to Santo Domingo; Old Sonoyta was abandoned.[12]

New Sonoyta, like the Old Sonoyta, was positioned on the south bank of the Sonoyta River, and residents rebuilt their place and lives around the new oasis, constructing a dam on the river above (east) town to collect water for diversion. For almost a decade, however, Santo Domingo downstream remained the central settlement of the area, and it was not until 1904, when Cipriano Ortega, the patriarch of the community, died that the once thriving hacienda languished. In time, New Sonoyta became simply Sonoyta, and the oasis village emerged as the principal settlement along this stretch of the Sonora, Mexico, border.

When Hornaday's expedition visited Sonoyta in 1907, the author sketched a map of the few principal features of the town (fig. 6.2). The map revealed a veritable oasis along the river flanked by desert, with the main structures of the town—about a dozen adobe dwellings—situated south of the Sonoyta River.

Along the north, a fringe of compact, willowy jungle marks the course of the river. Beyond that lies a line of naked-November fields; then a long, hedge-like line of bushes starting in good form on the left, with a scattering of tall trees, and at the extreme right terminating in a lofty grove of dark-green foliage. Beyond the hedge-line there lies another procession of bare fields, another green string of hedge and more fields. As a border for the last series of fields there is a straggling growth of tall trees, and a string of adobe houses to number of a dozen or so. Then comes the desert once more. . . . Those three long green lines of hedge in the middle distance, that parallel the river, mark the courses of the three irrigating ditches of river water that give the Oasis its life. They are the arteries of Sonoyta. Burst the dam above them, and you break Sonoyta.[13]

Both Hornaday and Charles Lumholtz visited Sonoyta within a few years of each other, and each befriended the most prominent resident of the town, Traino Quiroz, the *comisario*, or local official, who presided over civil and criminal matters. Lumholtz

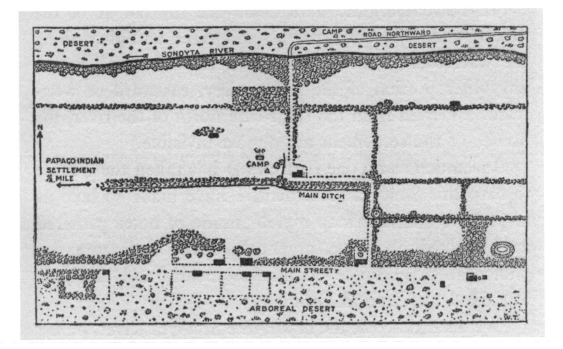

Figure 6.2. Sketch map of Sonoyta, 1907. The town sits on the south bank of the Sonoyta River, whereas the river bottom is cultivated and bordered by groves of trees and riverine brush. Hornaday, *Camp-Fires on Desert and Lava*, 85.

recalled, "Both he and his family delighted in showing me hospitality and attentions; he accompanied me to the place in which I was most interested here, the beginning of the Sonoita River."[14] Hornaday recollected "His house, his mill, his forge, and his little park [garden] behind the fence across the way, constitute a very interesting establishment; and we were graciously permitted to inspect everything."[15]

Sonoyta Townscape

Sonoyta transformed from a town of only a few streets and buildings hinged along the Sonoyta River in the early 1900s to a small but significant border town and gateway to its surrounding region by the 1950s. The town grew from circa one hundred to perhaps eight hundred residents in five decades and then exploded to almost two thousand between 1950 and 1960 (table 1.1). During this era, Sonoyta was situated chiefly south of the river, about two miles from the international boundary. Because there was no permanent bridge crossing the drainage, autos were forced to drive into the riverbed to reach town (fig. 6.3). In the winter dry season, fording the channel

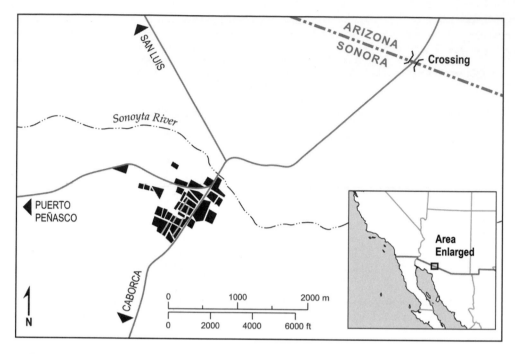

Figure 6.3. Sonoyta town plat circa 1950s. Adapted from Instituto Nacional de Estadística Geografía e Informatica, *Puerto Peñasco* (map). Cartography by Barbara Trapido-Lurie.

might be difficult but not impossible; in the wetter months of the summer, the river could rise as much as thirty feet, and Sonoyta could be inaccessible from the north for days at a time.[16]

A comparison of two photographs, one from 1907 and another from the 1940s, suggests the incremental change along Sonoyta's main street. Figure 6.4 is an image made by John M. Phillips, who accompanied the Hornaday expedition, showing the meager streetscape of the town. The wide, dirt main street is flanked by scattered adobe buildings with ramadas and attached corrals. The distinctive mountain outline on the northeastern horizon is the Sierra de Sonoita. Figure 6.5 is a photographic postcard taken in Sonoyta by J. Pacheco sometime in the 1940s. This view shows the main street of the desert oasis and how little changed from earlier in the same century. Before the 1950s, Sonoyta was a strategic location, situated approximately fifty to one hundred miles from Caborca, Sonora, to the southeast, San Luis Río Colorado, Sonora, to the northwest, Puerto Peñasco, Sonora, to the southwest, and Ajo, Arizona, to the north (fig. 6.1). At Sonoyta, auto travelers were likely to find a single gasoline pump to be the only fuel for miles around. In Pacheco's postcard image, we see Richfield Oil, an American petroleum company, as the only service in the town.

From a photograph by J. M. Phillips

"Main Street" in Sonoyta, Looking East

The House of "the Singing Bird" on the left; Señor Medina's store and mescal establishment first on the right

Figure 6.4. Main street in Sonoyta, 1907. John M. Phillips, in Hornaday, *Camp-Fires on Desert and Lava*, facing 86.

Figure 6.5. Main street in Sonoyta, 1940s. J. Pacheco Foto.

Further comparison of photographic images from 1936 and the 1950s illustrates how Sonoyta's main street emerged from a small-town village to an automotive gateway. Figure 6.6 shows a horse race down the town's main street as part of the Día de Guadalupe (December 12) celebration in 1936. Bystanders crowd the street margins as riders thunder past. The street is dirt, and single-story buildings are adobe, some with whitewashed exteriors. Figure 6.7 shows the changes to the commercial center of Sonoyta by the 1950s. The Y intersection marks the division of roads in town; to the left is the road southeast to Caborca (this would become Mexico 2, the primary border highway), and on the right is the road to Puerto Peñasco (later designated Mexico 8, fig 6.3). The diversity of retail establishments—eatery, automobile services, hotel, bar, package liquor, even a barbershop—suggests the importance of roadside businesses in Sonoyta's developing gateway identity.

While Sonoyta figured a strategic stop for highway travelers, most visitors seemed unaware that the town, like all Mexican settlements, contained landmarks critical to the local residents. Chief among these spaces is the town plaza. Close inspection of the land-use map of Old Sonoyta suggests that the early town lacked a formal plaza.[17] New Sonoyta created a plaza probably during the 1920s or later, because early twentieth-century visitor accounts fail to mention a plaza for the town. In 1921, Mexico City dispatched an official to Sonoyta to launch several construction projects, including a church, school, and federal administrative building.[18] Whether Sonoyta's plaza was constructed then is uncertain. Nevertheless, the town plaza, dedicated to Mexican president Benito Juárez, is captured in a 1940s postcard (fig. 6.8). Photographer J. Pacheco's early plaza view shows the small square fringed by adobe buildings and comprising an open dirt and grass area that appears to be flanked by a shallow berm and filled with varieties of palm trees and several tamarisk trees. There is not a *kiosco* (bandstand) so common to most Mexican border town plazas.[19] Another postcard view of Sonoyta's plaza from the 1950s illustrates the changes to the space with the addition of concrete walkways and benches and electrical lighting; still, the plaza lacked a *kiosco* (fig. 6.9).

Sonoyta's plaza is unusual in several ways. First, because the town evolved along roads that were irregular and not the conventional grid of streets intersecting at ninety-degree angles, the plaza is hidden behind the main street and not visible to passersby: it is located at an unidentified open space tucked among town blocks between the Puerto Peñasco and Caborca roads (fig. 6.3). Further, Plaza Benito Juárez does not front a church, also a traditional spatial alignment for Mexican towns although by no means universal. When geographer Ronald Ives visited Sonoyta in the 1930s, he noted that there was "no resident physician and no resident priest."[20] Sonoyta received sacrament on occasion from a visiting priest who traveled from Altar. Consequently, the first church, La Sagrada Familiar, would not appear until the

Figure 6.6. Horse race down main street, Sonoyta, 1936. Courtesy Arizona Historical Society, Tucson, Earl Fallis Photo Collection #43109.

Figure 6.7. Commercial zone with roadside services, Sonoyta, 1950s. México Fotográfico 3.

Figure 6.8. Sonoyta's plaza circa 1940s. J. Pacheco Foto., 23.

Figure 6.9. Sonoyta's plaza circa 1950s, showing the growth of trees (cf. fig. 6.8) and improvements to the space. México Fotográfico 1.

1940s, and its placement was blocks away from the plaza. Sonoyta's plaza, however, did attract a popular landmark to the northwest corner of the space during the 1940s: a *cine*, or movie theater.[21]

Tourist Places

From its earliest days, Sonoytense (Sonoyta residents) quenched their thirst for spirits by consuming locally produced mescal. Because vineyards were part of the irrigated farming along the Sonoyta River, local residents also manufactured primitive wines for local consumption.[22] By the 1920s, during U.S. Prohibition, several efforts were launched to attract visitors from nearby Ajo, Arizona, and beyond to the border at Sonoyta, where alcohol could be consumed outside of the jurisdiction of America's Volstead Act. Chiefly, however, drinking spots in Sonoyta were founded after Prohibition (post 1933), and two types of establishments emerged: clubs created by outside capital and typically operated by locals, and bars owned and operated by locals.

The earliest establishment organized in Sonoyta was the Cactus Club, founded in 1930 by an Ajo hotel owner who received approval from the town's *comisario* to build a hotel and nightclub on a hill just below the international boundary. The Cactus Club featured a "leviathan wooden bar" and adjoining dance floor as well as small rooms that functioned as lodging. Sometime after opening, the club was sold to another Ajo businessman, who changed the name to La Dorina and converted the operation to a hunting lodge. According to one account, affluent sportsmen from across the country were attracted to La Dorina, where they would be comfortably accommodated, plied with food and drink, and guided to hunting grounds in the nearby Sierra Pinta and the Pinacate Lava fields. Hunters were chauffeured to campsites in heavily sprung Dodge sedans, while local horseman rode ahead to spot for game, especially bighorn sheep, Sonoran pronghorn, and white-tailed and mule deer. When La Dorina passed again to new owners, the operation slowly faded and then failed as game became less plentiful and fewer clients appeared.[23]

Both outsiders and locals patronized several bars operated by Sonoytans. One of the longstanding establishments that became popular following Prohibition was the Alamo Bar, situated on the town's main street. A splendid photograph by Earl Fallis in 1936 captured some of the bar's celebratory regulars crowded around its entrance (fig. 6.10).

Another landmark enterprise in Sonoyta was Nacho's Bar and Café (fig. 6.11). Ygnacio Quiroz (1886–1962) was a prominent personality of Sonoyta and the border from the early 1900s to the 1950s. Born in Caborca, Sonora, he moved to Ajo,

Figure 6.10. Celebrating El Día de Guadalupe in front of the Alamo Bar, Sonoyta, 1936. Courtesy Arizona Historical Society, Tucson, Earl Fallis Photo Collection #43105.

Figure 6.11. Nacho's Bar and Café, Sonoyta, 1940s. Ygnacio "Nacho" Quiroz was a prominent figure operating several businesses in Sonoyta during the 1930s and 1940s. J. Pacheco Foto.

Arizona Territory, and opened a store to service the fledgling mining community. He and business partner M. G. Levy excavated the ruins of the Mission San Marcelo de Sonoydag, sharing findings with historian Herbert E. Bolton and ethnographer Carl Lumholtz. Fluent in Spanish, English, and O'odham, Quiroz served as a valuable interpreter for many fieldworkers and often guided visitors to historical and archeological sites in the Sonoyta borderland. He operated the first motorized mail route from Gila Bend to Ajo and later blazed auto routes between Ajo and Sonoyta, Sonoyta and Puerto Peñasco, and along the Camino del Diablo. During the Great Depression, he moved from Ajo to Sonoyta, served a term as the town's *comisario*, and operated a mill, a store, and a café and bar.[24]

The South of the Border Bar served Sonoyta during the 1940s and 1950s. A corner building with a distinctive entrance, the original structure was also a hotel in the 1930s. By the 1950s (fig. 6.12) the building was remodeled to accentuate a curving streamline moderne cornice with decorative window accents and block glass above the entrance.

During the 1940s and 1950s, park rangers who worked across the line at the Organ Pipe Cactus National Monument only a few miles from the border would frequent the eating and drinking establishments of Sonoyta. Following a plate of piquant enchiladas in a local eatery and in need of tepid beer, one ranger recalled how "we strode onto the

Figure 6.12. South of the Border Bar, Sonoyta, 1950s. México Fotográfico 6.

pueblo's streets, often as not northward to the Copacabana Night Club or westerly to an outdoor bar called La Selva (The Jungle) because of the dense growth of date palms around it . . . ordered beer in *caguamas*, meaning literally 'sea turtle.' But in Sonoran barroom jargon a *caguama* is a liter-sized beer. At 'Lico's place' [La Selva] old Mexican men, solitary and morose, wearing soiled hats, came to drink beer and to listen to the jukebox's mournful wails of *corridos* (ballad or narrative poems, from *occurido*, meaning 'happening') and the working-man's country/western ranchera music."[25]

Beyond dispensing libations, Mexican cantinas in some segregated districts of Mexican border towns developed reputations as zones of legal prostitution.[26] Sonoyta proved no different than other towns along the line. North of the Sonoyta River and isolated from the town proper, clustered behind a string of hills at the end of a graded and pockmarked road were a group of *casas de las muchachas* bearing the names El Molino, Carta Blanca, and, reputedly the most popular, La Copacabana. "Once in the club . . . *musica ranchera* and *Norteña* overpowered any but a shouting conversation. Here, mostly Anglo men and Mexican women mingle, trying to converse bilingually in simple declarative sentences as they drink at the bar or at tables surrounding the dance floor. Music blares alternately from a juke box and a local band. Any man who does not soon accost a girl is soon accosted by her and, per her job description she cadges drinks and entices visits to her back room. Her's [*sic*] is the world's oldest profession."[27]

As Sonoyta morphed into a gateway to the sport fishing activities at Puerto Peñasco, new roadside businesses appeared to cater to automobile travelers, including liquor stores and curio shops. Because the main street of the town—known by this time as Boulevard de las Américas—was also the road south and west to the Gulf of California, enterprising Sonoytans located their shops along this drag. One of the most celebrated of these establishments was the store owned and operated by Manuel Vasquez (fig. 6.13).

> Life and business in Sonoyta was seasonal. The cooler months lured tourism, traffic and commerce connecting California and Arizona with the Mexican interior. The town's main street, which Hornaday had walked praised [*sic*], was now wide and paved. It was called Boulevard de las Américas. On weekends, it hosted all manner of vehicles, most of them traveling the road to Puerto Peñasco. The boulevard's north side offered a *supermercado* (supermarket), a *botica* (drugstore)[,] a discount Corona beer outlet, a curio store or two, and a *peluquería* (barbershop). The street's centerpiece was Manual [*sic*] Vasquez's sprawling liquor store with an adjacent room of curios and furniture. We all knew the legendary Don Manuel whose adult life had been devoted to the distilling and selling of liquor, contraband and legal.[28]

Figure 6.13. Vasquez Liquor and Curios, Sonoyta, 1950s. México Fotográfico 13.

Vignette: Crossroads and Gateway Border Town

The historic isolation of the Sonoyta oasis in the western borderland created economic opportunity for the small town. From the late nineteenth century, travelers across the region secured local supplies and, of course, water at the strategic Mexican border location. Early visitors never failed to praise the production and variety of crops and specialty fruits and vegetables available from the irrigated farming along the margins of the Sonoyta River. Beyond staples such as corn, beans, and squash, Sonoytans produced various greens, peppers, onions, carrots, and other so-called kitchen garden crops, the surplus of which was sold to surrounding communities, including Ajo, Arizona.[29] In addition, various fruits such as figs, pomegranates, melons, and grapes were planted and harvested at the oasis. Sonoyta's access by road to communities in Sonora and Arizona enhanced its connectivity and gateway status in the region.

This crossroads condition worked both ways. Produce grown in Sonoyta and traded to other towns enabled places with greater connectivity beyond the border to supply Sonoyta with products it could not generate. One of the early traders who traveled through Sonoyta was Dona Liberate Rodrigues, who operated a freighting business along the Sonora border between 1896 and 1924. Horse-driven wagons hauled staples and merchandise between Hermosillo, Sonora, and Ajo, Arizona, passing through Sonoyta.[30] Other merchants, such as M. G. Levy, opened general stores in nearby towns, including Sonoyta and Ajo, and the Sonoyta stores were said to be stocked with American products supplied from Ajo.[31]

The business connections linking Sonoyta and Ajo created a symbiotic relationship where the Arizona mining town was the equivalent American border town to Sonoyta in spite of the forty-mile distance dividing the communities. As early as 1917, Sonoyta residents traveled to Ajo to participate and observe Christmas Eve ceremonies in the town plaza. During the 1920s to the 1940s, familial connections linked some Sonoyta residents with Mexican ancestry residents of Ajo. "At that time, the 20s and 30s, people migrated back and forth. They would work in the mines for a little while, and they would go back to Mexico."[32]

Crude trails were the precursors to later paved roads bringing Sonoytans and Ajoans together. The "Old Sonoita Road" extending almost due north from the international boundary to the Arizona mining town was abandoned in 1917. The "Ajo-Sonoita Road" that replaced the former one veered slightly west of the old trail to take advantage of known water wells along the route.[33] During the 1920s, various routes emerged between Ajo and Sonoyta, but whatever the trail followed, travel was one full day each way between the Mexican border and the Arizona town. Some grading improvements occurred in the early 1930s, but the Sonoyta-Ajo Road was not oiled and then paved until 1939.[34]

Sonoyta was also a strategic jump-off for travel west to the Colorado River and beyond. This stretch of the Gran Desierto had been blazed by Eusebio Kino in the Spanish colonial era and continued as a route through the nineteenth and into the twentieth centuries. One of the more daring travel connections across the desert south of the international boundary was the so-called Mexicali taxi. In 1935, Julian and Helen Hayden visited Sonoyta and witnessed one of these taxis as it prepared travelers for the 130-mile journey to San Luis Río Colorado. "There was a Studebaker sedan, the old square box type, probably a 1928 or so model, holding perhaps ten or twelve people, loading for a trip to San Luis, Mexico and Tia Juana. There were gasoline cans tied along the sides, racks on top held goats, chickens and baggage, children and adults leaning out every window, tires and spare axles tied on the rear and a great deafening racket as folks said farewells."[35] This transport system consisted of a fleet of sedans called *camioncitos* (little buses) that operated between 1928 and 1942. The sedans were typically Studebakers, Buicks, Cadillacs, and Dodges (fig. 6.14). The drivers were members of La Union de Choferes del Desierto (Desert Chauffer's Union). The route across the desert was a challenging excursion because roads were unpaved and the heat, sand, and wind made for treacherous conditions. Each stopover along the route had a nickname. Sonoyta was known as La antesala de Infierno (Hell's Waiting Room).[36]

Figure 6.14. The Mexicali taxi was one of a fleet of sedans called *camioncitos* (little buses) that ferried travelers across the desert between Sonoyta and the Colorado River. This photo, snapped by Ronald Ives circa 1930, is in front of the Oficina de Migración (Immigration Office) in Sonoyta. Courtesy Arizona Historical Society, Tucson, Ives Collection PC Bk5 2364.

The regional connection that transformed Sonoyta into a popular gateway settlement was the development of Puerto Peñasco (known as Rocky Point in Arizona), sixty miles south on the Gulf of California (known as the Sea of Cortez in Mexico). Puerto Peñasco was a remote fishing hamlet until American sport fishermen discovered its tourism potential in the late 1920s. When an early marine club development was anticipated in 1928, both Arizona governor George W. P. Hunt and Sonora governor Fausto Topete visited the site by plane because overland travel was so uncertain.[37] In 1941 and 1942, Mexico commenced construction of an oil-paved highway across the desert sands to connect Puerto Peñasco to Sonoyta. The oil arrived in Ajo by rail and was transferred to trucks and hauled across the border to surface the route. A consequence of the road construction was the erection of a wooden bridge across the Sonoyta River that greatly improved access between Sonoyta and Ajo.[38] The Sonoyta–Puerto Peñasco road was completed in 1946, by which time Rocky Point's population expanded to circa twenty-five hundred.[39]

With paved road surfaces connecting Sonoyta to Ajo and Puerto Peñasco, tourism boomed via the oasis gateway.[40] A port of entry crossing with customs gate was constructed on the international boundary north of Sonoyta (fig. 6.15). As traffic through

Figure 6.15. Looking north from the Mexican customs gate crossing on the international line during the 1950s. With paved roads linking Ajo, Arizona, with Puerto Peñasco, Sonora, via Sonoyta, the border town boomed as a popular gateway to recreational activities on the Gulf of California. México Fotográfico 9.

Figure 6.16. Roadside services in Sonoyta boom with the paving of the road to Puerto Peñasco. México Fotográfico 8.

the gateway increased, tourist services emerged to cater to visitors who would typically stop in Sonoyta to provision before continuing south to the gulf (fig. 6.16).

Sonoyta transformed significantly with the popularity of travel through this crossroads/gateway during the 1950s. The town population more than doubled as the old oasis integrated into the regional economy (table 1.1). Nevertheless, Sonoyta expanded beyond the tourist activity that became central to its modern identity. During the 1950s, a sociological study of Sonoyta revealed that approximately 35 percent of the adult male population migrated to the United States for work and an additional 30 percent of the remaining adults interviewed had visited the United States.[41] Thus, some two-thirds of adult Sonoytans had by then some contact with American culture, an extraordinary percentage not likely matched by any other Sonoran border town.

7

San Luis Río Colorado

ullfights came to San Luis, Mexico, in 1957. Before then, fight fans from the Colorado River border town and from Yuma, Arizona, across the line were forced to drive west to Mexicali, Baja California, to witness the popular Mexican spectacle. When the *plaza de toros* opened on June 30 for a special inauguration, it stood starkly in the desert sand some three miles east of town on the road to Sonoyta. The ring proved a salvation for locals because only two years before, the Mexicali plaza had burned in a fire and had not yet been repaired. The grounds surrounding the San Luis ring eventually included a restaurant, curio shops, and a cantina. Most unusual, however, was the construction of the plaza itself, a large arena with a seating capacity of seven thousand. The San Luis bullring did not rise out of the desert sand de novo; rather, it was assembled section by section from an older ring dismantled in Tijuana and moved by trucks over the mountains and across the desert to its new home in San Luis. The wooden structure had served many fight seasons in the Baja California border town but was being replaced by a new steel and concrete ring. When the 1957 bullfight season began, the San Luis bullring was the only one operating between Nogales and Tijuana.[1]

Bullfights, along with curio stores and cabarets, were some of the primary lures that began to attract visitors to the remote Mexican border town of San Luis Río Colorado. In the shadow of its larger Mexican border town neighbor Mexicali, San Luis proved a popular draw for Arizonans and especially for residents of Yuma, the American "border town" some twenty-five miles north of the boundary. Unlike other Sonora border towns, San Luis emerged from an agricultural colony that was transformed to a military encampment during the Mexican Revolution and was not even a formal town until the 1930s. As a proper border settlement, it began to take shape in the 1940s, and, like all Mexican border towns, it exploded in popularity during the 1950s and 1960s.

In this chapter I explore the newest and the westernmost Sonora border town by first tracing its geographical context and early history, then assess its tourist landscapes as captured in postcards, and conclude with a vignette using postcard photography to visualize selected streetscapes of the town's 1940s–1950s past.

Geographic and Historic Setting

When the U.S. and Mexico boundary resurvey team visited the Yuma area in the late nineteenth century, it described the valley south of the Arizona town toward the international boundary as inhabited only by Yuma, Cocopah, and Diegueño Indians.[2] Indeed, the map published by the commission showed only the Colorado River, the locations of boundary markers 204 and 205 along the international border, and a rancho on the Mexican side of the line (fig. 7.1). San Luis Río Colorado was nowhere to be found.

Mexican ranchos were created south of the boundary after 1867 and included approximately a dozen sites scattered along the east bank of the Colorado River. One of these ranchos, Colonia Lerdo, created in 1879, survived as a ranch and farm settlement into the late 1880s.[3] Colonia Lerdo was abandoned in 1913–1914 as settlers relocated to a site near the international border proximate to the U.S. boundary. During this period, Sonora and nearby Baja California were being contested by several Mexican Revolutionary groups. Colonia Lerdo residents reasoned that proximity to the United States would prove strategically safer, so they moved to the border and named their settlement San Luis. In 1917, San Luis was an agricultural colony, and authority was vested in a local military garrison and customs officials who monitored cross border traffic. New colonists continued to arrive at the site then still called a rancho. Residents created irrigation systems using water from the Colorado River to raise cotton, grains, and vegetables in the floodplain below the sand terrace where the town would eventually evolve.[4]

During the 1920s, San Luis was a small settlement of less than two hundred residents (table 1.1). It came to be governed by a local *comisario* (commissioner) replacing the previous military authority. The incipient town developed contractual arrangements with Yuma, Arizona, across the boundary to supply electricity and to truck water to the settlement. San Luis would not be supplied with electrical power from Mexico until 1960. Yuma thereby became a primary service and market center for the fledgling community, a true American border town despite its distance from San Luis.[5]

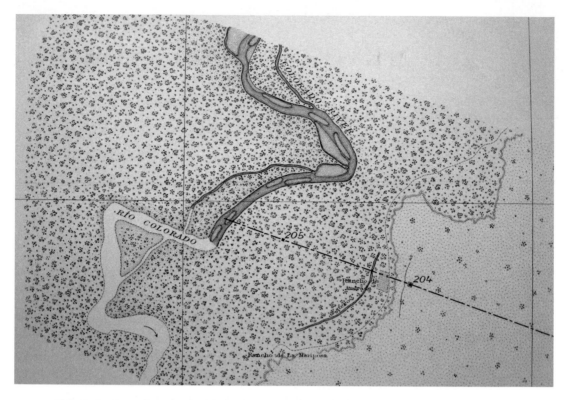

Figure 7.1. San Luis Río Colorado did not exist in 1889 when the U.S.-Mexico boundary was resurveyed east of the Colorado River. The town would later emerge opposite monument marker 204, built on the sand terrace above the Colorado River floodplain. International Boundary Commission, *Boundary between the United States and Mexico,* detail from map no. 4.

San Luis was remembered as a largely makeshift place in the 1920s. Most buildings were adobe and/or thatch construction and situated proximate to the international boundary, slightly northwest of the original residences that had been perched on the edge of the sand mesa overlooking the irrigated floodplain of the Colorado River. There were *las tiendas*, which consisted of a grocery, general store, drugstore, and a couple of curio shops. And, of course, there were cantinas. A few American-type houses owned by the commissioner, port authorities, and local businessmen could be found near the stores.[6]

San Luis crossed the threshold to become a formal town in its own *municipio* of the same name in 1939; previously, the town was included in the *municipio* of Caborca.[7] An influx of settlers drawn by colonization schemes in the Colorado River Delta initiated by Mexican president Lázaro Cardenas helped boost the population of the Sonora border town. The *fondo legal,* or official town plat, was a quadrangle of

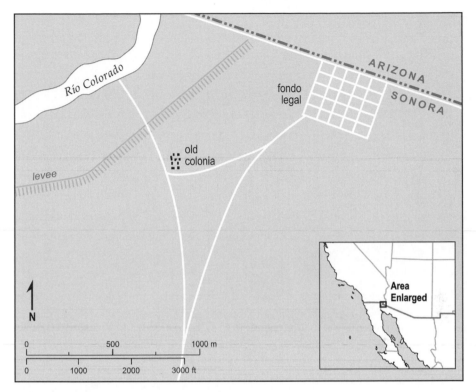

Figure 7.2. San Luis Río Colorado and surroundings circa 1937. After Eloy Méndez Sáinz, "De Tijuana a Matamoros," fig. 6. Cartography by Barbara Trapido-Lurie.

twenty-five blocks hinged against the international boundary and opposite border marker 204.[8] The town sat squarely on the sand terrace above the floodplain of the Colorado River with unpaved roads linking it to fields below the mesa (fig. 7.2).

Into the 1950s, San Luis remained a relatively compact town. It extended to perhaps thirty-eight blocks tight against the international boundary. The original twenty-five blocks in grid alignment on the east merged with an irregular series of triangular blocks on the west edge of the sand mesa overlooking the Colorado River floodplain (fig. 7.3). The entrance to the town from the United States was situated where Arizona Highway 95 from Yuma intersected the international boundary at Calle 1. West-to-east streets were named *calles* and included Calle Morelos followed by Calles 1–6; north-to-south streets were called *avenidas* and were named Internacional, Obregón, Madero, Juárez, Hidalgo, and Kino. Avenida Obregón was the principal commercial street of the town, and it connected east to Sonoyta, west to Mexicali, and via Calle 2 south to the Gulf (fig. 7.3). Several blocks southeast of the crossing were the town plaza and the principal church, developed in the mid-1950s (figs. 7.4, 7.5).

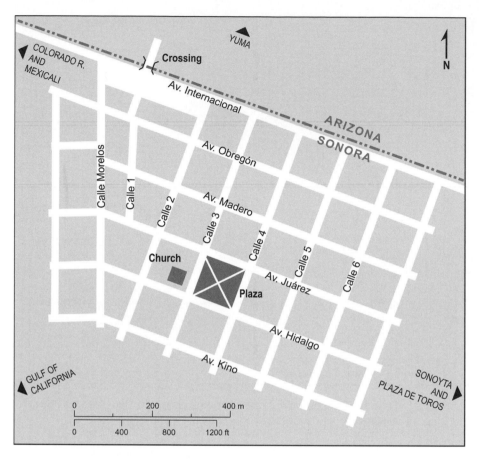

Figure 7.3. San Luis Río Colorado circa 1950s, illustrating the crossing, streets and avenues, and important landmarks. Adapted from Yuma Chamber of Commerce, "Yuma Arizona Sunshine Capital of the Nation." Cartography by Barbara Trapido-Lurie.

Tourist Places

The Prohibition era (1915–33) in Arizona and the United States brought cabaret and its associated vices to tiny San Luis as it had to every other Sonora border town. Given its small population, however, San Luis was not like Nogales or even Agua Prieta; rather, its entertainment establishments were more on the scale of what one found at Naco. The proximity to Mexicali and its abundance of cabarets tempered the extent of such activity in the westernmost Sonora border town. Nevertheless, like other border places, San Luis emerged as a center of curio shops and associated tourist venues, especially bullfights, in the post–World War II period. The 1950s and 1960s were the golden era of San Luis tourist attraction.

Figure 7.4. Plaza Benito Juárez with *kiosco* encircled by benches and walk paths lined with palms. The *kiosco* is dated 1955, which may suggest when the formal plaza was probably created. México Fotográfico 23, 1950s.

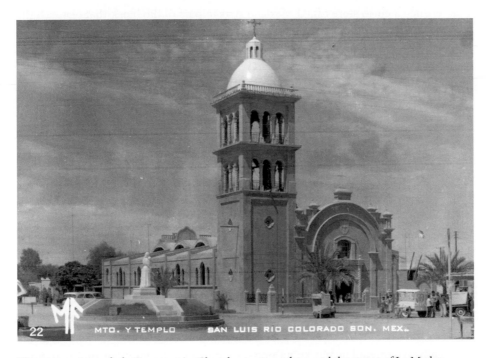

Figure 7.5. Imaculada Concepción Church, street vendors, and the statue of La Madre at the intersection of Calle 2 and Avenida Hidalgo in San Luis Río Colorado circa 1950s. México Fotográfico 22.

In the 1920s, American and Mexican investors formed La Compañía Comercial del Delta del Colorado, S. A., to purchase lots in and around San Luis. American Ethan Allan Washburn opened several establishments proximate to the border crossing in 1924.[9] Perhaps the most famous of Washburn's businesses was the International Club, which was featured frequently in the Yuma press in 1925. Advertisements declared the club only twenty-four miles from Yuma, all on paved roads. Pronouncements boasted about the club's Moorish style construction, jazz orchestra and dancing, delectable food, and perfect service. One full-page ad showed the exterior of the club and declared it would host a July 4 Independence Day celebration that provided a free barbecue (fig. 7.6). Dining specialties at the International Club included wild duck and quail in season and steak. During Prohibition, Jazz Age musicians played popular favorites such as "Yes Sir[,] That's My Baby," "Ain't She Sweet," "I Want to Be Happy," and "I'm Forever Blowing Bubbles."[10] The International Club continued to operate into the 1940s and became a regular local color site for out-of-town visitors, especially conventioneers in Yuma.[11] By the 1950s, various clubs were in operation in San Luis, but some of them, particularly adult venues that featured striptease, began to close by the end of the decade.[12]

Similar to what happened in Agua Prieta and Nogales, the closing of one entertainment created opportunity for another. During the 1940s, the International Club opened a curio store called Mexican Arts in part of the block that featured the restaurant, and that enterprise became one of the first such establishments in San Luis (figs. 7.7, 7.8).

The explosion of population in San Luis following World War II ushered the growth of tourism to the border. By 1955, San Luis counted fifteen thousand residents, more than tripling in size from only five years previously (table 1.1).[13] Tourist attractions such as stores that vended liquor, bars, and curio shops began to concentrate along the streets immediately next to the border crossing. Shops regaled visitors with handmade leather goods and linens, serapes, and blankets. Tourist shops depended on both pedestrian and auto traffic, but most became known through word of mouth and first encounter because few advertised in the Yuma press.[14] During this era, San Luis business groups made visits to Yuma to promote tourism in the Mexican border town, and the Yuma Chamber of Commerce regularly advertised San Luis as a place not to be missed when in Yuma, ever boastful of a visit to "romantic, colorful Old Mexico."[15]

Sporting events that typically involve wagering are part of the entertainment scene of Mexican border towns, and San Luis engaged a variety of these activities. In the 1920s, advertisements in the Yuma press announced cockfights in the then-small border community. In some border cities, specialized indoor arenas called *palenques*

Figure 7.6. The International Club in San Luis, located on the first block in from the border crossing, was a major attraction for American visitors from the 1920s through the 1940s. *Yuma Morning Sun*, "The International Club, San Luis, Sonora, Mexico," advertisement, July 3, 1925.

(palaces) were a regular feature of the sporting scene. In San Luis, the fights were staged at a "pitcock," but it is uncertain whether this was an enclosed *palenque* or an outdoor corral. One advertisement from 1923 was titled "Cocking Main" in San Luis, Sonora, Mexico, at 1 p.m. on Sunday, March 11, featuring Meyers and Moorman of California versus Vasquez and Martinez of San Luis. Presumably these were the owners of the fighting birds. The purse was $500, and the birds were said to be "bona-fide game fighters."[16]

Figure 7.7. The International Club block opened a curio shop to complement its dining and dancing tourist appeal. Foto Haro, 1940s.

Figure 7.8. Mexican Arts attached to the International Club block was one of the first curio stores in San Luis. Foto Haro, 1940s.

Far and away the most popular sport staged in San Luis during the 1950s and 1960s was bullfighting. The San Luis *plaza de toros* opened in 1957 and operated into the early 1960s. The fights were heavily promoted and reported in the Yuma newspapers during the especially popular winter season when each month featured two fight days, typically Sundays.[17] The San Luis arena drew known matadors who also fought in Mexico City as well as in Nogales and Tijuana. In addition, established *toreras* (female bullfighters) such as Patricia McCormick and Bette Ford performed in San Luis.[18] The bullring was also used to stage rodeos that featured Mexican *charro* (rodeo) performances, folk dancing, mariachi musicians, and fancy rope tricks.[19]

Vignette: Landscapes of San Luis Río Colorado

Postcard photographers documented the streets, landmarks, and social activities of San Luis Río Colorado from the 1940s to the 1960s. Their images enable a brief narration of the town's place identity, how San Luis looked to outsiders at the time. In a few instances, the landscapes framed in one period were snapped again in a later decade, and comparison of the images permit us to see changes in landscapes over time through informal repeat photography. Not surprisingly, most places captured in postcard images were chiefly within a few blocks of the international border, the primary spaces visited by tourists.

The formal crossing, or *aduana* (customs), at San Luis was not more than a simple structure, a house really, until the mid-1940s.[20] As the border town expanded in the 1950s, a three-story modern architectural structure with offices and two portals to accommodate vehicle entry and exit appeared on the international boundary. Figure 7.9 shows the crossing in the 1950s and the associated tourist landscape of liquor stores and curio shops flanking the main street—Calle 1—only a block from the boundary. In the previous decade the number of crossings into the United States from San Luis was estimated at two hundred thousand per month.[21] By the late 1960s, the *aduana* had been modified at street level to three vehicle portals, emphasizing how residents of the Mexican border town expanded cross border shopping in Arizona. In that decade a twelve thousand square foot supermarket opened in San Luis, Arizona, just sixty yards across the line from San Luis, Sonora. The American supermarket carried a greater variety of goods than was typically found in small Mexican stores. The supermarket appealed especially to pedestrian shoppers who could purchase a week's supply of groceries in Arizona; a free open-air shuttle bus ferried Mexican consumers from the supermarket to the border crossing, where groups of boys waited on the

Figure 7.9. Entrance to San Luis Río Colorado looking north from Avenida Obregón along Calle 1. The *aduana*, or Mexican customs, is the three-story modern building positioned on the border with portals for entering and exiting. By the 1950s, tourist attractions such as liquor stores, bars, and curio shops concentrated close to the border crossing. México Fotográfico 17, 1950s.

south side of the border to carry bags of groceries for clients into San Luis. On a busy weekend the shuttle would make up to one hundred trips a day.[22]

In San Luis, like in most Mexican border towns, shoppers from the United States were typically pedestrians who simply crossed the line to visit curio stores and related tourist services close to the boundary. Figure 7.10 shows the corner of Avenida Internacional and Calle Morelos looking east toward the crossing in the 1950s. Azteca Curios is visible on the corner property, and other tourist shops were found along this block during this time. Figure 7.11 is a similar view of the same corner in the 1960s, showing the same property now called Jalisco's but still a tourist shop. Additional curio stores as well as an office housing a customs agent who processes cross border commerce are visible across the street. In the same vicinity only a block beyond on Calle Morelos in the 1950s, businesses were chiefly wholesale liquor distributors

Figure 7.10. Azteca Curios, at the corner of Avenida Internacional and Calle Morelos, only a block from the border crossing, accommodates pedestrian shoppers from the Arizona side of the line. México Fotográfico 2, 1950s.

Figure 7.11. Regalos Jalisco, a tourist gift shop at the corner of Avenida Internacional and Calle Morelos. Compare this view of approximately a decade later with the view shown in figure 7.10. Mexfotocolor, 1960s.

Figure 7.12. Wholesale and retail businesses looking north along Calle Morelos near the intersection with Avenida Obregón, 1950s. México Fotográfico 6, 1950s.

Figure 7.13. Calle Morelos looking north, showing curio businesses that replaced wholesale enterprises from the previous decade. Compare with figure 7.12. Mexfotocolor, 1960s.

and other local services (fig. 7.12). By the 1960s, many of these operations closed and transformed into tourist retail outlets to capture the strategic advantage of proximity to the border crossing (fig. 7.13).

During the 1940s, when Calle 1 nearest the crossing was a streetscape of homes and small businesses, the Cine Maya, San Luis's only movie theater, was but a stone's throw from the boundary. Figure 7.14 illustrates the façade of the theater with ornate decorative columns, triple-door entrance, and lobby cards posted on wooden stands on the sidewalk in front of the building. Next door on the left is a dwelling suggesting how the main street then was chiefly residential. Figure 7.15 is a Calle 1 street-level view from a 1950s photographic postcard showing part of the façade of the Cine Maya with its art deco neon sign projecting from the modified building face. By the 1950s, most of Calle 1 had transformed to businesses, and residential spaces relocated south of Avenida Obregón (fig. 7.3). In the following decade even the Cine Maya would close down as newer and larger movie houses opened in San Luis flanking Benito Juárez Plaza.[23]

Another sign of the changing landscape along Calle 1 was the construction of the Hotel Dori at the intersection of Avenida Obregón in the 1940s (fig. 7.16). This corner became something of a peak land value intersection for San Luis by the 1950s because Avenida Obregón evolved as the principal commercial strip of the town over the next several decades. The building that was the Hotel Dori was renamed the Hotel Río Colorado, with rooms above and a furniture store, El Campesino, on the ground floor (fig. 7.17).

Figure 7.18 is a 1949 view of a street parade with a flatbed truck decorated as a float moving along Avenida Obregón. Seated on a raised platform at the rear of the truck float is a young woman in formal gown wearing a crown and draped in a cloak suggesting a coronation event, perhaps the queen of a patriotic celebration, because there are five additional young women dressed formally seated below her. Local residents line the street and walk alongside the truck float. In the background is a landmark building that may have been unknown to the photographer, yet its presence signals the early days of San Luis. This adobe and stucco wall enclosure with tile parapet is the Cuartel de la Guarnición, the original home of the military garrison that dates to the founding of San Luis in the first decades of the twentieth century.[24] When governmental authority in the town passed from military to municipal in the late 1930s, the building became a school. In this postcard view, the building appears to have evolved into a commercial enterprise specializing in electrical and appliance repair.

San Luis emerged in the twentieth-century automotive era, so vehicles appear in almost every postcard image. Figure 7.19 shows a gas station in the town circa 1940s. The house and canopy form with gas pump on an island under the canopy

Figure 7.14. Cine Maya was San Luis's only movie theater in the 1940s. Foto Haro, 1940s.

Figure 7.15. Cine Maya visible on Calle 1 on the right with its art deco neon sign in the 1950s.

Figure 7.16. Hotel Dori was under construction in the 1940s at the corner of Calle 1, on the right, and Avenida Obregón on the left. Obregón would become the major commercial strip of San Luis in the following decades. Foto Haro, 1940s.

Figure 7.17. Hotel Río Colorado, formerly the Hotel Dori, as it appeared in the late 1940s. Hotel rooms were on the second floor, and ground-level shops included the Mueblería (furniture store) El Campesino. The art deco façade building El Campesino Mueblería shown in figure 7.15 was the converted Hotel Río Colorado of a few years earlier. Attributed to Haro, 1940s.

Figure 7.18. Parade in San Luis along Avenida Obregón in 1949. The stucco-tiled building to the right of the truck float with entourage is the original Cuartel de la Guarnición, the garrison home of the military authority that governed San Luis in the early years of the twentieth century.

was introduced in the 1910s and quickly adopted by stations in the United States and Mexico into the 1920s.[25] The postcard image captures an attendant servicing an auto in front with carwash and lubrication bays behind. One truck on the left is stacked with bales of cotton harvested and ginned in the Colorado River delta fields below San Luis, suggesting that the station was likely located on the edge of town along Avenida Obregón.

As San Luis expanded during the 1920s, residential districts were built south of the border crossing onto the expansive sand terrace that is the primary site of the town to this day. Figure 7.20 captures a view of Calle Morelos, the diagonal street on the western edge of town and south of Obregón, in the 1940s (fig. 7.3). Land use along this street is mixed residential and small neighborhood commercial businesses such as the *botica* (drug store) and *clinica* (doctor's office) pictured in figure 7.21. Dwellings shown in figure 7.20 appear to be 1940s architectural styles, probably adobe construction with stucco exteriors, and enclosed by front property fences so typical of housing found in many Mexican border cities.[26] Several structures show evaporative cooler boxes mounted on platforms at window openings. Large trees visible at the backs of

Figure 7.19. Gasolinera San Luis circa 1940s. Cotton baled on the truck at left signals how San Luis participated in the agricultural boom of the nearby Colorado River delta farming economy. This station was probably located along Avenida Obregón on the western outskirts of town. Foto Haro, 1940s.

Figure 7.20. Street scene along Calle Morelos south of Avenida Obregón. Fence-enclosed dwellings that mixed with neighborhood businesses along streets of compacted sand were common residential landscapes of San Luis in the 1940s and 1950s. Foto Haro, 1940s.

Figure 7.21. Small shops such as a drug store (*botica*) and doctor's office (*clinica*) were part of the mixed business and residential townscape of San Luis in the 1940s. To the left of the *botica* building is a glimpse of the fields along the Colorado River floodplain below the sand terrace on which most of San Luis was built. Foto Haro, 1940s.

Figure 7.22. Palacio municipal (city hall) was a small building in keeping with the modest population of San Luis in the 1940s. Nevertheless, the structure incorporated modernist flair with streamline moderne façade, block glass, and large plate-glass windows. Foto Haro, 1940s.

several properties appear to be salt cedar, a nonnative plant that spread extensively in the Colorado River delta area when native vegetation was cleared to introduce crop plants in the 1920s.[27] The street is unpaved and consists of compacted sand; during the 1950s, only a few streets—those near the crossing—were paved.[28] Beyond the residential landscape, the left edge of figure 7.21 reveals the agricultural land along the floodplain of the Colorado River below the sand mesa where the town is located.

When San Luis transitioned to municipal government in 1939, the Palacio municipal (city hall) was a single building in keeping with the town's modest population of less than one thousand (fig. 7.22). A prominent sign and a flagpole at the front of the building were the only clues that this was the seat of municipal authority in the border town during the 1940s. Nevertheless, the streamline moderne façade with period block glass flanking the entrance and abundant plate-glass windows suggest that San Luis was architecturally au courant. In the 1950s and the 1960s, when the town population exploded, a new and extensive government complex that showcased modern buildings of International style was constructed immediately east of the main plaza. The original city hall building was converted to a bank when the municipal government relocated to new quarters.[29]

Part III

Sonora Border Revisited

8

Seeing Place Through a Popular Lens

This project has been an exercise in the use of vintage historic postcards to reconstruct the visual past of Sonora, Mexico, border towns. Photographic postcards are a form of popular media that enables visual documentation of twentieth-century places because there were millions produced in the early decades of that century, and they continued to be made and distributed through the 1950s. Mass popularity often meant that tourist locales were pictured and photographed repeatedly, decade after decade, often illustrating the same streets, landmarks, and attractions for a particular location. That repetition of pictured sites creates an image density for a place that can facilitate its visual interpretation where greater numbers of images enhance the potential to see a place through time. This quality may be unique to postcards among other forms of popular media.

Postcards from the Sonora Border presents a historical and geographic analysis of five towns along the Arizona boundary and their individual place personalities during the first half of the twentieth century. Sonora border towns emerged and developed in the context of larger historical events such as the Mexican Revolution, U.S. local and national Prohibition, and the economic boom that followed World War II. At the same time, circumstances particular to each town shaped specific patterns of growth and change. Geographical considerations such as access by railroad and highway and proximity to larger places combined with the local efforts of individual residents and entrepreneurs who contributed to the success or lack of success for the towns. Agua Prieta, Naco, Nogales, Sonoyta, and San Luis Río Colorado are all border towns, yet each developed its own identity in the first five decades of the twentieth century. That identity is revealed, in part, through popular visualization, and the photographic postcard is a critical agent in that representation. Postcard analysis, combined with historical geographic interpretation, permits a popular visual narrative of these places that is unique as a way to see the past. In this chapter I discuss the findings of this project, both the use of visual method to understand border places and the patterns of place representation in the Sonora border towns.

Visual Method

Buried in the notes of Erik Larson's award-winning book *Issac's Storm*, an excruciatingly detailed yet compelling account of the famous 1900 hurricane that devastated Galveston Island on the Texas shore—still to this day the single greatest natural disaster in American history—is a testimony to the value of the photograph as an instrument of historical research. "The single most valuable trove of documents on the hurricane . . . lies in Galveston's Rosenberg Library. . . . The library has . . . over four thousand photographs. . . . I used photographs as original documents and spent hours studying them with a magnifying glass. I used details of these photographs to decorate the scenes in *Issac's Storm*. For example, I describe in one section what Issac saw from his house where he and his daughters came ashore the night of the storm. Incredibly, the Rosenberg archive has a photograph of exactly that view."[1]

Multiple methods have been used to explore the place identity of Sonora border towns. *Postcards from the Sonora Border* follows in the spirit of other geographical explorations of the Mexican border urban scene where landscape or townscape is the thematic focus of understanding place, and the case study method is employed to excavate sources and to contextualize the story for each border town discussed.[2] This project is informed especially by those few studies that have wed historical and visual narratives to understanding Mexican and American border places.[3] In these projects, the visual as much as the text steers the narrative. The historic and contemporary image is given equal footing with the written document as a source of evidence: it is an original document, as Larson explains. In this approach, a photograph becomes more than illustration; it stands as witness, testimony, memory, *la cara del tiempo*—the face of time—as Miguel Ángel Berumen calls it.[4] Serial assembly of many images for a place creates the potential to see changes in place, an aging of that face of time.

One way to assess visual method is to analyze the photographic postcard as a lens to place popularity. Unlike historic photographic material used in so many studies, the photographic postcard differs in its purpose as a visual form—the photographer likely never intended it as documentary evidence. That innocence, in retrospect, enables a certain gauge of image popularity and thereby provides a baseline for assessing how a place or part of a place was represented. The postcard, therefore, is not simply a commercial artifact; it becomes a visual medium that can be appreciated for its documentary revelations.

In *Postcards from the Sonora Border*, we see how more populated places such as Nogales and Agua Prieta were more visually attractive to the postcard photographer, resulting in a greater frequency of imagery than for smaller border towns such as Naco, Sonoyta, and San Luis Río Colorado. This is so even where a town like Sonoyta is more than a century older than places many times larger. Popularity is, in large measure, a product of a place's identity and how knowledge about that place is communicated to outsiders. Nogales and Agua Prieta were not only better known to Arizona residents and visitors from other locations through the common media of the era—newspapers—but they were also better connected by multiple forms of transportation and situated on major state, national, and international highways.

Figure 8.1, an advertising postcard, illustrates how U.S. 80 linked Nogales and Douglas, Arizona, during the 1920s, thereby giving principal access to the Sonora border towns of Nogales and Agua Prieta, respectively, and indirectly via Bisbee to Naco, Sonora. This same highway continued east to El Paso, Texas, and Ciudad Juárez, Chihuahua, a major railroad junction during the early twentieth century. While U.S. 80 also entered Arizona from California over the Colorado River and would give secondary access to both San Luis Río Colorado via Yuma, Arizona, and Sonoyta via Gila Bend and Ajo, Arizona, auto traffic into that part of the Arizona-Sonora borderlands was considerably reduced compared with traffic south and east of Tucson. Beyond the proximity of the southeastern Arizona border towns to Tucson, substantial tourist visitor traffic flowed south to Nogales from Phoenix, the largest place in Arizona by 1920.[5] Further, the Southern Pacific railroad paralleled U.S. 80 with a substantial depot at Douglas, across from Agua Prieta.

One of the findings following the use of photographic postcard imagery for each town is the variability of imagery by era, not simply the total number of images but the relationship between image frequency and time period. Because larger towns such as Agua Prieta and Nogales counted many more postcard images than smaller border places, we can use those towns as examples to illustrate this variability of imagery by time. Figure 8.2 shows the frequency of postcards for these towns in the Arreola Collection. Nogales is represented in some 530 individual postcards between the 1900s and 1950s, whereas Agua Prieta was captured in 238 separate postcards during the same time period. Given the population size of Nogales during the period of study and the border town's importance as a gateway connecting the American borderland to the west coast of Mexico, the frequency difference is not surprising.

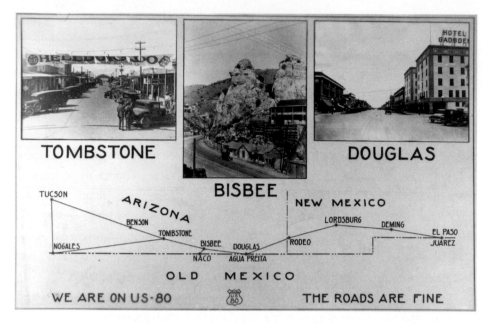

Figure 8.1. In the first decades of the twentieth century, place popularity was enhanced by accessibility to highways. In this 1920s advertising postcard, southeast Arizona towns such as Tombstone, Bisbee, and Douglas are shown connected to larger regional centers such as Tucson and El Paso. As a consequence, Sonora, Mexico, border towns such as Agua Prieta and Nogales benefited from their proximity to American border towns integrated to U.S. 80.

While Agua Prieta was a popular Sonora border town in the first half of the twentieth century, Nogales appears to be more than two times as popular if postcard frequency is an indicator.

When we compare the postcard frequency of these Sonora border towns by segments of the entire fifty-year interval, however, variations appear. Agua Prieta, like Nogales, sees a small measure of postcard popularity in the first decade of the 1900s. During the 1910s, however, there is an explosion of postcard production for the two towns. This captures the early fascination with the photographic postcard especially because it was novel during this period and most of the postcards produced for the Sonora border towns in that era were photographic formats. This is in keeping with the national popularity of photo postcards all across the United States during the first decade of the century.[6] The towns, especially Agua Prieta, were also buoyed by the Mexican Revolution and the pull of postcard photographers to the Mexican border to capture the events for a popular audience. Postcard production declines in the 1920s for both Agua Prieta and Nogales, yet the decline appears steeper in Nogales than in Agua Prieta. The 1920s was the prime era of American Prohibition, and whereas

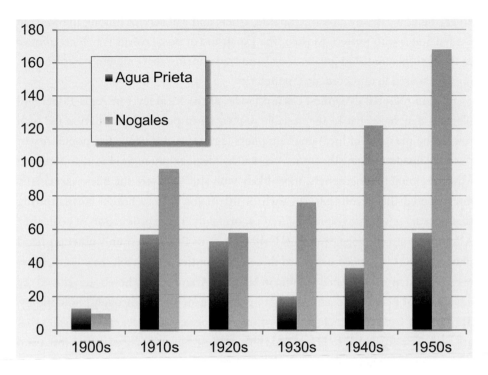

Figure 8.2. Postcard frequency for Agua Prieta and Nogales, 1900s–1950s. Arreola Collection.

each town experienced attraction resulting from the accessibility to alcohol in Mexico, population growth for each town during the decade was modest; Nogales grew by less than one thousand and Agua Prieta by less than fifteen hundred (table 1.1). Why Nogales postcard production would decline so much during this era is hard to explain. Part of the reason may be fewer local photographers who were active in the decade or that the abundance of postcard photography for the 1910s could not be matched in the next decade. In the 1930s, both towns actually lost population (table 1.1), yet postcard production in Agua Prieta plummeted while it expanded in Nogales. This may suggest that Agua Prieta was more severely crippled as a tourist destination during the Great Depression because of the region's dependence on copper mining, which retracted considerably during the era. Nogales, by comparison, was less dependent on a single industrial economy and its proximity to Tucson, Arizona, and Hermosillo, Sonora, likely sustained it as a transaction node for regional travel and exchange, thereby enabling greater exposure, including postcard representation. In the 1940s and 1950s, border towns in general boomed, and Nogales and Agua Prieta more than doubled and tripled populations, respectively (table 1.1). Not surprisingly, both towns rebound from the 1920s and 1930s, with Nogales especially emerging as a gateway crossing for auto, truck, and rail service linking the western United States with western Mexico. The expansion of post–World War II economies in the region stimulated greater travel and trade during that era, and postcard production soared to unprecedented popularity.[7]

Beyond regional dynamics, circumstances at the local level in Agua Prieta and Nogales may have shaped the variable popularity of postcard production for each town. The presence of local photographers appears to influence the popularity of postcard imagery during the 1910s. As noted by Mexican photographic historian John Mraz, regional photographers, most likely with studios, were the ones who chiefly documented the Revolution.[8] In each of the major Sonora border towns during that decade, one photographer figured prominently in the production of postcards: Alfred W. Lohn for Nogales and Cal Osbon for Agua Prieta. Certainly other postcard photographers produced images of these towns in the 1910s (table 2.1). Lohn, however, resided in and operated a studio in Nogales, Arizona, and thereby developed the advantage of being on location daily to record observations through photography. The Arreola Collection includes forty-three photographic postcards of Nogales that are signed or attributed to Lohn, and most of these were produced in the 1910s and 1920s. Lohn may have been nearly the exclusive postcard photographer of Nogales during the 1910s.[9] Osbon likely stayed for extended periods in Douglas during the era of Revolutionary battles in Agua Prieta, although there is no evidence that he operated a studio in the American border town. The Arreola Collection includes thirty-five photographic postcards of Agua Prieta in the 1910s and 1920s that are signed by or attributed to Osbon. He was the premier postcard photographer of the Revolutionary battles in Agua Prieta, and his images were popular chiefly during that time. Other studio photographers resident in Douglas also made postcards of Agua Prieta, but none appears to have been as prolific as Osbon.

During the decades of the 1930s, 1940s, and 1950s, independent postcard photographers in Nogales and Agua Prieta were transcended by a single postcard company, La Compañia México Fotográfico, based in Mexico City. México Fotográfico hired stringer photographers across the country and became the major producer of photo postcards in Mexico including the border region (see chap. 2). The Arreola Collection includes 218 photo postcards of Nogales identified by the distinctive MF logo that attributes the image to México Fotográfico, and the collection includes eighty-seven postcards of Agua Prieta with the same attribution. For Agua Prieta, 76 percent of all the postcards counted in the Arreola Collection for the 1930s through the 1950s were produced by México Fotográfico; similarly, for Nogales, 41 percent of all the postcards counted for the same three decades were issued by MF (fig. 8.2). The popularity of postcard production and representation of the two largest Sonora border towns was chiefly the result of México Fotográfico's linking photographic postcard production of unattributed local and regional photographers to a national and international distribution network.

Local postcard producers appear to play a similar role in the early photographic postcards for Sonoyta and San Luis Río Colorado, although the exact studio location of these photographers is not known. The Arreola Collection includes ten Sonoyta photographic postcards signed and attributed to J. Pacheco, all taken during the 1940s. For San Luis, the collection includes thirteen photographic postcards signed or attributed to Haro, and all are from the 1940s. By the 1950s, México Fotográfico photo postcards began to appear for Sonoyta and San Luis, and the Arreola Collection includes sixteen MF postcards for those towns.

Postcards from the Sonora Border demonstrates that visual method can enhance our view of place when sufficient image density is organized for a locale. Generally, the larger the place the greater the likelihood that robust postcard imagery will be available for analysis. Periodicity can temper visual inspection, as popularity of a place as well as its representation through photographic postcards is subject to variability over time. A place's visual identity, however, is enhanced when a studio photographer who embraces postcard photography is resident in that place, and a national postcard company intent on popularizing towns and regions can bring even greater exposure.

Border Places

Using postcards as a visual method to assess the popularity of places is furthered when the postcards individually shed light on the changing nature of border places. In *Postcards from the Sonora Border*, postcards illustrate similarities and differences among five separate towns. Comparisons of images for towns over a half century allow visualization of the principal landscape elements of these places, including crossings, streets, landmarks, tourist locations, and historic events.

Agua Prieta, Naco, Nogales, Sonoyta, and San Luis Río Colorado, like all Mexican border towns, exhibit qualities of townscape. Each border town contains one or more crossings, streets, tourist spaces, and distinctive landmarks captured by postcard photographers. Visual analysis reveals equally subtle differences that characterize some places and not others. Sonoyta is not joined to a formal American border town, and its crossing is more than a mile from the town center. Nogales has a distinctive topographic setting that promotes panoramic views of the borderline, which resulted in dozens of postcard images of the international boundary. Agua Prieta and Naco were celebrated locales under repeated siege during the Mexican Revolution, and photographers emphasized imagery about those events in their postcards. Using this framework, what do findings for this project reveal about the nature of Sonora border town places?

The greatest commonality of townscape elements revealed by postcard photography is the international border crossing. Every Sonora border town is represented by postcard views of the crossing or, in the case of Nogales, multiple crossings. The crossing landscape is a symbolic feature of the boundary where Mexican (and American) officials sanction entry and exit. Postcard photographers have been intuitive to the significance of that space, and it is, therefore, inevitably recorded as the first step into Mexico. Larger towns experience greater attention to the changing nature of that element of townscape, and, as a consequence, the crossings at places such as Nogales and Agua Prieta are well documented. Yet even smaller towns such as Naco and San Luis Río Colorado exhibit multiple views of the crossing through time. Only Sonoyta appears to lack multiple views of the crossing, and in this case the explanation may be that the crossing is some distance from the center of town, and there is no equivalent American border town that might contextualize the space as part of the international boundary.

Another common view captured by postcard photographers is a town's streets. Streets embody the physical and cultural qualities of places, and postcard photographers have recognized this and recorded it over many generations. In the Sonora border towns, Nogales and Agua Prieta commanded the greatest investment in street photography in large measure because they were bigger and more active places. In each instance, main streets such as Avenida Pan Americana in Agua Prieta or Calle Elías and Calle Arizpe/Avenida Obregón in Nogales became the focus of most postcard photography. These main streets captured the hustle and bustle of retail enterprise; they became the platforms for emergent tourist activities; and, typically, they situated significant landmarks along their alignments. This was true as well in smaller border towns such as Naco, Sonoyta, and San Luis Río Colorado, although the extent of those main streets was limited in keeping with their size.

Public spaces are another common townscape regularly featured by postcard photographers for the Sonora border towns. Every town, even tiny Sonoyta, has postcard images of the town plaza, and often plaza views picture the primary church, municipal palace, and surrounding activity spaces such as businesses and entertainment venues. This suggests that postcard photographers, even those who were not of Mexican ancestry, quickly learned the symbolic and everyday importance of public space in the border towns as part of the tradition of Mexican urban places. A particular landmark of the railroad border towns such as Nogales, Agua Prieta, and Naco was the *aduana*, or customs house, that represented the importance of crossing tariffs and the collection and holding of monetary accumulation from train traffic serving economic hinterlands on both sides of the border. That condition was especially important in border towns such as Agua Prieta and Naco, where Revolutionary conflicts sometimes pivoted on capturing or protecting the resources held in the customs house. The customs houses were typically grandiose architectural statements signaling the importance of a particular border town—Nogales and Agua Prieta are the best examples—and that quality elevated the stature of a town that might otherwise be seen as a peripheral border location.

Postcard views of cabaret landmarks are more varied by border town. In smaller places, such as Naco, Sonoyta, and San Luis Río Colorado, the notoriety of establishments was typically short lived if not fleeting. Even in Agua Prieta, the most celebrated establishments chiefly disappeared with the repeal of Prohibition. In Nogales, however, one place, La Caverna, or the Cavern, became legendary far into the late twentieth century, suggesting how the appeal of one enterprise can be sustained when there is a reputation and demand for its celebrity.

One important unanticipated finding related to the cabaret industry was the role of Chinese merchants in this economy during the first two decades of the twentieth century. Chinese merchants were present in early Nogales, Naco, and Sonoyta, but it was in Agua Prieta where their business acumen was most developed. Before the Sonora expulsion laws of the 1930s, Chinese dominated building ownership in Agua Prieta—an inheritance of early investments and control of the grocery business—and this lead to their capitalizing on property rents to chiefly Anglo businessmen who operated the town's burgeoning cabaret industry during Prohibition.

By contrast with cabaret businesses, curio establishments, although they appeared early in most Sonora border towns, chiefly flourished in the post–World War II economy. Every town engaged the curio trade, but once again the industry was best developed in the largest places, especially Nogales and Agua Prieta. The former town became the epitome of a Sonora tourist attraction as curio businesses hatched on one street—Calle Elías—transitioned to the post–World War II tourist drag, Avenida Obregón. Nogales remains the most important curio trade center on the Sonora border given its position at the end of a major American highway (Interstate 19) and traffic to the interior of Sonora via Mexico 15 as well as the border town's proximity to Tucson and Phoenix, which supply day-tripping visitors, especially in the winter.[10] Curio enterprises eventually faded in places such as Agua Prieta and Naco, in large measure because those towns previously accessible via U.S. 80 were bypassed as highway traffic routed north along Interstate 10. Further, the gateway status of those places evaporated with so little interior travel south of the border into northeast Sonora. Sonoyta and even San Luis Río Colorado, however, continued to facilitate travel to the interior of northwest Sonora, where tourist activities focused on the Gulf of California, especially at Puerto Peñasco, supported, if marginally, a curio store presence in those towns.

Another unanticipated yet important finding about the curio trade in Sonora border towns was the early pioneering role of female entrepreneurs at Agua Prieta and Nogales. American-born Alice Gatliff was a prominent personality in Agua Prieta. Her Curio Store Café was one of the earliest such businesses on the border in the 1900s, and the establishment continued until her death in 1936 as a tourist draw where visitors could eat, drink, and purchase Mexican arts and crafts. Gatliff embodied the entrepreneurial spirit of the border when she arranged to have postcards made from photographs of local sites in Agua Prieta and vended those products along with other tourist items in her store. In Nogales, Sonora-born Delfina Rochin de Vergobbi operated La Industria Mexicana, the first Mexican arts and crafts store in the city. Like Gatliff, Rochin de Vergobbi was an enterprising business owner who visited the Mexican interior to purchase art objects for her store and with an early partner produced photographic postcards of scenes in Nogales that could be sold to tourists.

Postcards from the Sonora Border suggests that places within and surrounding Agua Prieta, Naco, Nogales, Sonoyta, and San Luis Río Colorado were visually differentiated and selectively exhibited in convenient and compact display by postcard photographers before mass televised imagery. In the same way that a guidebook to a place selectively narrates the points of interest that might be visited, picture postcards attribute visual importance to select locations of the tourist experience. In this manner, border places—whether a crossing, a street, a space, a landmark business, or a public institution—can become codified into memory and part of collected consciousness.

Revisiting the Sonora Border Past

This story started with a recounting about recent popular efforts to revisit the past using visual evidence. The visual past is a particular form of greater historical inquiry where the visual material is not simply supplementary to textual narrative but rather becomes the narrative itself. *Postcards from the Sonora Border* explores one way that the visual past can be used systematically to reconstruct an informed view of the past. That view, or, more accurately, arrangement of views, can give insight to a vernacular past about place. Because the historic postcard is in large measure a document about place, its utility is especially valuable for geographical interpretation. The product of thousands of shutter releases, photographic postcards can create a blueprint for understanding the anatomy of a place at a particular time. When used in series, that view of time can become nearly cinematic, revealing how a place might change through time.

Still, "the past is a foreign country" as historical geographer David Lowenthal argued in his book of that very title. The notion of seeing the past, says Lowenthal, gained currency with the proliferation of book illustration that accustomed people to the past as a visual experience. Photography then made the material world accurate and ubiquitous so that memory was seemingly replaced by imagery. Photographer Walker Evans is said to have developed profound historical empathy for the things around him, the landscapes of everyday life and vernacular places, as destined for extinction, and therefore his photographs were intended as prospective relics.[11]

Photographic postcards enhanced the identity of Sonora border places between 1900 and the post–World War II era. Both the variety of place imagery—crossings, streets, landmarks—and the persistent and continued representation of those landscapes through time reinforced the place personality of border towns in the minds of tourist visitors and those who received postcards sent from Mexico. Postcard photographers who walked the streets, climbed to rooftops, pointed their cameras at the daily spaces and places of the Sonora border towns between the 1900s and 1950s leave an unintended legacy of visual information. In retrospect, that legacy tells us about places—the Sonora border towns—that have been foreign to Americans in so many ways and for so long despite the large body of rhetoric and exaggeration inscribed in our faded collective memory. The postcards, as Walker Evans believed, might be seen as a kind of prospective relic, a glimpse back that permits us to revisit a place. Agua Prieta, Naco, Nogales, Sonoyta, and San Luis Río Colorado live into the present through that imagery, a fascinating window of reflection to their pasts.

Notes

Introduction

1. *New York Times*, "Web Sites With a Historical Bent."
2. See Thunder Bay Press (http://www.thunderbaybooks.com) for examples of Then and Now series books and Arcadia Publishing and the History Press (http://www.arcadia publishing.com) for a list of hundreds of towns and cities featured in photo book format. *New York Times*, "Touch Screen," details the Ken Burns app and other online history sites.
3. Lowenthal, *Possessed by the Past.*
4. Sternbergh, "Positively Fourth Street."
5. Paumgarten, "Mannahatta Project."
6. Two researchers who use visual repetition and sequencing in photographic fieldwork are Charles R. Ames, "Along the Mexican Border," who repeats images of U.S. and Mexico border monuments using photographs from nineteenth-century surveys compared with 1960s images of those same monuments, and anthropologist Matilda Coxe Stevenson, who developed a format for sequencing images of native subjects to create visual narrative from still images; see Issac, "Re-observation and Recognition of Change."
7. For an explanation of image density in rephotography, see Klett, Manchester, and Verburg, *Second View*; Klett et al., *Third Views, Second Sights*; and Klett and Lundgren, *After the Ruins.*
8. Old NYC.
9. Lynch, *Image of the City, What Time Is This Place?*; Conzen, "Analytical Approaches to the Urban Landscape"; Jakle, *Visual Elements of Landscape*; Rose, *Visual Methodologies*; and Swartz and Ryan, *Picturing Place.*

10. Arreola and Burkhart, "Photographic Postcards and Visual Urban Landscape."

11. Jakle, *American Small Town, Postcards of the Night*; Meikle, *Postcard America.*

12. Vaule, *As We Were*, 67.

13. Bogdan and Weseloh, *Real Photo Postcard Guide.*

14. Jakle, *Postcards of the Night*, 14, 26.

15. Vanderwood and Samponaro, *Border Fury.*

16. Romo, *Ringside Seat to a Revolution*, 155.

17. Samponaro and Vanderwood, *War Scare on the Rio Grande.*

18. Sarber, "W. H. Horne and the Mexican War Photo Postcard Company."

19. Arreola, *Postcards from the Río Bravo Border.*

Chapter 1

1. Arreola and Curtis, *Mexican Border Cities.*

2. Officer, *Hispanic Arizona*, map, "Arizona-Sonora, 1700–1850," end papers; Weber, *Mexican Frontier*, map 2, "The United States of Mexico," p. 23; Voss, *On the Periphery of Nineteenth-Century Mexico*, map, "Political Composition of the Region of Sonora and Sinaloa," p. 36. Some of this section is based on Arreola, "Echoes in the Borderland."

3. Martínez, "Surveying and Marking the U.S.-Mexico Boundary"; Rittenhouse, *Disturnell's Treaty Map*; Bufkin, "Making of the Boundary Between the United States and Mexico."

4. Martínez, *Troublesome Border*, 9–23; Griswold del Castillo, *Treaty of Guadalupe Hidalgo*, 43–61.

5. Garber, *Gadsden Treaty*; Walker and Bufkin, *Historical Atlas of Arizona*, 22.

6. International Boundary Commission, *Report of the Boundary Commission.*

7. Rebert, *La gran línea*, 100–37; International Boundary Commission, *Boundary Between the United States and Mexico.*

8. Metz, *Border*, 95–116; Humphrey, *90 Years and 535 Miles*, 164–415.

9. Arreola and Curtis, *Mexican Border Cities*, table 2.1, p. 15.

10. Hall and Coerver, *Revolution on the Border*, 31.

11. Ibid., 107–25.

12. Martínez, *Troublesome Border*, 76; Hall and Coerver, *Revolution on the Border*, 126.

13. Hall and Coerver, *Revolution on the Border*, table 8.4, p. 136.

14. Martínez, *Troublesome Border*, 108–9; St. John, *Line in the Sand*, 150–58.

15. Arreola and Curtis, *Mexican Border Cities*, 77–96.

16. Arreola, "Across the Street Is Mexico."

17. Tenorio-Trillo, *Mexico at the World's Fairs.*

18. Delpar, *Enormous Vogue of Things Mexican*; Oles, *South of the Border*.

19. Berger, *Development of Mexico's Tourism Industry*.

20. Curtis and Arreola, "Through *Gringo* Eyes."

21. Arreola, "La Macarena."

22. West, *Sonora*, 92–134; Finn et al., "Puerto Peñasco."

23. Arreola and Madsen, "Variability of Tourist Attraction on an International Boundary."

24. International Boundary Commission, *Boundary Between the United States and Mexico*, map no. 11.

25. St. John, *Line in the Sand*, 98; Arreola and Curtis, *Mexican Border Cities*, 5; International Boundary Commission, *Report of the Boundary Commission*; Weisman and Dusard, *La frontera*, 145–46, where Weisman characterized Sásabe, Sonora, as "The Mexico that everyone who's never been there pictures when they think of Mexico. No pavement. Little chinked houses on cactus-covered hills. Burros, sloppy cantinas, sombreros, wooden saddles—la enchilada completa."

26. International Boundary Commission, *Boundary between the United States and Mexico*, map no. 12; Lochiel name changed from La Noria ca. 1890, when Scotsman Colin Cameron acquired land in the nearby San Rafael ranch and had the customs house crossing in Arizona changed to honor a place name from his homeland; see Valenzuela, "Lochiel."

Chapter 2

1. Evans, "Main Street Looking North from Courthouse Square," 102.

2. Rosenheim, *Walker Evans and the Picture Postcard*; Mendelson and Prochaska, "Introduction," xvi.

3. A summary of the postcard and its evolution is given in Arreola, *Postcards from the Río Bravo Border*, 45–47, 223–28.

4. Klamkin, *Picture Postcards*, 24–28.

5. Dotterrer and Cranz, "Picture Postcard," 44.

6. Ibid.; Miller, *Delaware Album*, 2.

7. Snow, *Coney Island*; Miller, *Delaware Album*, 2.

8. Miller and Miller, *Picture Postcards in the United States*, 22, 28.

9. Harrington, "Postal Carditis and Some Allied Manias," 565.

10. Steele, "Pernicious Picture Post Card," 288.

11. Harrington, "Postal Carditis and Some Allied Manias," 566.

12. Michas, *Real and Other Photos*, 16.

13. Stechschulte, *Detroit Publishing Company Postcards*, xi; see also Detroit Publishing Company Collection.

14. See, e.g., Grant, *Postales salvadoreñas del ayer*; Jakle and Sculle, *Picturing Illinois*; Khoo and Wade, *Penang Postcard Collection*; Schor, "*Cartes Postales*"; and Steiber, "Postcards and the Invention of Old Amsterdam."

15. DeBres and Sowers, "Emergence of Standardized, Idealized, and Placeless Landscapes"; Isenberg, "Fixing an Image of Commercial Dignity," 42–77.

16. Dotterer and Cranz, "Picture Postcard"; Jakle, *Postcards of the Night*.

17. Morgan and Brown, *Prairie Fires and Paper Moons*; Vaule, *As We Were*; Sante, *Folk Photography*; Bogdan and Weseloh, *Real Photo Postcard Guide*; Uribe Eguiluz, *Una aproximación a la Compañia México Fotográfico*.

18. Much of the technical and detailed information in this section is summarized from Miller, *Delaware Album*, 6, 173–77. George Miller is an authority on the history of postcards, and his discussion in this source is comprehensive. Both the Kodak 3A camera and the photographic postcard auto press machine are illustrated in this work. See also Wall and Ward, *Photographic Picture Post-Card*.

19. A complete protocol for dating real photo postcard backs can be found in Bogdan and Weseloh, *Real Photo Postcard Guide*, 217–33, and Rowe, *Arizona Real Photo Postcards*, 75–88.

20. The eleven real photo postcards in the Arreola Collection for Agua Prieta are numbered as follows: 28, 37, 41, 45, 49, 51, 52, 53, 104, 111, 134.

21. Miller, *Delaware Album*, 3–6.

22. García y Alva, *Album-directorio del estado de Sonora*. See the discussion about studio photographers who also produced postcards for the Río Bravo border towns in Arreola, *Postcards from the Río Bravo Border*, 48–55. For a complete discussion of photographic postcard photographers who operated in the United States, see Bogdan and Weseloh, *Real Photo Postcard Guide*, chap. 3, "Photographers and Careers," 56–94. For an inventory of photographers who worked in Mexico during the Mexican Revolution, see Berumen, *México: Fotografía y revolución*.

23. Sarber, "W. H. Horne and the Mexican War Photo Company."

24. See, e.g., the discussion about Walter M. Cline and his Chattanooga based postcard company in Arreola, *Postcards from the Río Bravo Border*, 53–55.

25. I am indebted to Cynthia Hayostek, a historian and resident of Douglas, Arizona, who extracted the names of Douglas and Agua Prieta photographers from Douglas city directories.

26. Fulton, *Arizona Postcard Checklist*, app. 7; Rowe, *Arizona Real Photo Postcards*, 72; *El Fronterizo*, "Fotografía Popular"; Mautz, *Biographies of Western Photographers*.

27. A similar famous Cal Osbon photo postcard, number 54, December 22, 1915, showing a U.S. soldier posed on one side of the border line and a Mexican soldier standing on

the opposite side, is reproduced in Fox, *Fence and the River*, 73, and in Truett, *Fugitive Landscapes*, front dust jacket. Fox also reproduces other Osbon images in her book.

28. *Nogales Daily Herald*, A. W. Lohn, advertisement, October 23, 1915; August 22, 1917; January 5, 1918.

29. Callarman, *Photographers of Nineteenth Century Los Angeles*.

30. William Manger, who is researching the life of Lohn for a book about the postcard photographer, has determined from newspaper accounts that Lohn probably arrived in Nogales circa 1913 from Los Angeles; Manger, personal communication, February 17, 2014, March 30, 2016, and July 27, 2016. See also Manger and Arreola, "Photographic Postcards of A. W. Lohn."

31. Manger, personal communication, February 17, 2014, March 30, 2016, and July 27, 2016; Manger and Arreola, "Photographic Postcards of A. W. Lohn." See also A. W. Lohn Papers.

32. Camaras de Comercio, *Folleto de recuerdos*, 30.

33. One particular Lohn photo postcard, number 56, titled "Market: Nogales Sonora México," and produced in the 1920s, was reproduced by Curt Teich Company of Chicago as a black-and-white printed white-border postcard number 109583 and titled "Muicipal [*sic*] Market, Nogales, Sonora, Mexico." E. A. Werdall ordered one thousand copies of this printed postcard from Curt Teich in May 1926. See, Curt Teich Postcard Archives, "Nogales, Sonora."

34. "About the Frasher Foto Postcard Digitization Project at the Pomona Public Library," Pomona Public Library; Rowe, "Have Camera, Will Travel," 343.

35. Dawson, Stein, and Watts, "Wishing You Were Here"; Rowe, "Have Camera, Will Travel," 344.

36. Some years after the death of Burton Frasher in 1955, the Frasher family donated approximately one hundred thousand items, including postcards, from the Frasher Fotos Company to the Pomona Public Library. See, Rowe, "Have Camera, Will Travel," 352. About five thousand photo postcards are accessible on the library's Burton Frasher Collection website. Sixteen Frasher Foto postcards of Nogales, Sonora, are posted to this website. See "About the Frasher Foto Postcard Digitization Project at the Pomona Public Library," Pomona Public Library.

37. The history of the company México Fotográfico is summarized in Arreola, *Postcards from the Río Bravo Border*, 55–56. See also Uribe Eguiluz, *Una aproximación a la Compañía México Fotográfico*.

38. Fernández Tejedo, *Memories of Mexico*, 29–42.

39. *Chrome postcards* refer to modern postcards that have a shiny paper surface like a color photograph. The term is said to derive from *photochrome*, the word used by the

234 | Notes to Pages 42–49

Union Oil Company of California, which began to produce this type of postcard in 1939; the glossy surface is based on a color photograph converted to a printed format. Although the chrome postcard is attributed to the modern era (post-1945), chromes became increasingly popular in the 1950s and 1960s, both in the United States and Mexico. See Smith, *Postcard Companion*, 13, and Uribe Eguiluz, *Una aproximación a la Compañía México Fotográfico*, 84–87. Today, most postcards found on racks anywhere in the world are likely to be chrome cards.

40. The general discussion that follows closely parallels my rationale about postcard views selected and used in a previous project. See Arreola, *Postcards from the Río Bravo Border*, 56–63.

Chapter 3

1. *Douglas Daily Dispatch*, "Agua Prieta Wins Name of Cleanest Mexican City on Border."
2. *Bisbee Daily Review*, "Agua Prieta Is to Have Buildings."
3. *Douglas Daily International*, "Agua Prieta, Springing from a Tiny Trading Post."
4. *Douglas Daily International*, "Ruins of Old Bull Ring at Agua Prieta Removed."
5. *Bisbee Daily Review*, "Initial Opening of the Bull Ring"; "A Watercolor Sketch of Ring"; "Agua Prieta Building to Be Better Than That at Naco"; "Sunday Amusement at Smelter City"; Hadley, "Border Boom Town," 31; *Douglas Daily Dispatch*, "Greatest Entertainment of the Season a Band of Women Bull Fighters," advertisement, August 23, 1904.
6. *Douglas Daily International*, "Agua Prieta, Springing from a Tiny Trading Post."
7. Ibid. *Douglas Daily International*, "Old Agua Prieat [*sic*] Bull Ring."
8. Surface water is largely absent in this area today, but east of Douglas and Agua Prieta, near the historic Slaughter Ranch, is the San Bernardino *cienega*, a spring-fed surface water area that historically sustained livestock and today is considered a prized wildlife refuge along both sides of the boundary. See, Gehlbach, *Mountain Islands and Desert Seas*, 8, 167, and Wilson, *Islands in the Desert*, 201.
9. International Boundary Commission, *Report of the Boundary Commission*, map no. 14.
10. Sandomingo, *Historia de Agua Prieta*, 56–58; Hadley, "Border Boom Town," 4–5, 31. Mexican teamsters and freighters had been operating in this region before the railroad, and it is likely that the water at Agua Prieta was a principal stop for cross border traffic; see Heyman, *Life and Labor on the Border*, 27; *Bisbee Daily Review*, "Agua Prieta Is To Have Buildings."
11. Hadley, "Border Boom Town," 5–12; Truett, *Fugitive Landscapes*, 78–83; Heyman, *Life and Labor on the Border*, 27–29.

12. When Agua Prieta was surveyed in 1903, many of the older street names were simpli-fied to numbers, see Sandomingo, *Historia de Agua Prieta*, 58, 72–73; Méndez Sáinz, "De Tijuana a Matamoros," 50, 58. An early attempt to rename Agua Prieta Ciudad Corral to honor former Sonora governor Ramón Corral never took hold; see *Bisbee Daily Review*, "Ciudad Corral."

13. Sandomingo, *Historia de Agua Prieta*, 111; *Douglas Daily Dispatch*, "Agua Prieta May Claim Few Months of Age over Douglas."

14. *Douglas Daily Dispatch*, "Agua Prieta Wins Name of Cleanest Mexican City on Border."

15. Heyman, *Life and Labor on the Border*, 7, 9, 28.

16. Hadley, "Border Boom Town," 30–31.

17. The E. D. Newcomer photograph collection consists of fifty-nine boxes of visual materials, chiefly black-and-white prints. Newcomer also made many photographs of Nogales, Sonora.

18. *Douglas Daily Dispatch*, "Name Is Changed to Pan-American."

19. Quotation from *Douglas Daily Dispatch*, "Much Building Activity Seen in Agua Prieta." See also *Douglas Daily Dispatch*, "Architect Here to Direct Work on Social Club."

20. Arreola and Curtis, *Mexican Border Cities*, 165–74.

21. Vanderwood and Samponaro, *Border Fury*, 123.

22. *Bisbee Daily Review*, "Agua Prieta Is to Have Buildings"; "Fire Destroys Custom House."

23. *Douglas Daily Dispatch*, "Brookhill to be Opened for Business Soon"; "Contract Is Let for $5,000 Improvement to International Club."

24. Hayostek, "Two Exceptional Men," 16. The mill was owned and operated by a Mormon family; Cynthia Hayostek, personal communication, July 25, 2015.

25. *Arizona Republic*, "U.S.-Mexican Amity Shown on Flag Day"; *Tucson Daily Citizen*, "Agua Prieta, Sonora."

26. Hayostek, "Alice Gatliff," 16.

27. *Douglas Daily International*, "Cine Alhambra Opens Tonight."

28. A complete discussion of plazas in Mexican border towns is given in Arreola and Curtis, *Mexican Border Cities*, 133–43; the naming of Plaza Azueta is discussed in San-domingo, *Historia de Agua Prieta*, 81.

29. Details about plaza and church renovations are cited in Sandomingo, *Historia de Agua Prieta*, 83, 100–101; quotation from *Douglas Daily Dispatch*, "Agua Prieta School and Church Repaired to Beautify Plaza."

30. McCool, "Agua Prieta, Sonora"; Hall and Coerver, *Revolution on the Border*, 142–43, discuss how Mexican Revolutionaries traded and smuggled arms into Mexico that were acquired in the United States.

31. Brenner, *Wind That Swept Mexico*.

32. Hayostek, "Medal of Honor Winner in Douglas, Julien Gaujot."

33. Christiansen, "Bullets Across the Border. Part I," 12.

34. Hayostek, "From Out of the North: The Mexican Revolution"; Christiansen, "Bullets Across the Border. Part I," 20.

35. Hall and Coerver, *Revolution on the Border*, 28–43.

36. Batallas del 1 y 2 de noviembre 1915, croquis de Agua Prieta y sus fortificaciones" (map).

37. Estimates of the size of Villa's army at the 1915 Battle of Agua Prieta vary from twenty-six hundred to thirteen thousand; see Cole, "Douglas Under Fire." Hall and Coerver, *Revolution on the Border*, 34–35, give a U.S. Army estimate of circa five thousand.

38. Ramírez Zavala, *La participación de los Yaquis en la Revolución*.

39. Cobb, *Douglas, Arizona, U.S.A.* Agua Prieta, about five blocks in from the boundary, is shown at the lower left of the map. The following bars and cabarets appear on the Agua Prieta part of the map: White House Club, White Horse Cabaret, Golden Gate, Silver Dollar, and Curio Café.

40. Douglas Borderland Climate Club, *On the Romantic Mexican Border*, 3, 15.

41. *Douglas Daily Dispatch*, "Flames Destroy White House Club."

42. *Douglas City Directory 1930*, 143–46; *Douglas City Directory 1938*, 140.

43. *Douglas Daily Dispatch*, "Extensive Improvement Program Goes Forward"; "Agua Prieta Cabaret Changes Owners"; "International Club Bar and Cabaret Destroyed by Fire Friday Morning."

44. Romero, *Chinese in Mexico*, 24–25, fig. 3.1.

45. *Douglas Daily Dispatch*, "80 Per Cent Mexican-Help Rule"; "Jim Joe, Back from the West, Greets Friends"; "Jim Joe's Place in Agua Prieta Burns in Early Morning Fire"; "$5,000 Insurance on Silver Dollar Destroyed by Fire"; *Douglas Daily International*, "Jim Joe Plans Large Ballroom."

46. Romero, *Chinese in Mexico*, 157, 172–73.

47. *Douglas City Directory 1930*; *Douglas City Directory 1935*; Sandomingo, *Historia de Agua Prieta*, 72, lists the names of thirty-eight Chinese merchants who resided in Agua Prieta before the Sonoran exclusion laws were decreed.

48. *Douglas Daily Dispatch*, "Brookhill Café Opens to Trade in Agua Prieta."

49. *Douglas Daily Dispatch*, "Sammarcelli and Williams Started Business Together in 1921."

50. *Douglas Daily Dispatch*, "Flames Destroy White House Club"; "Troops Guard Ruin Where Popular Club Burned to Ground"; "Total Loss in Resort Fire Mounts."

51. *Douglas Daily Dispatch*, "Architect Here to Direct Work on Social Club"; "New White House Club Opens Tonight."

52. *Douglas Daily Dispatch*, "Only Night Club in Agua Prieta Is Finally Closed." Combating vice industries in Agua Prieta chiefly involved raiding clubs that permitted gambling when state of Sonora edicts prohibited such activity. Prostitution and drug

consumption—essentially opium use among Chinese—was condemned and occasionally confronted but received less press than gambling busts. *Douglas Daily International*, "Sonora Confiscates Thousands in Gambling Den"; *Douglas Daily Dispatch*, "Gambling in Agua Prieta May Close"; "Mexican Governor Orders Gambling Closed in Agua Prieta."

53. The Royal Night Club opened in 1944, offering the first modern cabaret in Agua Prieta since the end of Prohibition. It was located on Pan Americana, the main street known formerly as Avenida 3, and across the street from the customs house. The club included a dining room and a dance floor with live orchestra, and it was furnished with chrome chairs and tables; its windows were block glass in keeping with its art moderne style. *Douglas Daily Dispatch*, "Finishing Touches Being Placed on Royal Night Club."

54. Most of the information presented here about Gatliff and the Curio Café can be found in Hayostek, "Alice Gatliff."

55. Ibid.

56. *El Paso Herald-Post*, "Friend of Mexican Statesmen Is Dead."

57. Botica Ramos, a pharmacy, advertised "Post Cards and Curios," and the cigar stand of Eduardo Arevalo announced "Handsome Post Cards" in a 1930 directory. *Douglas City Directory 1930*, 139–40.

58. *Douglas Daily Dispatch*, "La Azteca Is Opening in New Building."

59. *Douglas Daily Dispatch*, "Agua Prieta Invites Residents of City to Shop."

60. *Douglas City Directory 1940*, 212–16.

61. *Arizona Republic*, "Citizens Make Bid For New Business," mentions that curio shopping is good in Agua Prieta.

Chapter 4

1. Simpich, "Along Our Side of the Mexican Border," 71. On the origin of the town name, see Sandomingo, *Historia de Agua Prieta*, 43; *Herald-Dispatch*, "Naco Wasn't Always That Sleepy Little Border Town." Yet another interpretation is that of Arizona cattle rancher B. A. Packard, who claims that he recommended to the railroad engineers who laid out the town that they call the town Naco, after the first four letters of the original destination for the rail line, Nacozari. See, Myrick, *Railroads of Arizona*, 194.

2. Ring, "Naco Café Thrives with 'Hospitality.'"

3. *Herald-Dispatch*, "Naco Wasn't Always That Sleepy Little Border Town."

4. Peterson, "Naco, Arizona's Accidental Place in History."

5. Heyman, *Life and Labor on the Border*, 27, cites C. L. Sonnichson's, *Colonel Greene and the Copper Rocket* (1974), noting nine hundred animal teams. Fred Valenzuela, a U.S. Customs officer at Naco, recalls from a 1929 transcript that the number was five hundred teams; see "District of Nogales Papers, 1892–1977," box 10, folder 97.

6. The Phelps Dodge Company then recognized the advantage of building south from Nacozari to Agua Prieta and Douglas through the Agua Prieta Valley, a flatter terrain with sufficient water; see Truett, *Fugitive Landscapes*, 82–83. For the history of the El Paso and Southwestern Railroad, see Myrick, *Railroads of Arizona*, 199–242.

7. Trennert, "Southern Pacific Railroad of Mexico," 267.

8. Truett, *Fugitive Landscapes*, 83–103; Heyman, *Life and Labor on the Border*, 28–30.

9. Tinker Salas, *In the Shadow of Eagles*, 162–63; *Bisbee Daily Review*, "Bisbee-Naco Gives Water to Naco."

10. Greene obtained a second concession in 1901 to build extension rail lines from his Naco-Cananea railroad to the interior of Sonora, and in 1902 he named this line the Cananea, Yaqui River and Pacific Railroad; see Trennert, "Southern Pacific Railroad of Mexico," 267.

11. Tinker Salas, *In the Shadow of Eagles*, 162–63.

12. Sanborn Map Company, *Naco, Cochise County, Ariz., 1904*.

13. Tinker Salas, *In the Shadow of Eagles*, 164; Thiel, *Archaeological Testing of the Naco, Arizona Port of Entry*, 2.

14. "District of Nogales Papers, 1892–1977"; Thiel, *Archaeological Testing of the Naco, Arizona Port of Entry*, 2.

15. Tully, "Bullets for Breakfast," 8.

16. *Bisbee Daily Review*, "Collector Jiminez Says New Custom House Sure"; *Arizona Republic*, "Naco Balks at Enforcing New Border Law," 31.

17. Epler, "Prohibition Promised Prosperity for Naco, Sonora."

18. Valenzuela, "Border Memories of Fred Valenzuela" (interview); *Bisbee Daily Review*, "Announcing the Opening of the White House Café Naco, Sonora," advertisement, December 15, 1922; "Naco, Wide Open Attracts Big Gathering."

19. *Bisbee Daily Review*, "Prohibition Affected Naco Economy."

20. *Herald-Dispatch*, "Naco Wasn't Always That Sleepy Little Border Town"; *Bisbee Daily Review*, "Bull Fights! Plaza de Toros, Mazzantini, Naco, Sonora," advertisement, December 21, 1901; "An Event Never Equaled in the Southwest," advertisement, June 11, 1904; Sandomingo, *Historia de Agua Prieta*, 45.

21. *Bisbee Daily Review*, "Prohibition Affected Naco Economy."

22. Ibid. *Bisbee Daily Review*, "The Three Republics Naco, Sonora, Mexico: Just Across the Line," advertisement, August 13, 1907.

23. "District of Nogales Papers, 1892–1977."

24. Arreola and Curtis, *Mexican Border Cities*, table 5.1.

25. *Tucson Daily Citizen*, "Cinco de Mayo Is Being Celebrated."

26. Vanderwood and Samponaro, *Border Fury*.

27. *Herald-Dispatch*, "Naco Wasn't Always That Sleepy Little Border Town"; *Bisbee Daily Review*, "Rumors of an Attack Calls Guard to Naco"; *El Paso Herald*, "Naco Is Under Military Guard"; *Bisbee Daily Review*, "Soldiers Now in Control at Naco, Sonora"; *Arizona Republican*, "Customs House at Naco Is Opened."

28. Hall and Coerver, *Revolution on the Border*, 31. Rather than surrender to Calles and Bracamonte, Ojeda abandoned his army by crossing the border and surrendering to American military stationed at Naco, Arizona. See, Christiansen, "Bullets Across the Border. Part II," 27–36. On bombing the town, including the customs house, see *El Paso Herald*, "Ojeda Holds Naco Until His Last Bullet Is Fired." Homer Scott filmed "The Battle of Naco" and released a two-reel documentary that was featured in El Paso in 1913; see *El Paso Herald*, "The Battle of Naco." advertisement, July 15, 1913.

29. Gilliam, "Military Aviation's Revolutionary Beginnings," 58.

30. Mumme, "Battle of Naco Factionalism and Conflict in Sonora"; Hall, "Mexican Revolution and the Crisis at Naco."

31. Quotation from Mumme, "Battle of Naco Factionalism and Conflict in Sonora," 165. News accounts of the siege at Naco include the following: *Bisbee Daily Review*, "Hill's Forces Preparing to Defend Naco"; "Hill Fires More Shots into U.S."; "Statement on Occupation of Naco"; "Naco's Doom Sealed in Rise of Sun This Morning."

32. Ortigoza, *Ciento catorce días de sitio*; Mumme, "Battle of Naco Factionalism and Conflict in Sonora," 169–70. A redrafted version of the Calles map (fig. 4.22) by Don Bufkin showing the position of trenches defending Naco appears in Mumme.

33. Several photographic postcards from the 1914–1915 Battle of Naco can be viewed in the collections of the Arizona Historical Society, Tucson. The following are especially noteworthy: Hill's trenches—AHS #92238, AHS #100021; Hill's *cuartel* or garrison—AHS #100019; Naco, Sonora, residents fleeing to Naco, Arizona, in anticipation of the battle—AHS #100038.

34. Hall and Coerver, *Revolution on the Border*, 33–35; *Bisbee Daily Review*, "Breton New Prefect at Naco, Sonora."

35. Buchenau, "Plutarco Elías Calles and the *Maximato* in Revolutionary Mexico," 236.

36. Cited in Ragsdale, *Wings over the Mexican Border*, 15.

37. Sheppard, "One View of the 1929 Battle at Naco."

38. *Bisbee Daily Review*, "Fire Destroys Railroad Shops."

39. "District of Nogales Papers, 1892–1977"; Ragsdale, *Wings over the Mexican Border*, 46.

40. See photographic postcard titled "Car Bombed by Rebels on U. S. Soil, Naco, Arizona," Arizona Historical Society #15146; The postcard is reproduced in Sheppard, "One View of the 1929 Battle at Naco," and Peterson, "Naco, Arizona's Accidental Place in History."

41. See Ragsdale, *Wings over the Mexican Border*, 43.

42. Fisher, "When a Rebel Force Bombed Naco."

43. "District of Nogales Papers, 1892–1977"; McKinney, "1929 Revolution Was Big Show."

Chapter 5

1. Flores García, *Nogales*, 14–15; Tinker Salas, *In the Shadow of Eagles*, 147–55; Ready, *Nogales Arizona 1880–1980*, 6; Sokata, *Ambos Nogales, On the Border*, 2.

2. Tinker Salas, *In the Shadow of Eagles*, 147.

3. West, *Sonora*, 94.

4. Trennert, "Southern Pacific Railroad of Mexico," 265–66.

5. Southworth, *El Estado de Sonora, México*, 29; Flores García, *Nogales*, 30–33; Suárez Barnett, "Municipio de Nogales, Sonora, Mexico" (website) reproduces the details by property block and ownership that allowed the creation of the 1884 Nogales, Sonora, townsite.

6. Dávila, *Sonora Histórico y Descriptivo*, 303.

7. Ready, *Nogales Arizona 1880–1980*, 93.

8. Camaras de Comercio de Nogales, Mexico, *Folleto de recuerdos*.

9. *Nogales Daily Herald, Trade Territory of Nogales* (map).

10. Suárez Barnett, "Municipio de Nogales, Sonora, Mexico" (website).

11. Arreola, "La cerca y las garitas de ambos Nogales," figs. 7, 8, 15. Beyond the official crossing sites, there were numerous informal neighborhood crossings between Nogales, Sonora, and Nogales, Arizona; see, Mascareñas, "Reflejos historicos de mi pueblo Nogales" (website).

12. Nogales Wonderland Club, *Nogales and Santa Cruz County, Arizona*, 3.

13. Captions based largely on the following sources: Rochlin and Rochlin, "Heart of Ambos Nogales"; Arreola, "La cerca y las garitas de ambos Nogales"; Parra, "*Valientes Nogalenses*"; Suárez Barnett, "Municipio de Nogales, Sonora, Mexico" (website).

14. Postcard dating is explained in Bogdon and Weseloh, *Real Photo Postcard Guide*.

15. Flores García, *Nogales*, 44; Scott, "Nogales, the Picturesque," 7.

16. Hu-DeHart, "Racism and Anti-Chinese Persecution in Sonora, Mexico, 1876–1932," 10.

17. *Nogales Daily Herald*, "Ventas por Mayor y Menor Juan Lung Tain y Cia Sucursal Comerciantes y Importadores," advertisement, Sixth Anniversary and Industrial Edition, 1920. Mascareñas, "Reflejos historicos de mi pueblo Nogales" (website), lists the names and business locations for some of the Chinese merchants in Nogales.

18. Paulsen, "The Yellow Peril at Nogales"; Hansen, "Chinese Six Companies of San Francisco"; Yang, "In Search of a Homeland."

19. For details on the Municipal Palace, Purísima Concepción (the church), and the Escuela Pesstalozzi, see Suárez Barnett, "Municipio de Nogales, Sonora, Mexico" (website),

and Mascareñas, "Reflejos historicos de mi pueblo Nogales" (website). See also Flores García, *Nogales*, 67. The Pestalozzi schoolhouse was built in the architectural spirit of Richardsonian Romanesque, a style especially popular in America between 1880 and the early twentieth century. Although lacking the distinctive Roman arches of the style, the school building exhibits the telling red masonry combined with a rough-faced, squared stonework. See McAlester and McAlester, *Field Guide to American Houses*, 301–2.

20. Colonia Moderna was built in 1916–1917; see *Nogales Daily Herald*, "Nogales, Sonora"; Flores García, *Nogales*, 77.

21. *Nogales Daily Herald*, "Nogales, Sonora"; Flores García, *Nogales*, 77.

22. Sanborn-Perris Map Company, *Nogales, Pima Co., Ariz. T., 1893*; *Nogales, Ariz., Pima Co., 1898*; *Nogales, Pima Co., Ariz. & Sonora, Mex., 1901*.

23. Municipio de Nogales, "Cronología de hechos históricos, 1889, 13 de Julio" (website).

24. Programa Nacional Fronterizo, *Nogales, Son.*

25. Arreola and Curtis, *Mexican Border Cities*, 137.

26. Dávila, *Sonora histórico y descriptivo*, 304; *Nogales Daily Herald*, "Nogales, Sonora"; Tinker Salas, *In the Shadow of Eagles*, 118, 151.

27. Flores García, *Nogales*, 39, notes that the Nogales customs house building was inaugurated in 1893; however, the Gustavo Cox map for 1888 (fig. 5.4) shows the distinctive footprint of the building, and photographs from 1889 show the structure already part of the border town landscape. Alberto Suárez Barnett, the *cronista* (chronicler) of Nogales, gives 1887 as the date of completion and is the source for the cost of construction; see Suárez Barnett, "Municipio de Nogales, Sonora, Mexico" (website). José Ramón García, personal communication, August 4, 2015.

28. McAlester and McAlester, *Field Guide to American Houses*, 241, 343–44.

29. Sanborn Map Company, *Nogales, Santa Cruz County, Ariz., 1917*.

30. *Arizona Daily Star*, "Nogales Eager for New Role."

31. *Tucson Daily Citizen*, "Sonora Hopes to Finish Road Work"; Sokata, *Ambos Nogales, On the Border*; Ready, *Nogales, Arizona 1880–1980*, 109.

32. *Arizona Republic*, "Nogales Will Have New Tourist Hotel."

33. *Nogales Daily Herald*, "Nogales Pictorial"; Details about architects and contractors can be found in Suárez Barnett, "Municipio de Nogales, Sonora, Mexico" (website), and Mascareñas, "Reflejos historicos de mi pueblo Nogales" (website).

34. *Arizona Republic*, "Fray Marcos de Niza Hotel," advertisement, May 11, 1952; *Nogales Daily Herald*, "Hotel Fray Marcos de Niza," advertisement, November 21, 1950.

35. *Nogales Daily Herald*, "Dine and Dance Thanksgiving," advertisement, November 22, 1950; "Mexican Supper Every Wednesday," advertisement, November 1, 1950.

36. Nogales Wonderland Club, *You'll Like Nogales*.

37. *Nogales Daily Herald*, "Nogales, Sonora."

38. Southworth, *El Estado de Sonora, México*, 33; Moreno Castro, *Comerciantes emergentes de la frontera entre Sonora y Arizona 1880–1910*, 74.

39. Sanborn-Perris Map Company, *Nogales, Ariz., Pima Co., 1898*.

40. *Arizona Daily Star*, "Nogales, Gateway to Two Nations."

41. *Nogales Daily Herald*, "C. of C. Advertising Draws Many Tourists."

42. *Tucson Daily Citizen*, "No Red Tape in Crossing the Border into Mexico," advertisement, February 20, 1942; "For Entertainment, Excitement and a Foreign Atmosphere Visit Picturesque Nogales," advertisement, January 1, 1942.

43. *Arizona Republic*, "Plan a Visit to Nogales, Sonora Enchanting—Exciting—Different," advertisement, January 26, 1941; "Let's Go 'Abroad' This Winter in Romantic, Exciting Nogales, Sonora," advertisement, February 2, 1941.

44. *Arizona Daily Star*, "Nogales Visitors Find Romance South of the Border."

45. *Arizona Republic*, "And Here Is Mexico," advertisement, February 9, 1936.

46. *Nogales International*, "Mexican Social Life"; *Polk's Arizona Pictorial Gazetteer and Business Directory*. The Arreola Collection contains a handful of early Nogales, Sonora, postcards published by Rochin y Méndez.

47. *Arizona Republic*, "Let's Go 'Abroad' This Winter in Romantic, Exciting Nogales, Sonora." advertisement, February 1, 1941.

48. *City of Nogales Old Mexico Tourist Guide*; Harvill, *Newcomer's Guide to Nogales, Sonora, Mexico*; *Tucson Daily Citizen*, "Tourists Find Old Mexico's Attractions Close, Varied."

49. "Nogales, Sonora Mexico Manual de Trafico."

50. *Arizona Daily Star*, "Nogales, Son., to Move Red-Light Zone"; Arreola and Curtis, *Mexican Border Cities*, 106–9; Mascareñas, "Reflejos historicos de mi pueblo Nogales" (website) lists Canal Street as the Nogales zone of tolerance since 1928.

51. *Nogales Daily Herald*, "Bull Fight! Juanita Cruz and José (Pepete) Olivera at the Nogales Bull Ring," advertisement, January 27, 1939.

52. *Arizona Daily Star*, "New Bullring South of Nogales Will Mean Return of Corridas." Mascareñas, "Reflejos historicos de mi pueblo Nogales" (website), gives 1948 as the date for the construction of the first concrete bullring.

53. *Tucson Daily Citizen*, "Bullfights Top Tourist Fare"; "Trip to Nogales Is a 'Must' for Visitors"; "Horseback Bull Fighting."

54. Frontain, *Bullfighting in Nogales*.

55. Moreno Castro, *Comerciantes emergentes de la frontera entre Sonora y Arizona 1880–1910*, 66.

56. The story of Enrique Donnadieu is reported by his daughter Marie Donnadieu. See *Arizona Daily Star*, "Nogales' Fire-Ravaged Caverna Being Rebuilt." For an account of the variety of liquors regularly imported by Los Hermanos Donnadieu, see Moreno Castro, *Comerciantes emergentes de la frontera entre Sonora y Arizona 1880–1910*, 67.

57. *Nogales Daily Herald*, "When in Nogales, Sonora, Visit The Cave," advertisement, December 25, 1922; see also Nogales Wonderland Club, *Nogales and Santa Cruz County, Arizona.*

58. *Nogales Daily Herald*, "Dancing at the Cave Tonight."

59. *Nogales International*, "Border Beat by Don Smith"; an invitation letter held in the Arizona Historical Society Library and Archives dated November 7, 1937, signed by Jim P. and Nick P. Kerson, with letterhead given as "The Aristocratic & Famous Cavern Café Tenth Anniversary Celebration, An International Border Event, Nogales—Sonora—Mexico" explains the expansion of a single cave to create multiple cave rooms. See also Gonzalez, "La Caverna, Un Lugar Que Resurge de Sus Cenizas." For a list of the many celebrities and politicos who visited The Cavern, see Mascareñas, "Reflejos historicos de mi pueblo Nogales" (website). I am indebted to José Ramón García, personal communication, August 4, 2015, for some of the details about La Caverna.

60. *Nogales Daily Herald*, "International Floor Show Drawing Crowds The Cavern Café Nogales, Sonora, Mexico," advertisement, December 17, 1936; "The Cavern Café New Year's Eve Dinner," advertisement, December 31, 1936; "Dine . . . in Old Mexico at the Famous Cavern Café," advertisement, October 23, 1945; "Cavern Café for Your Thanksgiving Dinner," advertisement, November 21, 1950.

61. The menu is featured in a personal historic recollection video; see Larsen, "La Caverna (the Caverns [sic]) Café in Nogales, Sonora" (website).

62. *Arizona Daily Star*, "La Caverna Reopening Planned Within a Month"; "La Caverna Will Be Back"; "Nogales' Fire-Ravaged Caverna Being Rebuilt"; "Rebuilding Lapses on Cave Eatery in Nogales, Son."; *Tucson Daily Citizen*, "Reopening of La Caverna Not Scheduled Until May"

63. *Arizona Daily Star*, "La Caverna to Reopen Next Year."

64. *Arizona Daily Star*, "Nogales' Fire-Ravaged Caverna Being Rebuilt."

Chapter 6

1. Hornaday, *Camp-Fires on Desert and Lava*, 84.

2. Lumholtz, *New Trails in Mexico.*

3. Two companion explorers who accompanied Hornaday on his expedition were Daniel Trembly MacDougal and Godfrey Sykes, each of whom published articles about the Sonora borderland including references to Sonoyta. See MacDougal, "Across Papagueria," and Sykes, "Camino Del Diablo." See also Ronald L. Ives, a prolific chronicler of the Sonoyta environs, especially "Origins of the Sonoyta Townsite," "Sonoyta Oasis," and "Mission San Marcelo De Sonoyta."

4. Kurath, "Note on 'Arizona,'" 21; Ives, "Sonoyta Oasis," 2.

5. Lumholtz, *New Trails in Mexico*, 174; MacDougal, "Across Papagueria," 709; Ives, "Sonoyta Oasis," 2.

6. Ives, "Origins of the Sonoyta Townsite," 21.

7. Lumholtz, *New Trails in Mexico*, 176.

8. Ives, "Mission San Marcelo De Sonoyta"; Lumholtz, *New Trails in Mexico*, 176; Hoy, "Sonoyta and Santo Domingo." Zoñi and Altar are Sonoran towns southeast of Quitovac and east of Caborca, respectively. See Don Bufkin map in Hoy, "Sonoyta and Santo Domingo," 119.

9. Gray, *A. B. Gray Report*, 85–87.

10. International Boundary Commission, *Boundary between the United States and Mexico*, map no. 9; Hoy, "Sonoyta and Santo Domingo"; McGee, "Old Yuma Trail," 129–30.

11. Hoy, "Sonoyta and Santo Domingo," 125, includes a detailed map of land use and property ownership in Old Sonoyta drafted by Don Bufkin.

12. Greene, *Historic Resource Study*, 23–24. Greene cites accounts made by members of the U.S.-Mexico Boundary Resurvey team who visited Sonoyta in the 1890s; Hoy, "Sonoyta and Santo Domingo"; "First Sonoyta"; Lumholtz, *New Trails in Mexico*, 179.

13. Hornaday, *Camp-Fires on Desert and Lava*, 85–86.

14. Lumholtz, *New Trails in Mexico*, 178.

15. Hornaday, *Camp-Fires on Desert and Lava*, 88. Carl Lumholtz also photographed the Quiroz *molino* in 1909–1910, but the image was not reproduced for his book, *New Trails in Mexico*. The image, archived in the Lumholtz Photography Collection, Museum of Cultural History, at the University of Oslo, appears in a recent publication: see Ann Christine Eek, "Secret of the Cigar Box."

16. In "Sonoyta Oasis," Ives notes that during the early months of the wet season, vehicles were hauled across the river by use of a cable pulled by a tractor; see fig. 5. In 1950, he estimated that construction of a bridge at the site would cost more than the assessed value of all the buildings in Sonoyta. Apparently, a bridge spanning the Sonoyta River was built in the 1940s, but it was washed away in a flood and not rebuilt during this era. See Hoy, "Dry Hope," 65.

17. Hoy, "Sonoyta and Santo Domingo," 125. Don Bufkin's map of Old Sonoyta was originally sketched by Don Arturo Quiroz (1885–1970), who was born in Old Sonoyta and was the son of Traino Quiroz, who welcomed both Hornaday and Lumholtz to Sonoyta in 1907 and 1909. See also, Hoy, "Dry Hope," 17–19.

18. *Ajo Copper News*, "Capt. R. J. Molino Building Up Sonoyta."

19. Arreola and Curtis, *Mexican Border Cities*, table 5.1.

20. Ives, "Sonoyta Oasis," 49.

21. Hoy, "Dry Hope," 56, 66, 71.

22. Ibid., 72–73.

23. *Ajo Copper News*, "Sonoyta Has New Club"; Hoy, "Dry Hope," 73–74. La Dorina is also referenced by some Sonoytans as a onetime refuge on the border for the Al Capone gang, but that claim has never been substantiated. See Miller, "Sonoyta Interlude," 181–84.

24. Ives, "Ygnacio C. Quiroz"; *Ajo Copper News*, "Ignacio Quiroz"; Rutman, "Oral History of Norma Walker."

25. Hoy, "Dry Hope," 174–75.

26. Curtis and Arreola, "Zonas de Tolerancia on the Northern Mexican Border."

27. Hoy, "Dry Hope," 175.

28. Ibid., 173.

29. Ives, "Sonoyta Oasis," 7; *Ajo Copper News*, "Sonoyta Truck Farm Great Adjunct to Ajo."

30. Rutman, "Oral Histories: Margaret Ross and Ed Havens," 68.

31. Rutman and Rheaume, "Manuel G. Levy"; *Ajo Copper News*, "Sonoyta Truck Farm Great Adjunct to Ajo."

32. Montijo, "Ajo, Arizona Mexican Town Model 1934–1942." Montijo's map model shows the family names of resident households in Ajo's segregated Mexican town, and some of these residents were related to Sonoytans; International Sonoran Desert Alliance, *Ajo Memory Project Photo Album*, 11.

33. Greene, *Historic Resource Study*, 117–18.

34. Rickard, *Development of Ajo, Arizona*, 92, 222, 270; Rutman, "George M. Potter," 14, 270.

35. Hoy, "Dry Hope," 68–69.

36. Ibid., 69; Barrios Matrecito, "Ecos del desierto," 34–36.

37. *Ajo Copper News*, "Governor Hunt And Party to Fly to Gulf Next Fri."; "Gov. Topete of Sonora to Inspect Marine Club at Rocky Point."

38. Rickard, *Development of Ajo, Arizona*, 285.

39. Ives, "Puerto Peñasco, Sonora."

40. Finn et al., "Puerto Peñasco."

41. Form and Rivera, "Work Contacts and International Evaluations."

Chapter 7

1. *Yuma Daily Sun*, "Mexicali Bullfight Scheduled Sunday"; "A Los Toros"; "Yumans Introduced to an Ancient Art"; "Bull Fight Sunday Lists McCormick."

2. International Boundary Commission, *Report of the Boundary Commission*, pt. 2, p. 27.

3. Iglesias Serafin, *Monumento 204*, 7–11.

4. Verdugo Fimbres, *Frontera en el Dersierto*, 31–34, 45–50, 64; Flores, *Nuestra Herencia*, 82–84.

5. Verdugo Fimbres, *Frontera en el desierto*, 64–68.

6. George, "En San Luis Otros Tiempos."

7. Iglesias Serafin, *Monumento 204*, 22–23.

8. Méndez Sáinz, "De Tijuana a Matamoros," 49; Verdugo Fimbres, *Frontera en el desierto*, 81–92.

9. Verdugo Fimbres, *Frontera en el desierto*, 65.

10. *Yuma Morning Sun*, "The International Club San Luis, Sonora, Mexico," advertisement, January 11, 18, and July 3, 8, 1925; George, "En San Luis Otros Tiempos."

11. *Yuma Daily Sun*, "Arizona Knights of Columbus Convention to Open Here Saturday."

12. *Yuma Daily Sun*, "Jesus Martinez New Police Chief at San Luis," reports that the San Diego and La Tapatía clubs that featured strippers closed in 1957.

13. Verdugo Fimbres, *Frontera en el desierto*, 105–6.

14. *Yuma Daily Sun*, "Casa-Aurora Gift Shop, San Luis, Sonora, Mexico," advertisement, December 21, 1956.

15. *Yuma Daily Sun*, "News of Senior Citizens," mentions San Luis businessmen who visit Yuma; quotation drawn from Yuma Chamber of Commerce, "Yuma in the Land of Opportunity"; see also, Yuma Chamber of Commerce, "Territorial Trails Tours and Selected Points of Interest."

16. *Yuma Morning Sun*, "Cocking Main, San Luis, Sonora, Mexico," advertisement, March 8, 1923.

17. *Yuma Daily Sun*, "Winter Bullfight Season Opens at San Luis Today." See also the following advertisements in the *Yuma Daily Sun*: "Bull Fights!! Sunday, Feb. 2nd, 3:30 P.M. San Luis, Mexico," January 31, 1958; "Bullfights San Luis, Sonora Sunday Sept. 6, 5 P.M.," September 3, 1959; "Bullfights Sunday, February 5, 1961 at 3 p.m. Ariz. Time Bull Ring, San Luis, Sonora, Mexico," February 3, 1961; "Bull Fights Sunday, December 8, 1963 at 3:30 P.M. in San Luis Sonora, Mexico," December 4, 1963; Bullfights Sunday, Oct. 13th 4:30 P.M. San Luis, Mexico," October 13, 1957.

18. *Yuma Daily Sun*, "Bette Ford Tops Fight Card in San Luis Bull Ring Today"; "Bull Fight Sunday Lists McCormick." Arreola, "La Macarena," discusses the careers and bullfight performances of McCormick and Ford.

19. *Yuma Daily Sun*, "For the First Time on This Frontier a Real Mexican Rodeo at the Plaza de Toros, San Luis, Sonora Mexico Sunday Dec. 20, 1959 at 3 P.M. (Ariz. Time)," advertisement, December 18, 1959.

20. Verdugo Fimbres, *Frontera en el desierto*, anexo 4, "Mapas y fotográphias," includes a photograph of the *aduana*; Guillermo Lizarraga moved to San Luis Río Colorado in 1949 and began crossing the border to work in San Luis, Arizona, in 1959. He recalls the *aduana* as no more than a house. See Tovar and Lizarraga, "Oral History with Guillermo Lizarraga."

21. *Arizona Days and Ways* (brochure).

22. *Arizona Republic*, "Super 'Services' Market."

23. Morgan, "Take the Nickel Tour of San Luis."

24. Iglesias Serafin, *Monumento 204*, 23; Verdugo Fimbres, *Frontera en el desierto*, anexo 4, "Mapas y fotográphias."

25. Jakle and Sculle, *Gas Station in America*, 141.

26. Arreola and Curtis, *Mexican Border Cities*, 157–74.

27. Webster, "Reconnaissance of the Flora and Vegetation of *La Frontera*," 24.

28. Robles Payán, "Una visión retrospectiva."

29. Verdugo Fimbres, *Frontera en el desierto*, anexo 4, "Mapas y fotográphias."

Chapter 8

1. Larson, *Issac's Storm*, 276.

2. Herzog, *From Aztec to High Tech*; Arreola and Curtis, *Mexican Border Cities*.

3. Arreola, *Postcards from the Río Bravo Border*; Berumen, *La cara del tiempo*; Johnson and Gusky, *Bordertown*; Romo, *Ringside Seat to a Revolution*.

4. Berumen, *La cara del tiempo*, 13.

5. Whereas Tucson counted 13,200 people and was the largest population center in Arizona in 1910, by 1920, Phoenix's population (29,100) exceeded Tucson's (20,300). Douglas, Arizona, in 1920 was a town of 9,500 people, while Yuma counted 4,250, and Ajo just 2,300. Sargent, *Metro Arizona*, 51.

6. Bogden and Weseloh, *Real Photographic Postcard Guide*; Vaule, *As We Were*; Michas, *Real and Other Photos*.

7. Cadava, *Standing on Common Ground*, 73–87.

8. Mraz, *Photographing the Mexican Revolution*, 4.

9. In the Arreola Collection, the only other photographic postcards produced in the 1910s for Nogales were the few distinctive oval format images by an unknown photographer and attributed to Rochin y Méndez of La Industria Mexicana arts and crafts store in the town; see figs. 5.12, 5.14, and 5.50. In the 1920s, the Nogales postcard photographer Francisco Saenz Aguilar (who signed his cards P. M. A.) began to produce photo postcards and print postcards that competed with Lohn's postcards.

10. Arreola and Madsen, "Variability of Tourist Attraction on an International Boundary."

11. Lowenthal, *The Past Is a Foreign Country*, 257.

Bibliography

Archives and Collections

Arreola Collection. Placitas, NM.

A. W. Lohn Papers. Arizona Historical Society, Tucson, AZ.

Curt Teich Postcard Archives. "Nogales Sonora." Lake County Discovery Museum, Wauconda, IL.

Detroit Publishing Company Collection. Prints and Photographs Reading Room, Library of Congress. Washington, DC. http://www.loc.gov/rr/print/coll/202_detr.html.

"District of Nogales Papers, 1892–1977." MS 1136. United States Customs Service. Arizona Historical Society, Tucson, AZ.

E. D. Newcomer Photograph Collection. Arizona Historical Society, Tempe, AZ.

Old NYC: Mapping Historical Photos from the NYPL. New York Public Library. http://www.oldnyc.org.

Rochlin Collection. University of Arizona Library Special Collections. University of Arizona, Tucson, AZ.

Newspapers

Ajo Copper News

Arizona Daily Star

Arizona Republic

Arizona Republican

Bisbee Daily Review

Bisbee Gazette

Douglas Daily Dispatch

Douglas Daily International

El Fronterizo (Tucson)

El Imparcial (Hermosillo)

El Paso Herald

El Paso Herald-Post

Herald-Dispatch (Sierra Vista, AZ)

Nogales Daily Herald

Nogales International

Tucson Daily Citizen

Yuma Daily Sun [*Yuma Sun*]

Yuma Morning Sun

Websites

"About the Frasher Foto Postcard Digitization Project at the Pomona Public Library." Pomona Public Library, Pomona, CA. http://content.ci.pomona.ca.us/cdm4/about_frasher.php.

Dawson, Michael, Sally Stein, Jennifer Watts. "Wishing You Were Here: Frasher Fotos Postcards and the American West 1920–1950." Accessed August 29, 2015 (no longer posted). http://www1.youseemore.com/pomona/about.asp?p=46.

Larsen, Chris. "La Caverna (the Caverns [*sic*]) Café in Nogales, Sonora." June 3, 2013. https://www.youtube.com/watch?v=Oo3FpmfJY6s.

Mascareñas, Enrique. "Reflejos historicos de mi pueblo Nogales." http://musicaehistoria.com/index.htm.

Municipio de Nogales. "Cronología de hechos históricos. 1889. 13 de julio." http://web.archive.org/web/20070504191527/http://www.sonora.gob.mx/portal/Runscript.asp?p=ASP%5cpg212.asp.

Suárez Barnett, Fernando Alberto. "Municipio de Nogales, Sonora, Mexico. Historia, Geografía, Medio Natural, Sociedad, Cultura, Economia." http://www.municipiodenogales.org.

Government Documents

Elías Calles, Plutarco. *Informe relativo al sitio de Naco, 1914–1915.* Mexico City, 1932.

Emory, William H. *Report on the United States and Mexican Boundary Survey, Made Under the Direction of the Secretary of the Interior.* 3 vols. Austin: Texas State Historical Association, 1987. First published 1857–1859 by C. Wendell.

Greene, Jerome A. *Historic Resource Study, Organ Pipe Cactus National Monument Arizona.* Denver: Denver Service Center, Historic Preservation Division, National Park Service, U.S. Department of the Interior, 1977.

International Boundary Commission, United States and Mexico. *Boundary Between the United States and Mexico, as Surveyed and Marked by the International Boundary Commission under the Convention of July 29th, 1882: Revived February 18th, 1889*. Washington, DC: Government Printing Office, 1899.

———. *Proceedings Relating to the Placing of Additional Monuments to More Perfectly Mark the International Boundary Line Through the Town of Naco, Arizona-Sonora*. N.p., 1907.

———. *Report of the Boundary Commission upon the Survey and Re-marking of the Boundary Between the United States and Mexico West of the Rio Grande, 1891 to 1896*. Senate Document, 55th Congress, no. 247. Washington, DC: Government Printing Office, 1898.

McCleneghan, Thomas J., and Charles R. Gildersleeve. *Land Use Contrasts in a Border Economy*. Special Study no. 23, Bureau of Business and Public Research. Tucson, AZ: Bureau of Business and Public Research, University of Arizona, 1964.

Programa Nacional Fronterizo. *Nogales, Son*. Mexico City: PRONAF, 1963.

Maps, Directories, Guides, Ephemera

Arizona Days and Ways. Brochure. April 20, 1958.

"Batallas del 1 y 2 de noviembre 1915, croquis de Agua Prieta y sus fortificaciones." In *Compendio de datos históricos de la familia Elías*, edited by Armando Elías Chomina. Hermosillo, Sonora: privately printed, 1986.

Cámara de Comercio de Nogales, Mexico. *Folleto de recuerdos*. Nogales, AZ, 1919.

City of Nogales Old Mexico Tourist Guide. Arizona Collection. Department of Archives and Manuscripts, Arizona State University Libraries, n.d.

Cobb, Emory. *Douglas, Arizona, U.S.A.* Phoenix: printed by author, 1928.

Douglas Borderland Climate Club. *On the Romantic Mexican Border—Douglas, Arizona; All-Year Sunshine, Health* and *Opportunity*. [Douglas?], [1925?].

Douglas City Directory 1923. Long Beach, CA: Western Directory, 1923.

Douglas City Directory 1930. Long Beach, CA: Western Directory, 1930.

Douglas City Directory 1935. Long Beach, CA: Western Directory, 1935.

Douglas City Directory 1938. Bisbee, AZ: Douglas Directory Company, 1938.

Douglas City Directory 1940. Douglas, AZ: Mullin-Kille, *Douglas Daily Dispatch*, and F. A. McKinney, 1940.

Douglas City Directory 1948–49. Phoenix, AZ: Southwick, 1948–49.

García y Alva, Federico. *Album-directorio del estado de Sonora*. Hermosillo: Antonio B. Monteverde, 1905–7.

Harvill, George C. *A Newcomer's Guide to Nogales, Sonora, Mexico*. Tucson: University of Arizona, 1968.

Instituto Nacional de Estadística Geografía e Informatica. *Puerto Peñasco*. Mexico: 1992.

Kerson, Jim P., and Nick P. Kerson. Invitation letter to "The Aristocratic and Famous Cavern Café Tenth Anniversary Celebration, An International Border Event, Nogales—Sonora—Mexico." November 7, 1937. Ephemera file, Arizona Historical Society, Tucson.

Montijo, Horacio L. "Ajo, Arizona Mexican Town Model 1934–1942." Model map. Ajo Historical Museum.

"Nogales, Sonora Mexico Manual de Trafico." Pamphlet, 1950s. Places-Mexico-Sonora-Nogales, Ephemera File. Tucson, Arizona Historical Society Library and Archive.

Nogales Wonderland Club. *Nogales and Santa Cruz County, Arizona*. Nogales, AZ: Nogales Wonderland Club, 1927.

———. *You'll Like Nogales, on the Border*. Nogales, AZ: Wonderland Club and Nogales Chamber of Commerce, 1929.

Polk's Arizona Pictorial Gazetteer and Business Directory. St. Paul, MN: R. L. Polk, 1912. http://www.usgwarchives.net/az/santacruz/directories.html.

Sanborn Map Company. *Agua Prieta, Sonora, Mexico, 1929*. New York: Sanborn Map Company, 1929.

———. *Naco, Cochise County, Ariz., 1904*. New York: Sanborn Map Company, 1904.

———. *Nogales, Santa Cruz County, Ariz., Including Nogales, Mexico, 1917*. New York: Sanborn Map Company, 1917.

Sanborn-Perris Map Company. *Nogales, Ariz., Pima Co., 1898*. New York: Sanborn-Perris Map Company, 1898.

———. *Nogales, Pima Co., Ariz.*, and *Sonora, Mex., 1901*. New York: Sanborn-Perris Map Company, 1901.

———. *Nogales, Pima Co., Ariz. T., 1893*. New York: Sanborn-Perris Map Company, 1893.

"The Trade Territory of Nogales, 'The Wonderful West Coast of Mexico.'" In *Sixth Anniversary and Industrial Edition*, suppl. to the *Nogales Daily Herald*, 1920.

Yuma Chamber of Commerce. "Territorial Trail Tours and Selected Points of Interest." [Yuma, AZ?]: [Yuma Chamber of Commerce?], 1969.

———. "Yuma Arizona Sunshine Capital of the Nation." [Yuma, AZ?]: [Yuma Chamber of Commerce?], 1958.

———. "Yuma in the Land of Opportunity." [Yuma, AZ?]: [Yuma Chamber of Commerce?], 1950–51.

Books

Alarcón Cantú, Eduardo. *Estructura urbana en ciudades fronterizas: Nuevo Laredo-Laredo, Reynosa-McAllen, Matamoros-Brownsville*. Tijuana: El Colegio de la Frontera Norte, 2000.

Arreola, Daniel D. *Postcards from the Río Bravo Border: Picturing the Place, Placing the Picture, 1900s–1950s*. Austin: University of Texas Press, 2013.

Arreola, Daniel D., and James R. Curtis. *The Mexican Border Cities: Landscape Anatomy and Place Personality*. Tucson: University of Arizona Press, 1993.

Berger, Dina. *The Development of Mexico's Tourism Industry: Pyramids by Day, Martinis by Night*. New York: Palgrave Macmillan, 2006.

Berumen, Miguel Ángel. *La cara del tiempo: La fotografía en Ciudad Juárez y El Paso (1870–1930)*. Ciudad Juárez, Chihuahua: Cuadro por Cuadro, Imagen y Palabra, Berument y Muñoz Editores, 2002.

———. *México: Fotografía y revolución*. Mexico City: Fundación Televisa, 2009.

Bogdan, Robert, and Todd Weseloh. *Real Photo Postcard Guide: The People's Photography*. Syracuse, NY: Syracuse University Press, 2006.

Brenner, Anita. *The Wind That Swept Mexico: The History of the Mexican Revolution of 1910–1942*. Austin: University of Texas Press, 1971.

Cadava, Geraldo L. *Standing on Common Ground: The Making of the Sunbelt Borderland*. Cambridge, MA: Harvard University Press, 2013.

Callarman, Barbara Dye. *Photographers of Nineteenth Century Los Angeles: A Directory*. Los Angeles: Hacienda Gateway, 1993.

Cuen Gamboa, Manuel, comp. *La frontera, el río y el desierto: Lecturas para reconstruir la historia de San Luis Río Colorado*. Hermosillo: Dirección General de Culturas Populares Unidad Regional Sonora, 2000.

Dávila, F. T. *Sonora histórico y descriptivo*. Nogales, AZ: Tipografía de R. Bernal, 1894.

Delpar, Helen. *The Enormous Vogue of Things Mexican: Cultural Relations Between the United States and Mexico, 1920–1935*. Tuscaloosa: University of Alabama Press, 1992.

Fernández Tejedo, Isabel. *Memories of Mexico: Mexican Postcards, 1882–1930*. Mexico: Banco Nacional de Obras y Servicios Públicos, 1994.

Flores, Hermes. *Nuestra herencia: Recopilación histórico-regional de San Luis Río Colorado, Sonora*. San Luis Río Colorado: Comisión de Estudios Históricos, 1990.

Flores García, Silvia Raquel. *Nogales: Un siglo en la historia*. Hermosillo: INAH-SEP Centro Regional del Noroeste and Secretaria de Fomento Educativo y Cultura, 1987.

Fox, Claire F. *The Fence and the River: Culture and Politics at the U.S.-Mexico Border*. Minneapolis: University of Minnesota Press, 1999.

Frontain, Dick. *Bullfighting in Nogales*. Tucson, AZ: Los Amigos, 1965.

Fulton, Richard W. *Arizona Postcard Checklist*. Fairfax, VA: privately printed, 1994.

Ganster, Paul, and David E. Lorey. *The U.S.-Mexican Border into the Twenty-First Century*. 2nd ed. Lanham, MD: Rowman & Littlefield, 2008.

Garber, Paul Neff. *The Gadsden Treaty*. Philadelphia: University of Pennsylvania Press, 1923.

Gehlbach, Frederick R. *Mountain Islands and Desert Seas: A Natural History of the U.S.-Mexican Borderlands*. College Station: Texas A&M University Press, 1981.

Grant, Stephen. *Postales salvadoreñas del ayer—Early Salvadoran Postcards: 1900–1950*. El Salvador: Fundación María Escalón de Nuñez, Banco Cuscatlán, 1999.

Gray, A. B. *The A. B. Gray Report, and Including Reminiscences of Peter R. Brady Who Accompanied the Expedition*. Edited by L. R. Bailey. Los Angeles: Westernlore, 1963.

Griswold del Castillo, Richard. *The Treaty of Guadalupe Hidalgo: A Legacy of Conflict*. Norman: University of Oklahoma Press, 1990.

Hall, Linda B., and Don M. Coerver. *Revolution on the Border: The United States and Mexico, 1910–1920*. Albuquerque: University of New Mexico Press, 1988.

Herzog, Lawrence A. *From Aztec to High Tech: Architecture and Landscape Across the Mexico–United States Border*. Baltimore: Johns Hopkins University Press, 1999.

Heyman, Josiah McC. *Life and Labor on the Border: Working People of Northeastern Sonora, Mexico, 1886–1986*. Tucson: University of Arizona Press, 1991.

Hornaday, William T. *Camp-Fires on Desert and Lava*. New York: Charles Scribner's Sons, 1909.

Humphrey, Robert R. *90 Years and 535 Miles: Vegetation Changes Along the Mexican Border*. Albuquerque: University of New Mexico Press, 1987.

Iglesias Serafin, Federico. *Monumento 204: San Luis Río Colorado*. San Luis Río Colorado: Altec Publicaciones, 1992.

International Sonoran Desert Alliance. *The Ajo Memory Project Photo Album: Images and Stories from the Mexican Town and Indian Village Communities of Ajo, Arizona*. Ajo, AZ: International Sonoran Desert Alliance, 2010.

Jakle, John A. *The American Small Town: Twentieth-Century Place Images*. Hamden, CT: Archon Books, 1982.

———. *Postcards of the Night: Views of American Cities*. Santa Fe: Museum of New Mexico Press, 2003.

———. *The Visual Elements of Landscape*. Amherst: University of Massachusetts Press, 1987.

Jakle, John A., and Keith A. Sculle. *The Gas Station in America*. Baltimore: Johns Hopkins University Press, 1994.

———. *Picturing Illinois: Twentieth-Century Postcard Art from Chicago to Cairo*. Urbana: University of Illinois Press, 2012.

Johnson, Benjamin Heber, and Jeffrey Gusky. *Bordertown: The Odyssey of an American Place*. New Haven, CT: Yale University Press, 2008.

Khoo, Salma Naustion, and Malcolm Wade. *Penang Postcard Collection 1899–1930s*. Penang: Janus Print and Resources, 2003.

Klamkin, Marian. *Picture Postcards*. New York: Dodd, Mead, 1974.

Klett, Mark, Kyle Bajakian, William L. Fox, Michael Marshall, Toshi Ueshina, and Byron Wolfe. *Third Views, Second Sights: A Rephotographic Survey of the American West*. Santa Fe: Museum of New Mexico Press, 2004.

Klett, Mark, and Michael Lundgren. *After the Ruins, 1906 and 2006: Rephotographing the San Francisco Earthquake and Fire*. Berkeley: University of California Press and Museum of Fine Arts, 2006.

Klett, Mark, Ellen Manchester, and JoAnn Verburg. *Second View: The Rephotographic Survey Project*. Albuquerque: University of New Mexico Press, 1984.

Larson, Erik. *Issac's Storm: A Man, a Time, and the Deadliest Storm in History*. New York: Vintage Books, 2000.

Lowenthal, David. *The Past Is a Foreign Country*. Cambridge: Cambridge University Press, 1985.

———. *Possessed by the Past: The Heritage Crusade and the Spoils of History*. New York: Free Press, 1996.

Lumholtz, Carl. *New Trails in Mexico: An Account of One Year's Exploration in North-Western Sonora, Mexico, and South-Western Arizona 1909–1910*. New York: Charles Scribner's Sons, 1912.

Lynch, Kevin. *The Image of the City*. Cambridge, MA: MIT Press, 1960.

———. *What Time Is This Place?* Cambridge, MA: MIT Press, 1976.

Martínez, Oscar J. *Troublesome Border*. Rev. ed. Tucson: University of Arizona Press, 2006.

Mautz, Carl. *Biographies of Western Photographers: A Reference Guide to Photographers Working in the 19th Century American West*. Nevada City, CA: Carl Mautz, 1997.

McAlester, Virginia, and Lee McAlester. *A Field Guide to American Houses*. New York: Alfred A. Knopf, 1984.

Meikle, Jeffrey L. *Postcard America: Curt Teich and the Imaging of a Nation, 1931–1950*. Austin: University of Texas Press, 2015.

Metz, Leon C. *Border: The U.S.-Mexico Line*. El Paso: Mangan Books, 1989.

Michas, Aina. *Real and Other Photos: An Introduction to the History, Identification and Collectability of Early Photographic Postcards*. Rochester: Andrew W. Mellon Foundation, Advanced Residency Program, and Image Permanence Institute, 2007–9.

Miller, George. *The Delaware Album, 1900–1930*. Newark: University of Delaware Press, 2011.

Miller, George, and Dorothy Miller. *Picture Postcards in the United States, 1893–1918*. New York: Crown, 1975.

Moreno Castro, María Isabel. *Comerciantes emergentes de la frontera entre Sonora y Arizona 1880–1910: La casa comercial Donnadieu Hermanos*. Culiacán: Tesis Maestra en Historia, Universidad Autónoma de Sinaloa, 2010.

Morgan, Hal, and Andreas Brown. *Prairie Fires and Paper Moons: The American Photographic Postcard: 1900–1920*. Boston: David R. Godine, 1981.

Mraz, John. *Photographing the Mexican Revolution: Commitments, Testamonies, Icons*. Austin: University of Texas Press, 2012.

Myrick, David F. *Railroads of Arizona*, vol. 1, *The Roads of Southern Arizona*. Berkeley, CA: Howell-North Books, 1975.

Officer, James E. *Hispanic Arizona, 1536–1856*. Tucson: University of Arizona Press, 1987.

Oles, James. *South of the Border: Mexico in the American Imagination, 1914–1947*. Washington, DC: Smithsonian Institution Press, 1993.

Ortigoza, Manuel. *Ciento catorce días de sitio, la defensa de Naco*. Hermosillo: C. Gálvez, 1944.

Piñera Ramirez, David. *Caminando entre el pasado y el presente de Nogales*. Tijuana: Centro de Investigaciones Históricas, UNAM-UABC, 1985.

Ragsdale, Kenneth Baxter. *Wings over the Mexican Border: Pioneer Military Aviation in the Big Bend*. Austin: University of Texas Press, 1984.

Ramírez Zavala, Ana Luz. *La participación de los Yaquis en la Revolución, 1913–1920*. Hermosillo: Programa Editorial de Sonora, Instituto Sonorense de Cultura, 2012.

Ready, Alma, ed. *Nogales, Arizona, 1880–1980 Centennial Anniversary*. Nogales, AZ: Nogales Centennial Committee, 1980.

Rebert, Paula. *La gran línea: Mapping the United States–Mexico Boundary, 1849–1857*. Austin: University of Texas Press, 2001.

Rickard, Forrest R. *The Development of Ajo, Arizona (to Mid-Year 1942)*. Ajo: privately printed, 1996.

Rittenhouse, Jack D. *Disturnell's Treaty Map*. Santa Fe, NM: Stagecoach, 1965.

Romero, Robert Chao. *The Chinese in Mexico, 1882–1940*. Tucson: University of Arizona Press, 2010.

Romo, David Dorado. *Ringside Seat to a Revolution: An Underground Cultural History of El Paso and Ciudad Juárez: 1893–1923*. El Paso: Cinco Puntos, 2005.

Rose, Gillian. *Visual Methodologies: An Introduction to the Interpretation of Visual Materials*. London: Sage, 2001.

Rosenheim, Jeff L. *Walker Evans and the Picture Postcard*. New York: Metropolitan Museum of Art, 2009.

Rowe, Jeremy. *Arizona Real Photo Postcards: A History and Portfolio*. Nevada City, CA: Carl Mautz, 2007.

Samponaro, Frank N., and Paul J. Vanderwood. *War Scare on the Rio Grande: Robert Runyon's Photographs of the Border Conflict, 1913–1916*. Austin: Texas State Historical Association, 1992.

Sandomingo, Manuel. *Historia de Agua Prieta*. Agua Prieta: Tipógrafo Rafael Parra Araiza, 1951.

Sante, Luc. *Folk Photography: The American Real-Photo Postcard, 1905–1930*. Portland, OR: Yeti and Verse Chorus, 2009.

Sargent, Charles, ed. *Metro Arizona*. Phoenix: Biffington Books, 1988.

Smith, Jack H. *Postcard Companion: The Collector's Reference*. Randor, PA: Wallace-Homestead, 1989.

Snow, Richard. *Coney Island: A Postcard Journey to the City of Fire*. New York: Brightwaters, 1984.

Sokota, Ron. *Ambos Nogales, On the Border: A Chronology*. Tucson: University of Arizona, Udall Center for Public Policy, 1991.

Southworth, John R. *El Estado de Sonora, México: Sus industrias, comerciales, mineras y manufactureras*. Nogales, AZ: Oasis, 1897.

Stechschulte, Nancy Stickels. *The Detroit Publishing Company Postcards*. Big Rapids, MI: privately printed, 1994.

St. John, Rachael. *Line in the Sand: A History of the Western U.S.-Mexico Border*. Princeton, NJ: Princeton University Press, 2011.

Swartz, Joan M., and James R. Ryan. *Picturing Place: Photography and the Geographical Imagination*. London: I. B. Tauris, 2003.

Tenorio-Trillo, Mauricio. *Mexico at the World's Fairs: Crafting a Modern Nation*. Berkeley: University of California Press, 1996.

Thiel, J. Homer. *Archaeological Testing of the Naco, Arizona Port of Entry Expansion Property*. Technical Reports no. 94-8. Tucson, AZ: Center for Desert Archaeology, 1994.

Tinker Salas, Miguel. *In the Shadow of Eagles: Sonora and the Transformation of the Border During the Porfiriato*. Berkeley: University of California Press, 1997.

Truett, Samuel. *Fugitive Landscapes: The Forgotten History of the U.S.-Mexico Borderlands*. New Haven, CT: Yale University Press, 2006.

Uribe Eguiluz, Myra N. *Una aproximación a la Compañía México Fotográfico y la promoción del turismo a finales de los años veinte*. Mexico City: Universidad Nacional Autónoma de México, Facultad de Filosofía y Letras, 2011.

Vanderwood, Paul J., and Frank N. Samponaro. *Border Fury: A Picture Postcard Record of Mexico's Revolution and the U.S. War Preparedness, 1910–1917*. Albuquerque: University of New Mexico Press, 1988.

Vaule, Rosamond B. *As We Were: American Photographic Postcards, 1905–1930*. Boston: David R. Godine, 2004.

Verdugo Fimbres, Maria Isabel. *Frontera en el desierto, historia de San Luis Río Colorado*. Hermosillo: Instituto Nacional de Antropologia e Historia S. E. P., Centro Regional del Noroeste, 1983.

Voss, Stuart F. *On the Periphery of Nineteenth-Century Mexico: Sonora and Sinaloa, 1810–1877*. Tucson: University of Arizona Press, 1982.

Walker, Henry P., and Don Bufkin. *Historical Atlas of Arizona*. Norman: University of Oklahoma Press, 1979.

Wall, E. J., and H. Snowden Ward. *The Photographic Picture Post-Card*. London: Dawbarn and Ward, 1906.

Weber, David J. *The Mexican Frontier, 1821–1846: The American Southwest Under Mexico*. Albuquerque: University of New Mexico Press, 1982.

Weisman, Alan, and Jay Dusard. *La frontera: The United States Border with Mexico*. San Diego, CA: Harcourt Brace Jovanovich, 1986.

West, Robert C. *Sonora: Its Geographical Personality*. Austin: University of Texas Press, 1993.

Wilson, John P. *Islands in the Desert: A History of the Uplands of Southeastern Arizona*. Albuquerque: University of New Mexico Press, 1995.

Articles, Book Chapters, News Stories, Typescripts

(Newspaper advertisements do not appear here but are cited in full in the endnotes.)

Ajo Copper News. "Capt. R. J. Molino Building Up Sonoyta." September 24, 1921.

———. "Governor Hunt and Party to Fly to Gulf Next Fri." November 3, 1928.

———. "Gov. Topete of Sonora to Inspect Marine Club at Rocky Point." February 2, 1928.

———. "Ignacio Quiroz, 75, Passed Away Feb. 1." February 8, 1962.

———. "Sonoyta Has New Club." September 18, 1930.

———. "Sonoyta Truck Farm Great Adjunct to Ajo." April 16, 1921.

Ames, Charles R. "Along the Mexican Border: Then and Now." *Journal of Arizona History* 18, no. 4 (Winter 1977): 431–46.

Arizona Daily Star. "La Caverna Reopening Planned Within a Month." February 21, 1984.

———. "La Caverna to Reopen Next Year, Restaurant Owners Say Yet Again." November 3, 1987.

———. "La Caverna Will Be Back." April 7, 1985.

———. "New Bullring South of Nogales Will Mean Return of Corridas." July 6, 1975.

———. "Nogales Eager for New Role." March 20, 1955.

———. "Nogales' Fire-Ravaged Caverna Being Rebuilt." August 25, 1986.

———. "Nogales, Gateway to Two Nations, Playground for Mexico and U.S." April 14, 1929.

———. "Nogales, Son., to Move Red-Light Zone." August 16, 1987.

———. "Nogales Visitors Find Romance South of the Border." February 23, 1940.

———. "Rebuilding Lapses on Cave Eatery in Nogales, Son." November 25, 1986.

Arizona Republic. "Citizens Make Bid for New Business." February 23, 1958.

———. "Naco Balks at Enforcing New Border Law." November 19, 1953.

———. "Nogales Will Have New Tourist Hotel." January 26, 1941.

———. "Super 'Services' Market." May 29, 1966.

———. "U.S.-Mexican Amity Shown on Flag Day." June 20, 1943.

Arizona Republican. "Customs House at Naco Is Opened." February 3, 1915.

Arreola, Daniel D. "Across the Street Is Mexico: Invention and Persistence of the Border Town Curio Landscape." *Yearbook of the Association of Pacific Coast Geographers* 61 (1999): 9–41.

———. "Echoes in the Borderland, *Una Geografía Monumental*." In *Monuments* by David Taylor, 293–301. Santa Fe, NM: Radius, 2015.

———. "La cerca y las garitas de ambos Nogales: A Postcard Landscape Exploration." *Journal of the Southwest* 43, no. 4 (Winter 2001): 505–41.

———. "La Macarena: 'The Most Beautiful Place in the Best Town on the Border.'" *Image File* 18, no. 2 (2011): 3–7.

Arreola, Daniel D., and Nick Burkhart. "Photographic Postcards and Visual Urban Landscape." *Urban Geography* 31, no. 7 (2010): 885–904.

Arreola, Daniel D., and Kenneth Madsen. "Variability of Tourist Attraction on an International Boundary: Sonora, Mexico Border Towns." *Visions in Leisure and Business* 17, no. 4 (Winter 1999): 19–31.

Barrios Matrecito, Valdemar. "Ecos del desierto." In *La frontera, el río y el desierto: Lecturas para reconstuir la historia de San Luis Río Colorado*, edited by Manuel Cuen Gamboa, 34–36. Hermosillo: Dirección General de Culturas Populares, Unidad Regional de Sonora, 2000.

Bisbee Daily Review. "Agua Prieta Building to Be Better Than That at Naco." March 31, 1903.

———. "Agua Prieta Is to Have Buildings." July 16, 1903.

———. "Bisbee-Naco Gives Water to Naco." August 21, 1907.

———. "Breton New Prefect at Naco, Sonora: Man of New School in Republic to the South In Charge of Rejuvenation of Naco." February 2, 1915.

———. "Ciudad Corral." July 23, 1903.

———. "Collector Jiminez Says New Custom House Sure." April 20, 1906.

———. "Fire Destroys Custom House." May 21, 1903.

———. "Fire Destroys Railroad Shops." April 12, 1916.

———. "Hill Fires More Shots into U.S." October 7, 1914.

———. "Hill's Forces Preparing to Defend Naco Against Maytorena's Yaqui Army." September 27, 1914.

———. "Initial Opening of the Bull Ring." July 5, 1903.

———. "Naco's Doom Sealed in Rise of Sun This Morning: War Rages." October 17, 1914.

———. "Naco, Wide Open Attracts Big Gathering." February 16, 1915.

———. "Prohibition Affected Naco Economy." March 14, 1979.

———. "Rumors of an Attack Calls Guard to Naco." June 21, 1910.

———. "Soldiers Now in Control at Naco, Sonora." June 22, 1910.

———. "Statement on Occupation of Naco." July 25, 1915.

———. "Sunday Amusement at Smelter City." August 1, 1903.

———. "A Watercolor Sketch of Ring." April 7, 1903.

Buchenau, Jürgen. "Plutarco Elías Calles and the *Maximato* in Revolutionary Mexico: A Reinterpretation." *Jahrbuch für Geschichte Lateinamerikas* 43 (2006): 229–53.

Bufkin, Donald H. "The Making of the Boundary Between the United States and Mexico: A Study in Political Geography." *Cochise Quarterly* 13, no. 1/2 (Spring/Summer 1983): 3–29.

Christiansen, Larry D. "Bullets Across the Border. Part I: The Situation and the Beginning." *Cochise Quarterly* 4, no. 4 (1974): 3–20.

———. "Bullets Across the Border. Part II: The Revolution Rekindled." *Cochise Quarterly* 5, no. 1 (1975): 18–36.

Cole, Carl H. "Douglas Under Fire: An Account of Villa's Battle for Agua Prieta." *Cochise Quarterly* 14, no. 3 (1984): 3–12.

Conzen, Michael P. "Analytical Approaches to the Urban Landscape." In *Dimensions of Human Geography: Essays on Some Familiar and Neglected Themes*, edited by Karl W. Butzer, 128–65. Chicago: University of Chicago Press, 1978.

Curtis, James R., and Daniel D. Arreola. "Through *Gringo* Eyes: Tourist Districts in Mexican Border Cities as Other-Directed Places." *North American Culture* 5, no. 2 (1989): 19–32.

———. "Zonas de Tolerancia on the Northern Mexican Border." *Geographical Review* 81, no. 3 (1991): 333–46.

DeBres, Karen, and Jacob Sowers. "The Emergence of Standardized, Idealized, and Place-less Landscapes in Midwestern Main Street Postcards." *Professional Geographer* 61 (2009): 216–230.

Dotterrer, Steven, and Galen Cranz. "The Picture Postcard: Its Development and Role in American Urbanization." *Journal of American Culture* 5, no. 1 (Spring 1982): 44–50.

Douglas Daily Dispatch. "Agua Prieta Cabaret Changes Owners: Matt Medos Selling the International Club to Romaine, Allred and Germany." December 1, 1929.

———. "Agua Prieta Invites Residents of City to Shop; Entertainment Is Available and Warm Greeting Always Extended." August 30, 1942.

———. "Agua Prieta May Claim Few Months of Age over Douglas: Was Started in 1899 as Commerce Expanded." March 31, 1918.

———. "Agua Prieta School and Church Repaired to Beautify Plaza." November 1, 1929.

———. "Agua Prieta Wins Name of Cleanest Mexican City on Border: Has Fine Resorts." July 3, 1927.

———. "Architect Here to Direct Work on Social Club." August 11, 1928.

———. "Brookhill Café Opens to Trade in Agua Prieta." December 22, 1929.

———. "Brookhill to be Opened for Business Soon." May 30, 1929.

———. "Contract Is Let for $5,000 Improvement to International Club: Works Start Immediately." May 22, 1928.

———. "80 Per Cent Mexican-Help Rule Makes It Necessary [for] Some Agua Prieta Cafes to Close Temporarily to Meet Policy." July 22, 1931.

———. "Extensive Improvement Program Goes Forward in Agua Prieta on Banks, Resorts and Highways." July 20, 1928.

———. "Finishing Touches Being Placed on Royal Night Club." May 28, 1944.

———. "$5,000 Insurance on Silver Dollar Destroyed by Fire." February 12, 1932.

———. "Flames Destroy White House Club." September 2, 1930.

———. "Gambling in Agua Prieta May Close." January 17, 1924.

———. "International Club Bar and Cabaret Destroyed by Fire Friday Morning: Loss Reported Covered by Insurance." July 25, 1931.

———. "Jim Joe, Back from the West, Greets Friends." April 18, 1928.

———. "Jim Joe's Place in Agua Prieta Burns in Early Morning Fire, Requiring Aid from Douglas Department to Control It." December 27, 1930.

———. "La Azteca Is Opening in New Building." August 13, 1944.

———. "Mexican Governor Orders Gambling Closed in Agua Prieta and the Order Is Quickly Enforced by the Presidente." April 17, 1930.

———. "Much Building Activity Seen in Agua Prieta." April 24, 1928.

———. "Name Is Changed to Pan-American." September 15, 1942.

———. "New White House Club Opens Tonight." April 29, 1934.

———. "Only Night Club in Agua Prieta Is Finally Closed." January 5, 1932.

———. "Sammarcelli and Williams Started Business Together in 1921, Williams Buying Share of Ross and Wasserman." September 3, 1930.

———. "Total Loss In Resort Fire Mounts as Damage Is Estimated $70,000, Insurance on White House $51,000." September 8, 1930.

———. "Troops Guard Ruin Where Popular Club Burned to Ground." September 6, 1930.

Douglas Daily International. "Agua Prieta, Springing from a Tiny Trading Post, Now One of Prosperous Towns of No. Mex." July 2, 1926.

———. "Cine Alhambra Opens Tonight: Show House One of Finest in Sonora." June 22, 1946.

———. "Jim Joe Plans Large Ballroom." July 9, 1923.

———. "The Old Agua Prieat [sic] Bull Ring." August 26, 1913.

———. "Ruins of Old Bull Ring at Agua Prieta Removed: Gay Era of Early Day Recalled." December 1, 1917.

———. "Sonora Confiscates Thousands in Gambling Den." July 10, 1920.

Eek, Ann Christine. "The Secret of the Cigar Box: Carl Lumholtz and the Photographs from His Sonoran Desert Expedition, 1909–1910." Journal of the Southwest 49, no. 3 (2007): 369–418.

El Fronterizo. "Fotografia Popular." April 12, 1890.

El Paso Hearld. "Naco Is Under Military Guard." June 21, 1910.

———. "Ojeda Holds Naco Until His Last Bullet Is Fired." April 14, 1913.

El Paso Herald-Post. "Friend of Mexican Statesman Is Dead: Mrs. Alice Gatliff of Douglas Succumbs to Burns." April 9, 1936.

Epler, Bill. "Prohibition Promised Prosperity for Naco, Sonora." *Bisbee Gazette*, September 18, 1987.

Evans, Walker. "Main Street Looking North from Courthouse Square: A Portfolio of American Picture Postcards from the Trolley-Car Period." *Fortune*, May 1948, 102–6.

Finn, John, Arianna Fernandez, Lindsey Sutton, Daniel D. Arreola, Casey A. Allen, and Claire Smith. "Puerto Peñasco: Fishing Village to Tourist Mecca." *Geographical Review* 99, no. 4 (October 2009): 575–97.

Fisher, E. M. "When a Rebel Force Bombed Naco." *Tucson Citizen*, January 25, 1986.

Form, William H., and Julius Rivera. "Work Contacts and International Evaluations: The Case of a Mexican Border Village." *Social Forces* 37 (1958/59): 334–39.

Francaviglia, Richard V. "Streetcars to the Smelters: An Historical Overview of the Douglas Street Railways, 1902–1924." *Cochise Quarterly* 16, no. 1 (Spring 1986): 2–31.

George, Dorothy. "En San Luis Otros Tiempos, Otros Dias . . ." *Yuma Sun*, October 27, 1985.

Gilliam, Ronald R. "Military Aviation's Revolutionary Beginnings." *Aviation History* 10, no. 5 (May 2000): 52–58.

Gonzalez, Luis Orduno. "La Caverna, un lugar que resurge de sus cenizas." *El Imparcial* (Hermosillo), October 6, 1986.

Hadley, Diana. "Border Boom Town: Douglas, Arizona 1900–1920." *Cochise Quarterly* 17, no. 3 (Fall 1987): 3–47.

Hall, Linda B. "The Mexican Revolution and the Crisis in Naco: 1914–1915." *Journal of the West* 16 (October 1977): 27–35.

Hansen, Lawrence Douglas Taylor. "The Chinese Six Companies of San Francisco and the Smuggling of Chinese Immigrants Across the U.S.-Mexico Border, 1882–1930." *Journal of the Southwest* 48, no. 1 (Spring 2006): 37–61.

Harrington, John Walker. "Postal Carditis and Some Allied Manias." *American Illustrated Magazine* 61, no. 5 (March 1906): 562–67.

Hayostek, Cindy. "Alice Gatliff: Forgotten Woman of the Mexican Revolution." *Borderland Chronicles*, no. 1 (2008): 1–22.

———. "From Out of the North: The Mexican Revolution." *Borderland Chronicles*, no. 12 (2010): 1–26.

———. "Medal of Honor Winner in Douglas, Julien Gaujot." *Borderlands Chronicles*, no. 5 (2009): 1–30.

———. "Two Exceptional Men of the Borderlands and Electrical Power." *Borderlands Chronicles*, no. 11 (2010): 1–22.

Herald-Dispatch (Sierra Vista, AZ). "Naco Wasn't Always That Sleepy Little Border Town." April 12, 1972, A1, A2.

Hoy, Bill. "Dry Hope: Settlement of Sonoyta and Ajo." Typescript. Organ Pipe Cactus National Monument, 2000.

———. "The First Sonoyta: Its Setting and Settlers." Typescript. Organ Pipe Cactus National Monument, 1973.

———. "Sonoyta and Santo Domingo: A Story of Two Sonoran Towns and the River that Ran By." *Journal of Arizona History* 31, no. 2 (1990): 117–40.

Hu-DeHart, Evelyn. "Racism and Anti-Chinese Persecution in Sonora, Mexico, 1876–1932." *Amerasia* 9, no. 2 (1982): 1–28.

Isenberg, Alison. "Fixing an Image of Commercial Dignity: Postcards and the Business of Planning Main Street." In *Downtown America: A History of the Place and the People Who Made It*, 44–77. Chicago: University of Chicago Press, 2009.

Issac, Gwyneira. "Re-observation and Recognition of Change: The Photographs of Matilda Coxe Stevenson (1879–1915)." *Journal of the Southwest* 47, no. 3 (Autumn 2005): 411–55.

Ives, Ronald L. "Mission San Marcelo De Sonoyta." In *Land of Lava, Ash, and Sand: The Pinacate Region of Northwestern Mexico*, by Ronald L. Ives, compiled by James W. Byrkit, and edited by Karen J. Dahood, 99–114. Tucson: Arizona Historical Society, 1989.

———. "The Origin of the Sonoyta Townsite, Sonora, Mexico." *American Antiquity* 7, no. 1 (1941): 20–28.

———. "Puerto Peñasco, Sonora." *Journal of Geography* 49, no. 9 (1950): 349–61.

———. "The Sonoyta Oasis." *Journal of Geography* 49, no. 1 (1950): 1–14.

———. "Ygnacio C. Quiroz, 1886–1962." *Kiva* 28, no. 3 (February 1963): 33–34.

Kurath, William. "A Note on 'Arizona.'" *Kiva* 11, no. 2 (1946): 20–22.

MacDougal, D. T. "Across Papagueria." *Bulletin of the American Geographical Society* 40, no. 12 (1908): 705–25.

Manger, William F., and Daniel D. Arreola. "The Photographic Postcards of A. W. Lohn in Culiacán and Ambos Nogales." Paper presented at the 8° Congreso Mexicano de Tarjetas Postales, Mexico City, July 16–18, 2015.

Martínez, Oscar J. "Surveying and Marking the U.S.-Mexico Boundary: The Mexican Perspective." In *Drawing the Borderline: Artist-Explorers of the U.S.-Mexico Boundary Survey*, edited by Dawn Hall, 13–22. Albuquerque, NM: Albuquerque Museum, 1996.

McCool, Grace. "Agua Prieta, Sonora: Out of the Past." *Bisbee Observer*, August 31, 1988.

McGee, W. J. "The Old Yuma Trail." *National Geographic Magazine* 12 (March/April 1901): 129–30.

McKinney, Fred. "1929 Revolution Was Big Show." *Bisbee Gazette*, October 1, 1964.

Mendelson, Jordana, and David Prochaska. "Introduction." In *Postcards: Ephemeral Histories of Modernity*, edited by David Prochaska and Jordana Mendelson, xi–xix. University Park: Pennsylvania State University Press, 2010.

Méndez Sáinz, Eloy. "De Tijuana a Matamoros: Imágines y forma urbana." *Revisita El Colegio de Sonora* 4 (1993): 45–61.

Miller, Tom. "Sonoyta Interlude." In *On the Border: Portraits of America's Southwestern Frontier*. New York: Harper and Row, 1981.

Morgan, Neil. "Take the Nickel Tour of San Luis." *Redlands Daily Facts*, December 21, 1970.

Mumme, Stephen P. "The Battle of Naco Factionalism and Conflict in Sonora, 1914–1915." *Arizona and the West* 21, no. 2 (Summer 1979): 157–86.

New York Times. "A Touch Screen Becomes a Window to the Past." August 7, 2014.

———. "Web Sites with a Historical Bent Join a Place to an Image." September 6, 2012.

Nogales Daily Herald. "C. of C. Advertising Draws Many Tourists to Border Cities Here." September 29, 1939.

———. "Dancing at the Cave Tonight." August 16, 1924.

———. "Nogales Pictorial." December 30, 1950.

———. "Nogales, Sonora: Gem City, Rich in Resources and Commercial Possibilities: One of Old Mexico's Greatest Ports of Entry." Sixth Anniversary and Industrial Edition, 1920.

Nogales International. "Border Beat by Don Smith." June 25, 1986.

———. "Mexican Social Life as Described by Prominent Nogales, Sonora, Woman." March 27, 1940.

Parra, Carlos Francisco. "*Valientes Nogalenses*: The 1918 Battle Between the U.S. and Mexico that Transformed Ambos Nogales." *Journal of Arizona History* 51, no. 1 (Spring 2010): 1–32.

Paulsen, George E. "The Yellow Peril at Nogales: The Ordeal of Collector William M. Hoey." *Arizona and the West* 13, no. 2 (Summer 1971): 113–28.

Paumgarten, Nick. "The Mannahatta Project: What Did New York Look Like Before We Arrived?" *New Yorker*, October 1, 2007.

Peterson, C. O. "Naco, Arizona's Accidental Place in History." *American West* 20, no. 1 (January/February 1983): 46–47, 70.

Ring, R. H. "Naco Café Thrives with 'Hospitality.'" *Arizona Daily Star*, July 6, 1981.

Robles Payán, Patricia. "Una visión retrospectiva." In *La frontera, el río y el desierto*, Manuel Cuen Gamboa, comp., 59–64. Hermosillo: Dirección General de Culturas Populars Unidad Regional Sonora, 2000.

Rochlin, Fred, and Harriet Rochlin. "The Heart of Ambos Nogales: Boundary Monument 122." *Journal of Arizona History* 17, no. 2 (Summer 1976): 161–80.

Rowe, Jeremy. "Have Camera, Will Travel: Arizona Roadside Images by Burton Frasher." *Journal of Arizona History* 51 (Winter 2010): 337–66.

Rutman, Sue, and Ernest Rheaume. "Manuel G. Levy: Pioneer Miner and Merchant of Arizona." Typescript. 2012. In the author's possession.

Sarber, Mary. "W. H. Horne and the Mexican War Photo Company." *Password* 31 (1986): 6–12.

Schor, Naomi. "*Cartes Postales*: Representing Paris 1900." *Critical Inquiry* 18 (1992): 188–244.

Scott, G. S. "Nogales, the Picturesque: A Peep Through One of the Doorways to Mexico." *Arizona: The New State Magazine* 4, no. 4 (1914): 7–9.

Sheppard, Celina. "One View of the 1929 Battle of Naco." *Cochise Quarterly* 18, no. 4 (Winter 1988): 25–33.

Simpich, Frederick. "Along Our Side of the Mexican Border." *National Geographic Magazine* 38, no. 1 (July 1920): 61–80.

Steele, Rich. "The Pernicious Picture Post Card." *Atlantic* 98 (August 1906): 287–88.

Sternbergh, Adam. "Positively Fourth Street, All Over Again." *New York Times Magazine*, December 8, 2013.

Stieber, Nancy. "Postcards and the Invention of Old Amsterdam Around 1900." In *Postcards: Ephemeral Histories of Modernity*, edited by David Prochaska and Jordana Mendelson, 24–41. University Park: Pennsylvania State University Press, 2010.

Sykes, Godfrey. "The Camino del Diablo: With Notes on a Journey in 1925." *Geographical Review* 17, no. 1 (1927): 62–74.

Trennert, Robert A., Jr. "The Southern Pacific Railroad of Mexico." *Pacific Historical Review* 35, no. 3 (August 1966): 265–84.

Tucson Daily Citizen. "Agua Prieta, Sonora, Old Mexico, Gala Fiesta Sept. 12 thru 16, 1953." September 4, 1953.

———. "Bullfights Top Tourist Fare." February 11, 1955.

———. "Cinco de Mayo Is Being Celebrated." May 3, 1947.

———. "Horseback Bull Fighting: Ancient Survival of Art." May 1, 1954.

———. "Reopening of La Caverna Not Scheduled Until May." March 24, 1984.

———. "Sonora Hopes to Finish Road Work." March 4, 1942.

———. "Tourists Find Old Mexico's Attractions Close, Varied." February 19, 1954.

———. "Trip to Nogales Is a 'Must' for Visitors: Bullfights Featured in Border Ring." February 19, 1954.

Tully, Barbara. "Bullets for Breakfast." *True West* (June 1975): 6–12.

Valenzuela, Fred. "Lochiel: Oldest Gateway to Mexico." Typescript. Bisbee Mining and Historical Museum, Bisbee, Arizona, n.d.

Webster, Grady L. "Reconnaissance of the Flora and Vegetation of *La Frontera*." In *Changing Plant Life of La Frontera: Observations on Vegetation in the U.S./Mexico Borderlands*, edited by Grady L. Webster and Conrad J. Bahre, 6–38. Albuquerque: University of New Mexico Press, 2001.

Yang, Li. "In Search of a Homeland: Lai Ngan, a Pioneer Chinese Woman and Her Family on the U.S.-Mexico Border." *Journal of Arizona History* 52, no. 4 (Winter 2011): 337–54.

Yuma Daily Sun. "A Los Toros." May 12, 1957.

——. "Arizona Knights of Columbus Convention to Open Here Saturday." April 16, 1942.

——. "Bette Ford Tops Fight Card in San Luis Bull Ring Today." February 2, 1958.

——. "Bull Fight Sunday Lists McCormick." June 28, 1957.

——. "Jesus Martinez New Police Chief at San Luis." February 28, 1957.

——. "Mexicali Bullfight Scheduled Sunday." November 23, 1953.

——. "News of Senior Citizens." February 17, 1964.

——. "Winter Bullfight Season Opens at San Luis Today." November 27, 1960.

——. "Yumans Introduced to an Ancient Art." December 31, 1957.

Interviews, Personal Communication, Oral Histories

García, José Ramón (historian and board president, Pimería Alta Historical Society, Nogales, AZ), personal communication, August 4, 2015.

Hayostek, Cynthia (historian and archivist, Douglas Historical Society, Douglas, AZ), personal communication, July 25, 2015.

Manger, William F. (Mexico postcard collector, PhD), personal communication, February 17, 2014, March 30, 2016, and July 27, 2016.

Rutman, Sue. "George M. Potter: Stories of Early Ajo, Arizona." Typescript. Ajo, AZ: Salazar-Ajo Branch Library, 2001.

——. "Oral Histories: Margaret Ross and Ed Havins, Western Pima County, Arizona." Typescript. Ajo, AZ: Organ Pipe Cactus National Monument, 1999.

——. "Oral History of Norma Walker." Typescript. Ajo, AZ: Organ Pipe Cactus National Monument, 1999.

Tovar, Cecilia, and Guillermo Lizarraga. "Oral History with Guillermo Lizarraga." San Luis, AZ: Yuma County District Library, San Luis Branch, 2011.

Valenzuela, Fred. "Border Memoirs of Fred Valenzuela, Deputy Collector of Customs, Naco, Arizona." Vertical files. Bisbee Mining and Historical Museum, n.d.

Index

About the Author

Daniel D. Arreola is Professor Emeritus, School of Geographical Sciences and Urban Planning, at Arizona State University, Tempe. He is the recipient of the Carl O. Sauer Distinguished Scholarship Award and the Preston E. James Eminent Latin Americanist Career Award from the Conference of Latin Americanist Geographers. Arreola is the author of *The Mexican Border Cities: Landscape Anatomy and Place Personality* (with James R. Curtis); *Tejano South Texas: A Mexican American Cultural Province*; *Hispanic Spaces, Latino Places: Community and Cultural Diversity in Contemporary America*; and *Postcards from the Río Bravo Border: Picturing the Place, Placing the Picture, 1900s–1950s*.